Brian,

Enjoy

Digital

Trailblazer!!

Praise for *Digital Trailblazer: Essential Lessons to Jumpstart Transformation and Accelerate Your Technology Leadership*

"Isaac gives digital leaders a programmatic and comprehensive approach to tackling the ever-changing challenges in digital transformation. *Digital Trailblazer* is the must-go-to playbook for not only leadership advice, but also real-world stories on how to handle the toughest challenges in culture, process, and technology."

—R "Ray" Wang,
founder and CEO, Constellation Research, and two-time
best-selling author, *Disrupting Digital Business* and
Everybody Wants to Rule the World

"You'd be hard-pressed to find another author with a closer knowledge of both IT management and the underlying technology that powers enterprises. Isaac Sacolick has been there and done that as a CIO, so his advice is hard-bought—and thanks to his sharp writing skills, clear as a bell. Anyone involved in a transformational IT initiative would do well to read this book."

—Eric Knorr,
editor-in-chief, IDG

"Isaac Sacolick holds a unique vantage point in the CIO world. From individual contributor to board partner, he has seen and done it all. His latest book offers a roadmap to the opportunities and challenges of being a modern Chief Information Officer. It's a world where technology is the crucial enabler of transformation, and the CIO is a business leader first. Isaac's journey is personal, important, and offers valuable lessons to the rest of us. If you are a CIO or aspiring CIO, then read this book."

—Michael Krigsman,
publisher, CXOTalk

"*Digital Trailblazer* should be required reading for rising technology and business leaders. The candid stories and pragmatic lessons will help you take your career to the next level and prepare you for the many challenges you're bound to face in the future."

—Dan Roberts,
CEO, Ouellette & Associates Consulting,
and Host, *CIO Whisperers* Podcast

"I have had the pleasure of working with Isaac for several years in his role as a leader of numerous executive-level discussions for CIOs at the programs I run. His sessions are always the standout, must-join piece of content at our events. His first book, *Driving Digital*, was a revelation, and I regularly advise my CIO clientele to treat it as a bible for digital transformation. This next installment might just be even better. Don't miss it!"

—Ross Abbott,
CEO and founder, SINC USA

"If you're involved in any aspect of product development and digital transformation, you need to absorb the wide-ranging lessons Isaac Sacolick shares in *Digital Trailblazer*. Having served in many leadership roles in my career—including as CEO of a fintech company—his book gave me a new understanding and appreciation for the skills it takes to effectively lead transformations."

—Myles Suer,
facilitator of Twitter #CIOChat, top CIO influencer,
and eWeek Contributor

"Isaac's first book is an essential and pragmatic guide for technology leaders to drive tough, fast-paced digital transformation; this second book is a personal journey through a decorated career that blends relatable, real-world storytelling with that same exceptional practicality. It distills impactful lessons for everyone to adopt—from the individual contributor to the project manager all the way up to C-level leadership. All too often in the world of business and technology, we forget about the human experience—*Digital Trailblazer* does an exceptional job of using human experience to teach while entertaining the reader with situations to which I'd venture to say every person in this field has had some relatable interaction."

—Anthony Juliano,
general partner and CTO, Landmark Ventures

"Isaac has found a way to share relatable experiences that are entertaining and educational. They help drive home the key skills digital transformers need to make their organizations successful."

—Philippe Johnston,
national president, CIO Association of Canada

"Isaac reveals from his own career journey the many impediments that can derail digital and data transformation initiatives, particularly within technology teams and their leaders, with the goal of offering no-nonsense advice to drive, survive, and thrive beyond those career and project tripwires that we encounter along the way. With easy-to-read insights for current and future leaders, he will give you a healthy serving of advice, confidence, and lessons learned to guide your career journey to digital transformation leadership."

—Kirk Borne,
PhD, chief science officer, DataPrime

"You have in your hand (or on your screen) the most important business book you will read all year. Half memoir and half instruction manual, *Digital Trailblazer* is the truth you'll need to drive innovation in your workplace. I know, because I've been fortunate to have had Isaac Sacolick guide two of my teams through the digital transformation process—both with remarkable success."

—Larry Lieberman,
CEO, Mouse.org, and former COO, Charity Navigator

"It's rare to hear the real stories behind transformations. Rarely rosy—transformations almost always involve overcoming technology debt, disagreements about priorities, and other unexpected challenges that are largely impossible to plan for. Finally, someone is brave enough to show us what really goes on in executive meetings and boardrooms. Isaac Sacolick doesn't hold back in these personal stories and offers battle-tested lessons that leaders will get great benefit from, now and in the future. This is a book I know I'll be recommending often."

—Shelly Kramer,
founding partner and lead analyst, Futurum Research

"Digital transformation is a process that will make or break a company—regardless of size or scope of that transformation. It's a scary concept for any executive or product leader starting on this journey. Isaac Sacolick takes his formidable digital transformation experience and expertise and translates that for the 'rest of us' who need to understand what we don't know so we can successfully lead a digital transformation of our own."

—Kathy Greenler Sexton,
CEO and publisher, Subscription Insider

"Leading digital transformations requires winning over hearts and minds. Through descriptive stories, Isaac Sacolick's *Digital Trailblazer* teaches emerging leaders the ins and outs of how to secure support and successfully execute new ideas—big and small. This book is a must-read for technology and business leaders who want to encourage culture change in their organizations."

—Jay Ferro,
EVP and chief information and technology officer, Clario

"Finally, a comprehensive, 360-degree look at what it takes to be a hugely successful transformation technologist from someone who has observed it, taught it, and done it! *Digital Trailblazer* provides key lessons and real outcomes that every technology leader should know to successfully drive digital transformation—everything from how to speak to a Board of Directors, when to go deep, when to listen, and when to question."

—Adriana Karaboutis,
global CIO and chief digital officer at National Grid

"As a CIO, I've long been passionate about building a talent pipeline for the next generation of transformational leaders. The honest stories and lessons in *Digital Trailblazer* will help rising technology and business leaders leapfrog many of the challenges they'll encounter in their careers. CIOs should assign this book to their teams to speed up their journeys and allow them to become tomorrow's leaders today."

—Angelic Gibson,
CIO, AvidXchange

"Isaac Sacolick's advice is both timely and pragmatic. His insights are not theoretical or academic but based on his years of leadership within technology and are valuable for anyone starting their career in technology or seasoned leaders looking to improve and advance their careers."

—Jason James,
CIO, Net Health

"Isaac Sacolick has a history of positive disruption. His ability to walk you through a path of breaking down barriers and driving transformation through uncompromising storytelling is as distinctive as it is informative. No matter your place on the leadership evolution, his advice through lessons and relatable content is a page turner—not just another hard-to-finish instructional manual—that adds actionable intelligence to anyone's toolbelt."

—Jason T Burns Tilson,
CIO

"Practical and useful advice for transformational leaders at all levels. Isaac uses stories from his many years of experience to illustrate problems and guide the reader through a series of practical learnings to help them build and develop."

—Martin Davis,
CIO and managing partner, DUNELM Associates

"What got you here isn't what'll get you there. Sacolick takes technical folks on his own leadership journey and elicits relevant lessons for making the leap from technical expert to digital leader."

—Jonathan Feldman,
CIO, coach, and columnist

"Finally, a guide to career growth from techy to top dog. Isaac's story-led approach breaks down the imposter syndrome barrier new leaders face and imparts practical knowledge in a consumable way, saving the reader from experiencing the pain of making the same mistakes."

—Helen Wetherley Knight,
co-founder, TechForSocialGood.ca

"Empathy is one of today's most critical leadership skills. It's a trait that can make or break any digital transformation. In *Digital Trailblazer*, Isaac Sacolick provides a rare, well-rounded look into what it takes to be an empathetic leader."

—Jo Peterson,
vice president, cloud & security services, Clarify360

"Leading transformation is one of the most challenging jobs in business and technology. Isaac's book makes the journey less daunting by providing tactical advice that will be as useful in planning innovations as it is in the C-suite. *Digital Trailblazer* is the mentor professionals won't know they need until they experience a similar scenario. When they inevitably do, they can recall Isaac's entertaining stories and useful lessons to deftly navigate whatever is thrown their way."

—Robin Yeman,
CTO, Catalyst Campus, and strategic board member, Project & Team

DIGITAL TRAILBLAZER

DIGITAL TRAILBLAZER

Essential Lessons to Jumpstart Transformation and Accelerate Your Technology Leadership

ISAAC SACOLICK

WILEY

Published by John Wiley & Sons, Inc., Hoboken, New Jersey.
Published simultaneously in Canada.

For general information on our other products and services or for technical support, please contact our Customer Care Department within the United States at (800) 762-2974, outside the United States at (317) 572-3993 or fax (317) 572-4002.

Wiley also publishes its books in a variety of electronic formats. Some content that appears in print may not be available in electronic formats. For more information about Wiley products, visit our web site at www.wiley.com.

Library of Congress Cataloging-in-Publication Data

Names: Sacolick, Isaac, author.
Title: Digital trailblazer : essential lessons to jumpstart transformation
and accelerate your technology leadership / Isaac Sacolick.
Description: Hoboken, New Jersey : Wiley, [2022] | Includes index.
Identifiers: LCCN 2022007541 (print) | LCCN 2022007542 (ebook) | ISBN
9781119894537 (cloth) | ISBN 9781119894551 (adobe pdf) | ISBN
9781119894544 (epub)
Subjects: LCSH: Leadership. | Technological innovations.
Classification: LCC HD57.7 S226 2022 (print) | LCC HD57.7 (ebook) | DDC
658.4/092—dc23/eng/20220218
LC record available at https://lccn.loc.gov/2022007541
LC ebook record available at https://lccn.loc.gov/2022007542

Cover Design: Wiley
Cover Image: © tomertu/Shutterstock

SKY10034031_051122

To Michele, Ronan, Pietra, Jasper, Mom, Dad, Pam, Frank, Danny, Lisa, Allison, Langdon, Matthew, Brendan, Ilana, Jonathan, and Nova—my family's trailblazers.

In memory of Bill and Dean.

And a big thanks to all the great mentors I had during my journeys.

Table of Contents

Preface

A storm is brewing outside, and it's a perfect metaphor for today's workshop. I'm speaking to a room filled with business leaders, technologists, and innovators who seek my outside-in perspective on transforming their business. Some are eager to evolve their organization's digital strategies, while others are apprehensive about changing what works today.

I'm readying the group for the day's first collaborative exercise, and I need everyone's full participation. I'm on my toes, raise my hands, and shift my gaze from one leader to the next to get people's attention as I explain today's and tomorrow's realities. Outside the conference room windows, I see the sky darken.

"I know you're working harder and faster than you've ever had to before, and your teams are out of breath," I tell them. "You have the right instincts because the transformation initiatives you're leading are on a treadmill that must accelerate to remain competitive. What was emerging technology two years ago, for example, natural language processing, AR/VR experiences, and real-time data processing, is becoming mainstream.

"The pace of technology change is increasing, and you must reevaluate your digital strategy and priorities. Frequently. You will always be transforming, and your organization must establish transformational practices as essential core competencies."

I pause and look around the room. I need the message to sink in without me saying it. Today's innovations are great progress, but they will become tomorrow's legacy systems. They will need to transform again and again. The treadmill doesn't slow down, but the organization can build up the endurance to run marathons. That's why this next point is so important.

"And your business will need more transformation leaders—what I call Digital Trailblazers—who can lead teams, evolve sustainable ways of working, develop technologies as competitive differentiators, and deliver business outcomes."

I look around the room and wait till all eyes are on me, then ask everyone a fundamental question.

"Are you ready to take on a digital transformation leadership role in your organization?"

That's the question and advice I share with product management, technology, and data leaders aspiring for greater responsibilities. You must learn to become a Digital Trailblazer. You must develop the skills to define a vision for digital transformation initiatives, lead agile teams, and evolve technology practices. I wrote this book for you to read my stories and learn the lessons that can grow your responsibilities, guide you through handling a transformation's challenges, and accelerate your career.

You've probably already had roles in digital transformations. Maybe you're a product manager and launched digital products, improved customer experiences, and delivered financial results. Perhaps you're a software developer, DevOps engineer, work in IT Ops, or are an architect who has modernized application architectures, automated workflows, or developed customer-facing applications. You may also work in data science, DataOps, or data governance, paving your company's data-driven journey. Or maybe you're a business leader committed to learning the more technical aspects of digital transformation.

This book serves as a guide to help you expand your skills and confidence in leading transformation initiatives. Through my collection of stories and lessons, you will see some challenging scenarios unfold without waiting for them to happen to you. In writing this book, I intend to help current and future leaders accelerate their journeys in technology leadership by giving candid accounts of how I handled transformation's challenges.

Product management, agile development, DevOps, and proactive data governance are digital transformation's building blocks. From those starting points, I hope you want to expand your skills and confidence in leading transformation initiatives that will help evolve the business model, target new markets, and deliver innovations. But it's not easy, and program managers and scrum masters must help teams collaborate, improve productivity, and deliver quality results.

I hope you are one of these high-potential leaders—and maybe you've already experienced some of the challenges, such as addressing technical debt, getting buy-in for data governance programs, or winning over detractors who hold on to the status quo. I'll be sharing insights around these and many other transformation leadership issues in this book.

Or maybe you're already on your leadership journey. You oversee transformation initiatives and guide multidisciplinary teams but maybe have little experience presenting to the board or the strategic leadership team. When should you create a blow-up or shock-and-awe moment to help teams see opportunities from new perspectives? How do you balance innovation, self-organizing practices, and standards to evolve your organization's way of working?

You also might be a director, a vice president, or a senior vice president and striving to one day become a CIO, CTO, or CDO (both digital and data).

When I meet people like you in any of these roles, you tell me how hard it is to just keep up with the technical skills required to be employable. And now, you're faced with new leadership challenges that are hard to learn without direct experience.

Let me share how I got here and how my journey can help you accelerate your path to becoming a Digital Trailblazer.

After studying machine learning and medical image processing in graduate school at The University of Arizona, I take a job as a software engineer at a biotechnology company where I develop algorithms to compare genetic samples. I learn the basics of developing commercial software applications, but the Wild West of building internet applications at a startup lures me to New York City, and less than two years out of graduate school, I join this media startup as their director of software development. Back then, working at an "internet company" and joining a startup is a nontraditional career path, but I have a history of taking the off-beaten trail and just see an adventure into unchartered territory.

The founding CTO hires me to build a natural language processing engine to enable our search algorithms. We are having dinner where he tells me I won the job, then asks me if I want to hire the ex–Russian signal processing expert now cab driver sitting next to us. I do, and we go on to create the foundations of our software development lifecycle. But after a couple of years, several strategic investors come in and refinance the company. The founding CTO goes on to other opportunities, and I land the CTO job.

It's the late 1990s. I'm in my twenties and promoted to CTO of a growing and promising startup. It's still fairly uncommon to see young CTOs, but the internet is evolving from a technology tool to a disruptive business model, and it's my generation that's driving the innovation.

And now, I am the most senior technical leader in my startup and manage an office network, a colocated data center, and dozens of tech vendors. It isn't the first time I have had to figure out new technologies independently, and I am building confidence to manage the new responsibilities.

I report to the CEO and attend our board of directors meetings with highly seasoned executives. I must prove the organizational model and execute my strategy to grow the team, mature the development process, and scale the infrastructure. My responsibilities require creating multiple strategic plans and selling my strategies to colleagues, the CEO, and the board.

I'm young, cocky, and overly confident. Figuring out the technologies isn't the hard part. Managing the team has its challenges, but we're a small organization aligned to our vision. Partnering with other leaders and driving through the murky waters of growth, well, let's just say I have many hard lessons learned from the experience—and that's part of what I want to share with you.

Less than ten years later, I pivot my career and leave the world of being a CTO in startups to one leading transformation as a business unit CIO in an enterprise. Again, I am ahead of the times, a young CIO in his thirties, and entrusted to lead an organization through significant change. I go on to be a transformational CIO in three companies over the next ten years.

I had a front-row seat to industry transformation and disruption. I watched newspapers, magazines, banks, financial service companies, nonprofits, commercial construction contractors, manufacturers, tech startups, SaaS companies, universities, and other companies struggle with transformation.

I established several best practices during this period and started blogging in 2005 to share my insights. Today, I have over 800 articles published on leading publications for IT leaders, including CIO.com, InfoWorld, The Enterpriser's Project, and my blog, *Social, Agile, and Transformation*.

That led to my first book, *Driving Digital: The Leader's Guide to Transformation Through Technology*, an Amazon bestseller. This book shares detailed best practices on agile continuous planning, product management, citizen data science, and others instrumental to the transformations I led. You might have seen me keynote, speak, or moderate panels at one of the 150 events from 2017 through 2021.

I highlight several foundational practices in my roles as a CTO in startups, a CIO in transforming businesses, and now as CEO of StarCIO, a digital transformation consulting and services company.

Many organizational leaders understand top-down strategic planning. But transformation also requires "bottom-up" practices, knowledge sharing, innovation, and transformation management. Businesses need the ideas, innovations, and process improvements from everyone in the company to best adjust to market changes, excel with customer experience, and digitally enable the workforce. The essential transformational practices include continuous agile planning, DevOps, product management, becoming a data-driven organization, citizen technology capabilities, proactive data governance, hyperautomation, and culture transformation.

As I collaborate with more digital and technology leaders, it becomes apparent that as transformation grows in importance across more industries and businesses of all sizes, it is critically vital to groom new transformational leaders. My most vocal supporters are not just the CIOs, CTOs, CDOs, and product leaders but their direct reports and secondary reports. These leaders are challenged by the growing technical skill gaps, which are significant, but they also struggle with the leadership skill challenges and forming diverse leadership teams.

Let's consider how much has changed just over the last five years.

Five years ago, data scientists could get away with being data visualization experts and later learn fundamental statistics and analytics. Today, you need expertise in DataOps, predictive analytics, and machine learning. Organizations look for "full stack" software developers who can build applications from the front-end user experience all the way through their underlying database architectures. Operational engineers must not only keep the applications, databases, and networks reliable, secure, and high performing, business leaders expect you to automate most of the infrastructure and deployment processes. Product managers can no longer just prioritize backlogs, and you must learn how to research markets, capture customer needs, develop visions, and sell business cases.

But nowhere in these expectations, development needs, and mentoring is an easy path to learn transformation leadership skills. Classroom learning isn't sufficient to help you lead diverse, agile, and innovative teams that drive transformation management and change the culture. You will encounter challenges educating colleagues on leveraging data, intuition, and listening to others when making decisions. And when detractors emerge to transformation programs, how do you sell them on the vision, quell their fears, and win over their support?

And while organizations of all sizes often offer their own leadership programs—or funding for their people to learn leadership skills through conferences and classes—there's only so much you can cover. In fact, my company, StarCIO, has workshops in digital transformation, agile planning, DevOps culture, data-driven methods, and product management practices, and we help teams select a limited number of learning sessions to cover in any one workshop. But there are only so many stories that I can tell during a keynote, course, or workshop.

That's how the idea for this book came to me. I wanted to tell more of the stories behind my first book, *Driving Digital*. It's through stories that many of us learn and remember our best lessons. It is why Steve Jobs' presentations are so memorable and why TED Talks are so successful. Before we can learn from our actions, decisions, and mistakes, we learn largely through other people's experiences.

That's what I hope to do here. Each chapter is a mashup of stories from my career, and I jump back and forth in time to expose some of the key learning moments that remain relevant today. The names and characteristics have been changed, some events have been compressed, and some dialogue has been recreated. There are times when I am critical of people's behaviors and approaches—including my own. I mean no harm or disrespect to anyone and hope all will read this in the spirit of learning and improving.

Product, technology, data, and digital leadership are complex responsibilities requiring many skills, practices, and diverse perspectives. It's tough, fast, and can be unforgiving, and that's why I share some of these stories. At the end of each chapter, I conclude and share the underlying leadership lessons, and there are more than fifty transformation leadership lessons published in this book. You can also find more information about these lessons at https://www.starcio.com/digital-trailblazer/intro.

You will learn transformation leadership through your own experiences and hard lessons, but these stories and lessons will help you accelerate the journey to digital trailblazer.

Disclaimer

This book reflects the author's present recollections of experiences over time. Names and characteristics have been changed, some events have been compressed, and some dialogue has been recreated.

I'm not a frequent f-bomber, and I don't use profanity in the course of business. But I sometimes use this language in my head when I see or feel something terribly wrong, and the younger me was more emotionally reactive to my environment. Since this book has many of my personal stories, and I share them as I felt them at the time, you'll see me use some colorful language at times.

Acknowledgments

I went outside of my comfort zone in this second book, and it's been a three-year-long journey. A very special thanks to Ginny Hamilton, the "Chief Feedback Officer," editor, reader advocate, and inspiration over the last six weeks of finalizing the book. With her guidance, ten chapters of stories and lessons were transformed into the book you have today, and I hope you enjoyed and walked away with many lessons learned. Thank you, Ginny!

I want to thank the full cast of characters in *Digital Trailblazer,* including Adam, Alexandra, Alice, Bart, Bill, Blake, Boswell, Brian, Catherine, Charles, Clark, Craig, Daniel, Delores, Donna, Donovan, Elanor, Gracie, Henry, Hesam, Ilan, Jasper, Jerry, Johnathan, Jonah, Josh, Karina, Ken, Nagesh, Leo, Matt, Michele, Matthew, Niles, Pavel, Patrick, Phil, Pietra, Pranav, Ronan, Theresa, Warren, Wes, and Yasmine. Also thanks to many others whom I reference in the book without naming.

Thank you to everyone who contributed endorsements and quotes in the book: Ross Abbott, Kirk Borne, Jason T Burns, Martin Davis, Jonathan Feldman, Jay Ferro, Paige Francis, Angelic Gibson, Jason "JJ" James, Philippe Johnston, Anthony Juliano, Adriana Karaboutis, Helen Wetherley Knight, Eric Knorr, Shelly Kramer, Michael Krigsman, Larry Lieberman, Jo Peterson, Dan Roberts, Kathleen Greenler Sexton, Myles Suer, Kim Wales, R "Ray" Wang, and Robin Yeman.

A big thanks to several people who reviewed early versions of the book's chapters, including Michelle Fagan, Deb Gildersleeve, Roger

Neal, Wendi White, and Joanna Young. Specials thanks to Sheck Cho, Leslye Davidson, Dan Roberts. Thank you to everyone at Wiley who worked on *Digital Trailblazer*.

I've had a great team of people to collaborate and grow with at StarCIO and want to thank Jay Cohen, Ginny Hamilton, David Morgen, Mitch Schussler Anshul Goyal, Sandy McCarron, and Liz Martinez. A very special thanks to StarCIO partners, customers, and supporters. Thank you to my friends at CIO.com, #CIOChat, Foundry, #IDGTech-Talk, InfoWorld, SINC USA, nGage, CXOTalk, TechTarget, The Enterpriser's Project, DevOps.com, and Leadtail.

Thank you to all my mentors, including Adriaan Bouten, Linda Brennan, Brendan Burns, Jason T Burns, Bill Castagne, Jay Cohen, Keith Fox, Ginny Hamilton, Carter Hostelley, Sandra McCarron, Dean Kelly, Larry Lieberman, Alexa McCloughan, Mariella Montoni, and Roger Neal. Thank you to my health coaches, Brian Hollander and Nancy Regan, and to my pandemic support group, Helen Wetherley Knight and Jonathan Landon,

Most important, I also want to thank my family trailblazers: Michele, Ronan, Pietra, Jasper, Mom, Dad, Pam, Frank, Danny, Lisa, Allison, Langdon, Matthew, Brendan, Ilana, Jonathan, and Nova.

Chapter 1

Transitioning to Leadership: What's a Cookie?

"Fuck."

That's exactly how I feel today. I am the first one in the office, and getting in early before the crack of dawn is not something I do very often. The last software build failed, and I have to get it working before everyone gets here. Especially before Jessie gets in. Because once Jessie sees the problem du jour, well then, my day is freaking *over*.

I make a small change and start another software build. It's dark outside. Way too early to be here. I can't believe I started working on this problem before my first cup. But now, I have ten minutes to wait for this build to compile the code into runnable software. Plenty of time to fill the carafe and get a coffee drip going. Enough time to consider what music I will select to keep me inspired and moving. Maybe today it will be the new System of a Down CD because, well, I'm just in that head-banging mood. If I was more at peace, I might put on Pavarotti. Anything to help my concentration.

I think about how the rest of this difficult day will go. There's the 10 a.m. management meeting that I loathe attending, and I ponder how to best prepare for it. What should I report to the other leaders? Should I start with the root cause of the last issue—like I really have a freaking clue what it is—or should I focus on the status of this crazy important, better-hit-the-deadline, our-business-depends-on-it project that we're all working on?

What will the managers ask me this time? Probably the same things they always do. They almost always start by asking, "How's it going?" Then they get bolder. "When will the application be completed? Does it run fast enough? Do we have to buy more hardware? Did you hire another developer yet?"

I feel like the lead physician at a hospital that's in the middle of experimental surgery. No one quite understands what's going on, but they know the procedure is important. From their vantage point, if the tech works, then they can go back to their day-to-day business. So, the last thing I want is to make them nervous. That'll disrupt the meeting and get them solutioning. If they panic, they'll run around the office like chickens with their heads cut off, barking orders at everyone. That's the last thing I want.

This is how leadership meetings run every week, and as the coffee drips, I contemplate what happens to me during them. Why is it that everyone's eyes are always on me? And why is it that we're always talking about the underlying technology? Why aren't we talking about what we're selling, what customers we're winning, and why we're losing business? Why aren't we going over the financials to be ready for the next board meeting? What the hell are we getting out of all the money we're spending on marketing?

Most important, how do I answer questions that appease my colleagues? I can't shut down their questions, or they'll claim that I am not a team player and am being technically incomprehensible. But if I give them too much information, they'll dig deeper into the technical details. Their objective is to deflect the conversation off their areas of responsibility and onto another business area. Tech has a target on its back, and me being the youngest in the room makes that target sizeable and easy to hit.

Jessie is sure to zing me on something. She asks for twelve things. I commit to seven and deliver nine. Nope, that's not fucking good enough. She must deal with the salespeople who want the missing three that she should have said no to in the first place. She has incredible skills at navigating these meetings and sits next to the most influential leaders. She only shares the good news, and with such elaborate flare, it gets everyone raving. It's not just what she asks; it's when and how she goes about it. She picks the perfect time and gets everyone's attention. Her question missile is laser-guided and almost always aims at me, and I stand no chance. Especially when there are operational issues.

I'm too young, inexperienced, and not very confident. The 27-year-old chief technology officer (CTO) working at a pre-internet-bubble startup is easy pickings when the business isn't moving fast enough. And when the company is doing well, and we're signing up new customers, well then I'm the last in line to get a shitty bonus. Cheers for Sales! Marketing are heroes!

And where is Tech?

Where are the high-fives for the developers, testers, and systems engineers for a job well done? How come no one applauds the product managers for picking the right features or cheers the data analysts who quickly produced the new reporting dashboard?

I get it. The way they see it, there's always something broken, something slow, or something new that at least one executive team member expects. After a release, it always feels like we're out of the kitchen and into the fire.

And then that's when I hear that happy, whirling, swishing sound, bringing me back to the here and now.

Fabulous, the coffee is ready, and I pour myself a mug. Black. Just like in engineering school when we were studying for midterms. Some of those classes are still useful. The statistics, the physics, and the signal processing classes, but there was no way that the antenna theory class would ever be valuable. Why the hell was that a required class? Waste of my damn time. A communications, writing, or marketing class would have been far more useful.

3

Transitioning to Leadership: What's a Cookie?

I walk back to my desk, thinking about some of the lessons learned from my grad school days through today: the mistakes I made in pursuing overly elegant technology solutions, debating what should go into minimally viable products (MVPs), the collaboration skills needed to lead agile teams, and how to understand the business through its data. These are lessons people driving transformation need to know, learn, and adapt to their circumstances. And maybe, one day, I will share them with my teams and teach other leaders.

I look at my screen; thank goodness the build is done. Whenever I make a code change, I have to build the software to test it. It's one of those things Jessie and the others don't understand about developing software. I don't just code. I also have to deal with all the infrastructure that makes software run. It's the late 1990s, and as the internet is starting to boom, this means managing the complexities of running a data center, adding servers, and scaling networks. It requires the webserver software and the integration necessary to run the website. And on this day, it means packaging the software to integrate, deploy, and run within the server. This all takes time away from developing the bells and whistles that Jessie and others have on their mile-long list of requirements.

Today I'm trying to debug this nasty defect. How is it that two users can log into the same account, one being the real account owner and the second one getting access illegitimately? It's not their fault, and I've already determined that this isn't someone trying to hack into our login system. This is a software defect, and I have to figure out how two different people using two separate computers and browsers can access the same account.

I think about the problem from a technical perspective. We use cookies to remember the user, and that's the first thing the application checks to match a user to their account. Cookies. Who the hell came up with that term anyway?

I'm trying to focus on the problem, but thinking of the meaning of browser cookies brings me back to another time and place.

Six months ago, I was sitting in one of my first board meetings at the Conde Nast building in New York City. It's brand-new on 42nd Street in the heart of Manhattan, and an architectural standout, especially for Times Square. Just hours earlier, we meet Craig for breakfast in their expansive cafeteria that could live up to *Gourmet* magazine's high standards. Craig is an important board member and a member of "the family" that controls one of the largest media empires. I'm with our chief executive officer (CEO) previewing the primary news and decision points, and we hope Craig will help steer the discussions.

After breakfast, we ride the elevator to the top floor and start our first board meeting after the new round of investment. I'm sitting at the biggest freaking table I have ever seen. There's no way to reach across this table to shake someone's hand, and the room reminds me of the boardroom scene in the movie *Gung Ho*. In the movie, Michael Keaton's character asks his Japanese hosts, "Did you decorate this place yourself?" It's meant to be an ice-breaker, but it doesn't connect with the board and winds up being a disastrous way to start the presentation. I fully expect Brian, our CEO, who is sitting a few seats over from me, to pull out his death stare if I say the wrong thing.

We're working with hundreds of media websites. They publish newspapers, and we help bring their content and data to life on the World Wide Web. It's 1999, and the boom of the internet is in high gear—with nearly 250 million people logging onto it.[1] Napster is growing in popularity, eBay has gone public, and Craigslist incorporates as a for-profit business.

Our board, owners of thousands of newspapers, are antsy but not worried. They have been around a long time and weathered many storms. This internet thing is just another phase for them. Remember Compuserve and Prodigy? Blips in technology history. People won't abandon their local newspapers and the trust built up from reading the paper daily and weekly over generations.

So they thought.

Daniel, our ad sales leader, is explaining his new product concept, describing how we're going to put ads across all the newspaper websites. Everyone on the board is looking at him like he's Marie Curie trying to explain how she discovered polonium and radium.

The obvious question should have been, "How are you going to get those ads on *our* websites?" But no, one of our more technical board members is one step ahead and asks, "How are you going to track impressions and click-throughs across all of our websites?" To which Daniel replies, "Oh, we'll cookie the user."

That draws a moment of silence, and then Craig, who is usually quiet during these meetings, lifts his head from looking at the printout of the board presentation and asks, "What's a cookie?"

Instinctively, they all know to look at me. It's the executive radar that pops up when someone talks tech jargon at a business meeting.

I should point out that if I, as the chief technology officer (CTO), had used some form of tech terminology, then their radar would have triggered a devastating verbal missile attack. No one wants the CTO to go deep into technobabble or use overly complex buzzwords that would never appear in a business magazine. If I do such a thing, Brian would wait until after the meeting and give me more than an earful for dropping jargon and making the technology sound unnecessarily complicated.

Even worse is when a board member raises the issue with the CEO about having a CTO who can't talk "the language of the business." One missed word can launch an entire cycle of having to defend yourself from the barrage of MBA-fired warheads who want to monopolize the jargon and make sure it's their language that dominates the conversation.

Okay, so all eyes are on me. Now, if I were a little more experienced, then I probably wouldn't have been panic-stricken inside. My first "real" board meeting, and I'm asked an off-script question. And not just any question, but a somewhat technical one that is hard to answer without knowing how web browsers and web servers work. Eyes begin to look in my direction as I catch a glaze from Brian sending me a clear message.

He is saying, "This one is on you. And you better not fuck it up."

So, should I respond with the technically correct answer? "A cookie is a key value that a developer can store in the web browser's cache by utilizing the set-cookie header and then retrieving it on subsequent page views. Since web browsers are stateless clients that interface with a web server, setting a cookie is an easy way to retain the state from one page view to another and is commonly used to store user and session identifiers. The browser is smart enough to send cookies only from the domain of the web page the user is viewing."

Yeah, that would have been the right technical answer. In fact, I think the technology team back at the office would have been proud of how I explained a technical concept in such efficient language. But if I answered the question that way to the board of directors, I would be shown the virtual elevator down to the CTO morgue. That is where geeks with ties go when they can't explain technical concepts in simple language.

Here's how I actually answer the question: "A cookie is an identifier. We can track the ad across multiple websites by setting this identifier and having it sent back to our website even if the ad is on your newspaper's website."

I get a look back from Craig. It probably lasts for only three seconds, but it feels like an eternity. In the corner of my eye, I can see Brian's "oh, shit" face, fearing that we're going to take the meeting off the rails. Two days earlier, when we rehearsed the presentation at the senior leadership team meeting, he kept repeating to us, "We need to get these guys on board," and yes, the board was all men. And then he reminded us how dumbed-down we must make everything.

Craig opens his mouth and looks like he is getting ready to fire off another question. But his head turns, and he looks back over at Daniel to ask, "How do we make money doing this?" It's the right question and why I respect Craig.

Most important, I pass my first test.

And this is how I know the coffee I'm drinking today hasn't set in. I'm moving from one thought to the next. This problem is hard enough, and I need a clue before we meet this morning.

Two users. Two browsers. One cookie ID. How is that possible? How can a user get someone else's cookie ID in their own web browser? I'm not a security expert, and there are some fears that hackers may have infiltrated the website, especially after multiple users report this issue. And those users, Joe and Barbara, are not happy. In the early days of the consumer internet, most web surfers are unaware of privacy and security concerns when registering on websites. All Joe knows is he came back to his newspaper's website, and now the site thinks he is Barbara.

It was a crazy business idea back then, but not stupid enough. We are a Software-as-a-Service (SaaS) company before the invention of that acronym. Back then, the industry called it an Application Service Provider or ASP.

Our mission is to help newspapers go from print to digital, from paper to screens, from scanning paper to searching. We aim to help them save the stronghold newspapers have on classified advertisements. For the first time, newspapers face formidable competition from Craigslist, eBay, Monster.com, Cars.com, and other websites trying to chip away at their multi-billion-dollar business model. Newspapers can build a website, but they can't easily construct a search engine. Some can send emails to their subscribers, but they can't engineer an intelligent "AdHound" that creates personalized emails based on the cars, jobs, or homes people seek.

So, we build and host it for them. One multi-tenant web architecture hosts newspaper classified ads from thousands of newspapers. It is advanced for that time—a C++ application running off a multi-threaded web server with a Network Service Access Point Identifier (NSAPI) interface. We develop a natural language processing (NLP) engine to pull search terms from classified ads. It's helpful for real estate ads: We can find "BR" and then look one word earlier to see that it is a three-bedroom apartment. For car ads, we can locate Mustang in the ad's text and infer it is a Ford. It is a rudimentary natural language processor that leverages a word tokenizer, a dictionary of terms, and a rules engine. Back then, few people are trying to do this kind of knowledge extraction. *Artificial intelligence* is decades away from being a hyped buzzword that generates multi-million-dollar venture capital funding.

We feed the metadata in key-value pairs along with the text to a search index from AltaVista, and that was the back end to our website—all hosted on DEC AlphaServer 4100s. Of course, you can do key-value pair searching today with Lucene, Solr, and MongoDB, but this was all innovation back then. Most other CTOs at the time were still querying databases with SQL and keyword searching using *like* clauses.

We develop a proprietary tagging and configuration language to produce hundreds of newspaper sites, all with different designs and content configurations. Web page templates are preprocessed server-side and merged with content delivered from the search engine. The application then applies configuration settings specific to each newspaper before sending a completed web page back to the user.

An AdHound is just a simple agent. The user searches and registers the query with a name, and then AdHound emails them new results every day. If you are looking for a red 1969 Mustang under $10,000, you can save this query and only get results when AdHound finds matches.

Only somehow, Joe Catolover and Barbara Kleinersha have two registrations with the same cookie ID. This means one of two things. One possibility is that someone went into the database and changed the cookie ID for one of these users. While this was indeed possible, it would fail to explain how that cookie ID ends up in their browsers.

So, I pursue the second possibility. Could the system generate the same cookie ID for two different users?

The application that runs user registration uses Common Gateway Interface (CGI), a protocol that allows the webserver to execute a program, pass parameters to it, capture the results, and shut the program down. It isn't a technically efficient process by any means. Still, it is early in the internet days and an easy way to plug proprietary applications into webservers without coding complicated integrations.

The cookie ID it generates aggregates several parameters, including a code for the website the user is on and a time signature. That's all the programmer had instrumented in this "unique" ID. So, for two users to have the same identifier, they would have to register simultaneously on the same newspaper site. The server measures time in microseconds, and it seems like a longshot that two users on the same website would hit "submit" at the same time within 0.000001 seconds of each other.

I keep digging into the detailed manuals on C++, the standard template library, and DEC UNIX to make sure my assumptions are correct.

And there it is. Holy crap, this can't be right. It turns out that when the server is under heavy load, it doesn't update its clock every microsecond. What? Seriously? The mighty DEC AlphaServer doesn't have enough juice to update its clock? I had to simulate this and see if it was possible. So, I bombard my test web server with thousands of user registration requests and inspect the test database to see what unique registration IDs exist.

```
Select site_id, cookie_id, count(*) as count from t_userRegistrations  group
by site_id,  cookie_id having count > 1;
```

The database spits out:

```
news_nyy, 1098165, nyy_102102787, 2
news_njy, 1098213, njy_102102992, 2
```

The query results show two examples, one from news_nyy and the other from news_njy, that have duplicate IDs created: two for nyy_102102787 and two for njy_102102992.

And there it is. It is possible. Crap, a small oversight by the developer, and it is possible to compromise a user's account.

The only good news here is that we find the cause and have a way to fix it relatively quickly. Since the user registration application is a CGI, we can append a UNIX process ID and a random number to the cookies generated. We then encrypt the whole string, ensuring that the system will never generate two IDs again, even if the system is overloaded. Nowadays, this technique is known as salting.

We deploy this fix and then null the cookie IDs for the handful of affected users. The change creates a small annoyance, forcing them to log in and reset their password, resulting in the system generating a new and more secure cookie ID.

Coding is relatively easy compared to debugging. Debugging is always challenging but even more complex when issues arise from the impacts of load or volumes of disparate data. Developers quickly code and complete releases when trying to get functionality out the door. They can easily miss key details, especially when they make what appear to be reasonable assumptions about how the underlying systems perform. In this case, the developer assumed that requesting a time signature to the nearest microsecond would be sufficient to generate a unique ID.

I know for a fact that this developer didn't have the means to test this under load. Load testing tools didn't really exist then, and we launched the application when there was relatively low traffic across our websites. It would have taken much forward-thinking to decide to load test and then identify the duplicate identifiers.

> Being a CTO in a growing startup keeps you in the proverbial weeds where you have to dive into code, configuration, and data to understand how things work. It's a swamp, actually. And every time you feel ready to climb out to see the forest from the trees, something crazy and unexpected happens, and today's fire sucks you back into rapid problem-solving. But knowing your way through the weeds is a critical skill for a Digital Trailblazer.

I'm always going in and out of the swamp. I want to see the mess, then get a drone's view of the forest. If you can fly the drone in the sky, operate the airboat across the swamp, and pull out the machete to slash through the weeds, then that's the starting point of some of the transformational tools you need today. But it's just the start. Trust me.

Transformative Leadership Requires Working In and Out of the Weeds

It's roughly ten years later, and I'm at a construction industry conference moderating a panel of chief information officers (CIOs). I am the CIO of a media and analytics company that serves commercial general and subcontractors and building product manufacturers. I join the leadership team with Engineering News Record (ENR) editors who established this technology conference.

ENR is a premier media institution that published its first issue in April 1917.[2] Every year, this magazine hosts a black-tie awards dinner for leaders in the industry, and executives work hard to be on its top lists or win the Award of Excellence for a top construction project.

This conference is all about the technology construction companies use in the field and back office. There's a mix of emerging use cases showcasing augmented reality/virtual reality (AR/VR) technologies to aid architects during building, lidar for capturing accurate measurements during construction, and other field technologies to improve the productivity and safety of construction workers.

The conference committee agrees to let me moderate a panel of premier construction industry CIOs. Even though I was on the committee that founded this event, it did require some convincing that CIOs belonged on the agenda and that I should interview them. I then take one step further and invite these CIOs to a post-conference council to discuss technical challenges and opportunities. Never mind that I've never formed an executive council and that this is only the second time that I am moderating a panel at a big conference with hundreds of people attending. No worries. I'll get through it.

The panel kicks off fine. I ask questions about CIO priorities. What risks keep them up at night? What new technologies excite them? How do they work with their construction project managers on selecting technologies? It's all going well. Some ups and downs, but the audience looks engaged.

I then ask what I thought should be a simple question.

"So, when do you guys roll up the sleeves and get into the weeds working with project managers, forepersons, or your technology staff?"

Sadly, I call them *guys*. There are no women on the panel, and there are very few at the conference. Construction and technology are two industries poorly represented by minorities and women. I must change my language and thinking—a mental note I make to myself after recognizing my blunder.

My question is open-ended, and they could go anywhere with their responses. It was even on the list of questions I sent them to prepare for the conference, so it shouldn't have been a surprise.

But the room falls silent—dead silence for one, two, three seconds. Five seconds and it feels like an eternity. Since this conference, I've probably moderated hundreds of panels and never had a record-scratching moment like this one.

After a brief panic inside my gut, I pick my dignity off the floor and say, "Okay, no one's taking that one. Let's move on," and I get through the rest of the panel without complications.

But that moment sits with me for the rest of that conference and to this day.

How is it that these CIOs have no answer to this question? If I were on that panel, I'd have dozens of stories to tell. My challenge would be sticking to just one.

At the council meeting later that afternoon, I talk to the CIOs about their priorities. It's my second council meeting, and I come prepared with an agenda and a program. I have about ten CIOs attending and want to make sure their time is well spent. But as one CIO told me, "Isaac, you're working too hard. All we want to do is vent with our peers, without vendors around, and without repercussions."

So, I toss a softball question and let them loose. Some are upgrading their networks to handle their growing data needs better. A few are moving to the latest version of Microsoft Windows and Office while trying to get Microsoft SharePoint to work better for them. One is struggling to provide their legal teams with years of data for a lawsuit in discovery. I hear about one group experimenting with different security technologies that track who is coming on and off their job sites. We invest an hour hearing the complaints about difficult enterprise resource planning (ERP) upgrades, rogue IT in their organizations, and whether the chief financial officer (CFO) will increase their budgets.

It's 2010ish. No one is talking about *digital transformation* yet. It's not a trending keyword on Google, and the media isn't writing about it yet. Many of us have read Clayton Christensen's books on innovation, but much of the disruption is happening in select industries like media and with startups biting at the fringes. It's not happening in many other industries, including construction. Yet.

I'm irked by the discussion with the CIOs, and I'm still bothered by no one answering my question on getting in the weeds.

Years later, I put it all together.

At that time, these CIOs were only thinking about transitioning their organizations. Disruption hadn't hit the construction industry, and digital transformation was in its infancy. These CIOs were stepping up their games but hadn't gotten into the weeds on transforming—how their companies should use new technologies to drive business impacts, culture changes, growth, efficiencies, and quality differentiators. As one construction CIO recently told me, "All of us spent significant time in the job trailers talking to the workers and working hard to grow technology acceptance and then adoption. At the time, we were not relevant to boards, to Ops, only accounting."

Because transformation requires picking optimal moments to get your hands dirty, learn how the business runs today at detailed levels, and ask challenging questions, you want subject matter experts to see new opportunities to improve customer experiences or simplify operations and guide them on potential solutions.

What's happening in every industry will change who's on top and who's falling off the disruption cliff. Who are the new competitors likely to steal customers by offering winning experiences and capabilities? Where is the business using data to competitive advantage, and what data quality issues interfere with data-driven decision-making? Who should organizations partner with to deliver new customer-facing, digitally enabled capabilities? What customers are instrumental and can be early adopters to new business models? What other industries, companies, and leaders can people in your organizations learn from, get inspired by, and adopt their best practices?

These are outside-in examples of getting into the weeds and showcasing what's happening in the outside world that should influence the business's strategic direction. Sure, you can read about it or bring an analyst to the office to provide a digestible synopsis. But true intelligence and insights are best developed by getting out of the office and experiencing things for yourself.

The inside-out view is not about understanding code or improving your department's options. Ideally, you want to speak directly to customers and end-users to understand pain points, identify opportunities to deliver increased value, or discover ways to improve their experiences. You'll want to select stakeholders who are ready to partner on transforming the status quo and challenge how things work today. That partnership gives you the license to learn today's operations and pinpoint inefficient workflows, new ways to collaborate, and opportunities to hyperautomate—ways to use a combination of automation, apps, and machine learning to reduce manual tasks and enhance people's decision-making performance.

Getting into the *business* weeds can be very challenging for operational leaders. Sure, these technologists dive into the networks, systems, and applications hoping that business tools are operational, performing well, and secure. Some are risk-averse CIOs who track metrics like application uptime and the meantime to recover from production issues. These CIOs are more likely to be measured on cost savings and other operational metrics and are highly unlikely to think about customers, marketing, sales, and revenue growth.

There are analogies with product managers who focus on making incremental improvements to existing product lines. They manage mile-long backlogs of defects and small enhancements, mostly from internal stakeholders or the loudest customers complaining about their specific needs.

I also see similarities with data officers and the myriad data and analytic job roles that report to them. Yes, it's important to address data quality and iteratively improve existing reporting dashboards. It's also incredibly important to address gaps in data policies and security. But today's data and analytics officers must go beyond these basics. They should seek new datasets, consider partnerships, and review new platforms to increase the organization's intelligent capabilities.

Today's product, technology, data, and analytics leaders must aim much higher than the table stakes. Never heard that term? In casinos, it's the minimal bet to sit at the table and play a hand.

Playing to table stakes includes operational leaders who target minimal improvements in key performance indicators and are not taking many innovation bets. Table stake product managers act as administrative funnels and manage all the stakeholders' wish lists without looking at outside and inside opportunities to leapfrog the competition and drive business outcomes. The data officers chasing table stakes may be moving the data governance needle, but they aren't challenging the status quo or bringing in game-changing capabilities. The technology officers keep the lights on and manage risks but do not evaluate emerging technologies' threats and opportunities.

Table stake leaders don't challenge the organizational sacred cows that ground progress toward new business models. They expect that it's another leader's responsibility to drive culture change.

You have the skills to get into the weeds, and you likely have the adventurous spirit to thrash into the unknown. But it can be hard taking your first steps into the murky swamps of your industry or business.

Here's how I go hiking through the swamp and weeds, without a trail paving the path, but with a compass and other tools developed through past experiences.

I claw back to my experiences as a developer, engineer, data analyst, product owner, and architect as a means to get into the messy details buried in architecture, code, system, configuration, data models, and analytics. It's a skill all hands-on specialists must apply differently at the leadership level.

I use it to talk shop with the developers and better understand what's working well and where they face obstacles. I draw my intuitions on selecting technologies based on my skills to rapidly assess the differentiating qualities, ease of use, and scalability. And suppose there's a glaring implementation gap with no one stepping up to fill it. In that case, I just might roll up the sleeves and implement something in a low-code technology, data prep, or data visualization platform.

I talk to customers and go on sales calls. I attend the conferences that customers attend. I ask my peers in other industries what they are investing in and where they experience success.

I get my hands dirty with data. If no dashboard answers my questions, then I quickly develop one. I'll discuss proofs of concept (POCs) with a half dozen data scientist groups to learn and then place a bet to see what some can deliver.

I'll talk to technology partners, agencies, and freelancers. I'll write requests for proposals and sign on to do a handful of pilot projects.

At the same time, getting into the weeds means knowing which areas of the swamp to step into and which ones to avoid. You need to move fast and develop a plan to get out. Otherwise, you may just sink into the mud.

You don't want to be using these skills to stay in your comfort zone in operations, technology, product, or data. Worse case, this will mark you as a micromanager or someone not letting go of your previous responsibilities. You must venture into the uncharted swamps where you have little direct experience. However, you can still leverage your skills of asking questions, being detail-oriented, listening attentively, learning from diverse people, and making sense of conflicting data.

To grow beyond being a transitional leader and become transformational, you must know when to dive into the technical and operational details, and when to pull up, see the forest from the trees, and propose a vision and plan. You'll need to balance your time between building relationships with colleagues, exploring outside-in perspectives to strengthen these muscles, and selectively choosing when and how to use the inside-out muscles you've developed through your career.

And there are dangers in the swamp. Beyond just sinking, leadership snakes are lurking, ready to take a bite out of you for venturing into their territories. In fertile areas of the business, thick groves of institutional vines will slow down progress in efforts to maintain the status quo.

Then there are many existential threats, largely out of your control, that will either slow you down or require hard pivots. Pandemics, floods, and attacks are examples of events that drive externally driven transformations. It's not about having a plan for these situations. It's about developing the organizational structure, practices, and technologies to help organizations react, respond, and pivot appropriately.

Becoming a Digital Trailblazer and leading transformation is an incredible journey, but it's not for the faint of heart and mind. One day you'll feel like you are on top of the world, and the next, your colleagues will be coming at you with torches and pitchforks.

I hope you'll be more prepared through my stories. Enjoy the journey.

Digital Trailblazer Lessons

Transitioning to a Leadership Mindset

As you grow beyond your role from an individual contributor to leadership, you'll face new experiences and situations that require you to build on your knowledge and adapt to new environments.

Debugging applications, chasing customer issues, or fixing complex data problems are things you've done before. But solving them as a leader will require different approaches when you won't have all the background knowledge or the time to learn how everything works. You'll need to be leading and mentoring your staff while influencing colleagues. You may spend some time in the weeds to better understand a problem or opportunity, but don't get stuck in the mud trying to figure everything out. Delegate work to your teams so that they learn firsthand the problems and what types of solutions to recommend.

Other times, you'll be working in areas where you have no or limited experience and must figure out your role and voice in navigating them. Be brave, and don't let mistakes set you back. All leaders have their first experiences presenting to the board of directors, handling difficult situations while delivering presentations, and going on customer calls. Learn from them!

Enjoy the journey. Undoubtedly you will find mentors and remember learning experiences that will help develop your management and leadership skills. I hope the stories and lessons in this book also help mentor you as you blaze trails.

Here are five key takeaways from this chapter:

1. **Reflect on the skills that got you here won't get you there.** You don't become a leader by perfecting the technical, hands-on skills in areas where you are already an expert or just by building acumen on how to manage these functions. Your technical chops help you get by early in your career, but you will be a lot less hands-on as your responsibility increases. Your knowledge and experience will be critical when directing teams on problem-solving, using data to guide their investigations, and prioritizing where to focus their efforts. But leadership requires contributing to areas that you haven't worked in or directly managed by building skills, believing in yourself, and accepting that you'll make some mistakes. The primary skills you should develop include building trust with people who lead functional groups and asking questions to learn and challenge today's operating practices.
2. **Avoid solving technical problems with proprietary solutions.** Your prime objective as a digital leader is to solve customer and business problems. That's true for your team as well, and the more they develop proprietary solutions to technical challenges, the more you are creating a technical debt that will require ongoing support. When you have technical problems that aren't business capabilities, it's often better to seek out nonproprietary solutions through commercial technologies, open source platforms, partners, SaaS, web services, and low-code approaches. This is an especially important lesson for product managers who are quick to seek customized methods or data scientists who hard-code algorithms rather than leverage existing models. When you see developers

solving technical challenges, make sure you take the time to ask them if they've first explored third-party solutions.

3. **Recognize that communicating with the board and executives is a skill that requires practice.** There are some resounding do's and don'ts when communicating with board members and executive teammates. Do answer questions first, then follow up afterward with supporting facts, data, and essential details. Do come prepared to meetings with clear-cut summaries on the status of strategic initiatives because you don't know what board members will ask you. Don't go into technical details, and don't ramble when answering questions. Don't embarrass other executives or surprise them by sharing too much information. Share key decision points and supporting facts before the meeting. Never throw the CEO or your boss under the bus at a board meeting for not supporting your ideas or priorities. More on how to handle working with the strategic leadership team in Chapter 9, but the board meeting is not the place to air out these differences.

These are some of the basics. The art of navigating these meetings requires understanding their protocols and the personal motivations behind participants. Some call this politics, and to some extent, it is. But being successful in these environments is a skill you'll need if you want to grow as a leader.

4. **Understand the table stakes, then set broader goals.** Go ask your colleagues what they expect of you and your teams. When you do, I sincerely doubt that they'll tell you to keep doing what you're already doing, only better. Iteratively improving your operational metrics, increasing productivity, and addressing issues faster are all yesterday's table stakes. Today, business leaders expect innovation and new ways to

leverage technology and data, and more importantly, they seek Digital Trailblazers who will drive business outcomes. To get started, develop relationships with stakeholders who are likely supporters by scheduling one-on-one brainstorming sessions, sharing articles of mutual interest, or going to lunch when that's an option. Then partner on broader goals such as developing new digital experiences, integrating multiple data sources into real-time analytic systems, or creating a citizen development center of excellence.

5. **Step out of your comfort zone and broaden your perspective by seeking outside-in learning opportunities.** When a new opportunity or issue presents itself, the typical organizational response, especially from experienced leaders, is through their lenses of known knowns. As a Digital Trailblazer, your goal should be to share ideas and insights from outside your organization. You can learn from others by participating in social media, attending events outside of your industry, or learning from potential technology vendors and partners. When possible, visit customers and observe how they use your products and services. But make sure your learning is two-way and share your insights publicly with peers outside of your organization. You won't get important feedback if you keep your ideas to yourself, and Digital Trailblazers, including introverts, must extend their comfort zones to validate insights and ideas.

■ ■ ■

If you would like more specifics on these lessons learned and best practices, please visit https://www.starcio.com/digital-trailblazer/chapter-1.

Notes

1. Internetworldstats.com, 2021, "Internet Growth Statistics," https://www.internetworldstats.com/emarketing.htm.
2. Andrew G. Wright, Scott Lewis, Debra K. Rubin, and Scott Blair, "A Century of the ENR Banner," *Engineering News-Record,* April 13, 2017, https://www.enr.com/articles/41841-a-century-of-the-enr-banner.

Chapter 2

Dev: Technical Debt Is Now Your Problem

All developers know the feeling of sitting behind the screen and opening another developer's code. Or maybe you work in IT Ops and are reviewing a system administrator's automations, or a data scientist examining your colleague's machine learning model, or a product owner trying to understand a website's information architecture.

On the first inspection, it looks like a pile of spaghetti with three different sauces on top. One function calls another function that calls a third function of poorly structured code, with no consistent naming conventions, zero unit tests, and almost no documentation. You open five or more tabs to trace through the flow, reverse engineer the business logic, and hope that the modifications you need to make don't cause defects or introduce new issues.

Spaghetti code often happens when a developer, engineer, data scientist, or designer tries to get something done in too little time or with insufficient expertise. In some cases, it's written with zero care about what happens when the next person must review or improve on it. Other times, the code has been modified several times by different people, each imprinting their coding methods and style without cleaning up their predecessor's crafty work, again, often because management doesn't allocate sufficient time, direction, or priority to maintain and improve the code.

When you encounter spaghetti code, it's almost always because something of importance suddenly needs fixing. You rarely have the opportunity to clean up and refactor code. Usually, you come across it when you're under pressure to solve a problem. And that's why you do it. You ignore that pile of crappy code and come up with *your* way of implementing what is needed today.

You convince yourself that your code is better than your predecessor's. You will code with all the modernized components and standards, and it will take less time than pulling off an anthropological study of the coding fiasco that someone else left behind.

And in the back of your mind, you know that when your spaghetti code starts rotting and is causing heartache, there will be someone else responsible for cleaning up your mess.

Let me tell you about one colossal coding mess that I created. It was an Italian restaurant filled with bowls of spaghetti code held together with duct tape and Band-Aids. I must admit, it was a beast, and I never moved it entirely out of my responsibility for others to support it. It started with a simple problem that grew to layers of complexity over time. When it worked, you didn't know it even existed, but when it failed, it took a MacGyver to diagnose the problem and solve it before customers got angry.

Yeah, you've probably seen this before too.

Here I am, head of software development at the ripe age of 26 in the late 1990s. We have a simple problem of getting newspaper classified ads from their advertising systems into our search engine and available for users by dawn. That's when the paperboy—or papergirl—delivered the newspaper to doorsteps, so the assumption at that time was that readers who got their news from our website expected the same level of service.

But this wasn't easy. The newspaper's physical process of completing the print edition was developed and improved upon over decades. Sure, the editors can stop the printing presses for any number of reasons, but there are buttoned-down procedures to handle these disruptions. And although the printing press often supports multiple newspapers, there is a finite capacity limit given the sequential operations of printing and packaging newspapers, then loading them onto delivery trucks.

Our process for loading the digital version of the newspaper onto the website was still being worked out. More important, the process for publishing classified ads, a major source of revenue on a newspaper website, was our primary product and development challenge.

Gotta have those ads up. Must enable our users to search for that '73 red Mustang, the apartment with an amazing view of the park, the new job that pays better and is closer to home, or the house in a better school district. Our most dedicated users go treasure hunting in the "Buy, Sell, Trade" section, which eventually gets disrupted by eBay's and Craigslist's larger inventories and more convenient user experiences than hunting on individual newspaper websites.

But before eBay, Craigslist, Cars.com, HotJobs, and a slew of other websites decimate the newspaper classified ad business, I have the glorious job of running a software system that sucks all those ads in. Yeah, it is a file each newspaper FTP'ed to us almost every night on a schedule that matched the print newspaper's production workflow. Beyond that, it is a data dump in a format that looks nothing like a CSV, XML, or JSON output.

That's because it comes out of the newspaper's legacy ad systems, which do several things really well. They enable call centers of ad salespeople to sell classified ads on the phone. Yup, you used to call newspaper salespeople to tell them about that beautiful Camaro you want to sell. The ad reps would help you beautify a drab ad into something that someone was more likely to notice. Most important, this system calculates the advertisement's length in print ad lines and allows the ad salesperson to sell you on a whole bunch of add-on widgets. Want boldface in your ad? A small icon to catch people's attention? All that costs you extra and costs the newspaper next to nothing.

Now ask me, why did I care to work on this problem of searching classified ads? You're talented and can work on all sorts of different business opportunities? Why newspapers, and why classifieds?

When looking for problems to solve, consider your passions and interests. I loved newspapers and reading the Sunday paper. I still relish excellent journalism and am excited by any company that offers services, trust, and local community. But equally important, newspapers were ripe for digital disruption where the internet provided new product opportunities, better experiences, and greater efficiencies, all generating significant revenue that, ideally, leading newspapers would have used to invest in new digital business models.

Classified ads are cash cows for newspapers with $19.6 billion in newspaper revenue at its peak in 2000,[1] and their main costs are the call centers for selling the ads. The underlying systems are optimized to make the sales process efficient, produce the ads correctly, and calculate the cost accurately. Its last job is to spit out a file containing the classified ads with all the formatting required to print them on a newspaper page.

Until our website came along, the print systems were the only ones utilizing this output. And that's the file we get daily. It is a mix of funky codes signifying categories, line breaks, ad breaks, and other required formatting. Some of the markups are needed to place the ad in the right section and render it correctly in print, but most of the coding provides little metadata to make the ad searchable online, and a lot of it is totally useless for displaying the ad on a website.

Oh, yeah, and almost every newspaper's file is different. Sure, there are some similarities when they originate from the same underlying system. After that, the page formatting, the newspaper's categories, and the upselling ad enhancements are mostly different from paper to paper.

So with that as our starting point, here is how a pile of spaghetti code is created one application and script at a time.

My Recipe: Creating the Perfect Bowl of Spaghetti Code

First, we need an application to parse through all of these different file formats. So, the company's founding CTO, Ilan, whom I succeed two years later, develops a parser and calls it the "Universal Markup Conversion Utility." At least that's what I think it is called because we always referred to it by its acronym UMCU, pronounced *Uhm–Coo.* Ops uses this tool to extract the text, searchable categories, and other information from the classified ad files we receive. It has its own parsing language that, quite frankly, I never fully understand. But we have a small team in operations responsible for setting and maintaining these scripts, so it's out of sight, out of mind for me.

Back then, my brainchild is an NLP, an application that I appropriately name Babelfish. If you don't know what a Babel fish is, get yourself a copy of the Douglas Adams classic, *The Hitchhiker's Guide to the Galaxy*. It's a masterpiece that every engineer should read before acceptance into geekdom.

The Babelfish application opens one file at a time, reads one ad, parses out words, and looks to assign tags for searchable criteria. It makes it possible to extract key classified ad details such as makes and models of cars, job titles, number of bedrooms and bathrooms, and prices of anything. Apache Spark doesn't exist yet, and other parallel processing engines aren't affordable to startups. Sure, we experimented with parallelizing the jobs and even considered making the application multi-threaded. But our higher priority is always to improve the accuracy of the searchable tags extracted from these ads.

> **A critical skill for all engineers is to know when to invest more time and energy in solving a technical problem and when it's best to prioritize user experience. As you become a Digital Trailblazer, creating an agile, transparent, and collaborative culture ensures that people ask questions, challenge priorities, and invest time in the most pressing business, data, and technology opportunities.**

I'm super-proud of this creation called Babelfish, and in retrospect, it was short-sighted that we did not consider extending this into a product by itself. It is a legit NLP that we develop in the 1990s—15 years later and other NLP technologies I get the chance to use aren't all that much better. Yes, we had AI in the 1990s! Built on a fast, C++ engine and applied to data coming from thousands of customers. Why aren't we worth billions, damn it?

But I digress.

As good of a technology as this is, it is a very poorly architected application. You feed it dictionary and rule files that are all in proprietary file formats. It has minimal error checking and processes the data sequentially and at a snail's pace. While the rule engine is powerful, it isn't easy to learn, and it has no constructs to simplify implementations. As a result, if you develop a regular expression for parsing car prices out, you must copy and paste it into the real estate rules engine. It's not quite a mess, but it is poor architecture, bad coding, and technical debt.

So now we have a lot more contextual metadata about the ads and are ready to send this off to a search engine for indexing. We use the AltaVista search engine running on DEC AlphaServers, and we spend days visiting the DEC labs to test out these beasts, fast and cheaper than comparable servers from Sun Microsystems, but clunky to develop in DEC's flavor of UNIX.

We build another application that reads the file outputs from Babelfish and uses the AltaVista software development kit to create or update these index files. Of course, this is terribly inefficient, but this application is in its third version, having been used to work with other search technologies before we selected AltaVista. And, of course, we don't have time to better architect this with Babelfish's core capabilities. And keep in mind that APIs, service buses, and microservices don't exist yet. We're lucky to have web servers that allow us to plug in proprietary code and respond to web requests.

That's three applications: UMCU, Babelfish, and the Indexer. A fourth handles basic accounting, captures how many ads came from different newspapers, and stores this data in an Oracle database. Yup, that is a separate application.

But what makes this messy is less about the applications themselves and more about how we stitched them together. You see, every file must run through these applications, and we have limited hardware. We have cron jobs set up to run different applications on a cluster of servers. Don't know what a cron job is? It's what we use to schedule running applications before all the fancy schedulers and other utilities to kick off batch jobs.

Some of these cron jobs run independently, and others run on different servers. But they all leverage the same basic pattern:

1. Make sure no other instances of this application are running.
2. If there are new files, then run the application.
3. Check for errors when the application completes, and send out alerts if there is a failure.

This algorithm looks logical and simple, right? Its implementation is robust and should work without issues, right?

Well, this is far from reality, and plenty goes wrong.

There are many error conditions to check for and resolve. As we find one, we update the scripts to identify and resolve the issue.

If the application hangs and never completes for whatever reason, then the whole process grinds to a halt like someone jabbed an iron staff into the printing press. These disruptions happen more often than anyone wants to admit because the underlying infrastructure, databases we connect to, or services we rely on have their own faults. We develop more scripts to look for hung applications, stop them, and then restart them to resolve these issues.

As we grow customers, the processing time increases, and delays are even harder to recover from and get back on schedule. So, we add more hardware and more scripts to distribute the load across the infrastructure.

Load balancers distribute web traffic across multiple servers, but there aren't mainstream technologies to distribute batch processing applications. Maybe banks and insurance companies have them, but we're a startup and not seeking out these enterprise technologies. The scripts we develop to distribute the load need additional scripting to ensure robust operations, especially if one of the servers fails or is running slow.

The only thing going in our favor is that we instrument robust logging. Every application has a log, and every process, regardless of how many scripts are daisy-chained, also has a log. I become a wizard with UNIX tools like sed, awk, grep, and find to parse through these logs when seeking a root cause to a failed process.

By 2001, this jalopy is processing the classified ads from over 1,600 newspapers. We advance the scripting so much that it fails infrequently, but when it does, it's frustrating and challenging for the network operation center (NOC) to figure out the problem and the best route to solve it.

Once you write and support bad code, you attain a specialized skill set of detecting it in other people's code. Like any disease, you see the symptoms of it first. The application performing poorly or crashing could be an infrastructure or configuration issue, but I never rule out a coding problem as a possible root cause. When development teams are slow or even scared to make code changes, they're almost always inhibited by hard-to-read and trace code. Deployments that create production issues? You guessed it. It's probably bad code.

Bad code comes in many flavors, sizes, and impacts. And every time I walk into a new job or am involved in acquiring a company with proprietary software, I open my nostrils to sniff out where the code smells bad and what impact it's causing.

> It's almost always harder to fix someone else's code than to code something new, and management often only cares about solving the problem at hand. And when there are significant application performance or reliability issues, everyone wants the problem solved quickly and expects the team involved to address the root causes. But don't reward heroes who come in to save the day without transferring knowledge or contributing to more permanent solutions.

The technical debt, legacy systems, and half-developed integrations pile up. As people leave the company and others get reassigned to work on the next set of business priorities, fewer people are left behind with the knowledge to maintain these systems.

Knowledge transfer and enabling ongoing support may not be problems for you as a developer or technical lead. They might not be factors for you as a cloud or systems engineer when procedures are in place to recover from issues. Data scientists seek to move on to the next challenge, model, and insights. Product managers want to build products, deliver on customer expectations, deliver business impacts, and then move on to the next growth opportunity.

As you move up the ranks to director, vice president, or a CXO (anyone with a c-level title), you'll end up owning the mess. You'll struggle to find people to work on legacy systems, the time to address the root cause, and the budget to upgrade them. What's worse is, even with the best intentions, you're probably developing the next generation of legacy applications. You probably won't have robust standards in place or reinforced, and business leaders will be too demanding to release applications faster than the time required by developers and engineers to learn and implement best practices.

I am thinking back about those days when we were developing software without many of today's tools, platforms, and best practices. Today, your apps are either cloud-native or modernized to run in clouds and take advantage of the cloud's robust elastic infrastructure. Instead of just logging, there are standard practices for application observability. Instead of scripting and connecting applications with digital duct tape, you should leverage monitoring, automation, and AIOps platforms that analyze operational data in real-time, correlate alerts to incidents, and trigger automated responses. There are static and dynamic code analysis tools that can pinpoint bad code before developers check it into code repositories, and there is an oversupply of open source and commercial web services that developers and data scientists should leverage instead of developing technical solutions. Then there are low-code and no-code tools to create apps, application programming interfaces (APIs), integrations, dashboards, so you may be able to upgrade employee workflows and customer experiences without having to build code from scratch at all these days.

And yet, we develop more and will leave a new generation of technical debt and legacy systems behind, often because we try to do too much, too fast, and without sufficient investment in best practices.

Dramatize the Mess: Getting Leadership's Buy-In to Address Technical Debt

Let's time-warp to another point in my career and a new scenario where I confront a mess and must illustrate the magnitude of technical debt and spaghetti code to senior leaders.

This mess isn't my frankenarchitecture, but you can't pin the blame solely on the developers. After all, technology legacies start at the top and flow downstream into the implementations. The developer might have done all the coding, but they weren't the one layering on years of business rules and exceptions. The architect didn't create standards. The team leaders didn't conduct code reviews. And the managers didn't ensure knowledge sharing.

I'm sitting in a meeting one day with senior leaders of our transformation program, including the CEO. This company completely relies on technology. They collect data, process it, analyze it, and then sell analytics from it. Like most analytics companies I work with, they collect information on buyer behaviors and sell purchasing analytics back to the businesses that sell them products and services. Capturing data exists on the customer journey in every industry, especially retail, adtech, fintech, and other sectors where many interactions occur in digital modes. When the entire customer journey is digital, it's relatively easy to put hooks into the process and create A/B testing scenarios that collect data and use it to understand buying decisions. But when the journey is a mix of digital and physical steps, the data collection is more complex.

The CEO and the leadership team are frustrated because we had another data processing delay. It takes days to process data, and it requires weeks to deploy algorithm changes. These production and cycle times might have been acceptable five years ago, but today it's a barrier for this company.

One of the primary problems is that one developer manages this codebase. He's been at the company for a long time, and his peers like him for his business knowledge and understanding of the data. But relying on him frustrates the leadership group because there's no one else to step in and address issues.

Maybe they should have thought about the problem of code coverage while the developer was creating, improving, and growing the codebase. But chances are, the leadership team has little visibility on what the technology looks like underneath the hood. Maybe they need to.

My senses awake to the smell of bad code. I'm only at the company for a few months, and the developer has been with them for well over a decade. Data integrations, processing, and DataOps are the arteries of data and analytics companies, and the underlying technology supporting them is the beating heart. They deliver new and processed data across the organization for decision-making. When the arteries are clogged, it can slow the delivery of much-needed data to the brain, which we use to analyze, interpret, and identify insights. When the data arteries come to a halt, it's like a heart attack, and it starves a data-driven company, especially when analytics is the product.

The CEO looks over at me and says, "Isaac, we need to review the situation and come back with some recommendations."

I'm not surprised to be handed this assignment. But because no one addressed why one developer is maintaining the company's lifeblood, I already suspect I'm jumping into a messy code issue.

I schedule time with the developer to do a code walkthrough. It's mostly database stored procedures and reporting services that stitch together an end-to-end data flow. The developer never documented the codebase, and there are no high-level diagrams illustrating the data flows. Each procedure is a mix of data processing and computations and coded that way for performance considerations. Some of the code is in version control, but the rest is embedded in platforms that make it cumbersome to manage in external repositories. There's lots of code—certainly too much for me to understand in one sit-down. In fact, I'm still searching for how anyone would make their way through this codebase. It's like an overgrown jungle, but if you go in with a machete, you might actually hack something important.

I need more time to figure this one out, but I have to go back to the leadership team with an answer. So, I ask Phil to make a printout for me.

"A printout? That will take hundreds if not thousands of pages," he responds while giving me a you're-out-of-your-mind look. He thinks I'm going to read through all the code, and he also doesn't want to waste all that paper.

So, I let him know my intent, "You can print it double-sided in the smallest font available. I need to make a point. If it requires more than one package of paper, then you can stop."

I also hate the idea of wasting paper, but this is the most efficient way for me to make a point—dramatically. When asked for an update at the next meeting, I put the three-inch brick of paper down on the table. I pass it around and state emphatically that this will not be a simple problem to solve.

I look around the room for reaction and sense bewilderment. It's a shock-and-awe moment, and I hope the drama I created through this visual will convey the story and the magnitude of the problem. There's no anger or blame in their eyes—which is good—but I can sense that the weight of this problem (pun intended) is sinking in. Unfortunately, Digital Trailblazers are bound to hit legacy boulders in the road. The question becomes, which boulders should you focus on? You'll have to decide whether it's better to chip away at the problem or when it makes more sense to re-platform to a modernized solution, which often makes the most sense when the issue is business critical.

Over the next few months, we chip away at this problem. We put an extract, transform, and load (ETL) platform in for new data flows and refactor critical aspects of the legacy ones. But I never get to see this mess fully cleaned up.

Large codebases, managed by very few people, are one source of technical debt. I've seen 1.4 million lines of PERL code, HTML pages with tens of thousands of JavaScript code, stored procedures with thousands of lines of code, and databases with thousands of tables. I've seen a proprietary ERP developed as monolithic stored procedures running the back office of a large institution. Recently, I saw an organization with multiple service buses, each with multiple versions running production workloads.

So, while there is smelly code that needs fixing and technical debt that needs support, there are also what I call burning fires.

Burning fires take down the business. And not just once, often multiple times. Once the fire starts burning, a team assembles in a war room to determine root causes. Burning fires bring together people from the networks operations center, incident managers, and IT services management. If the fire is burning out of control, the war rooms may also require developers, testers, and business managers. Their collective work results in the problem being identified and resolved, but the fire is still smoldering. Soon, another fire flares up, and the team assembles again in another war room to put out a fire that's only slightly different than previous ones.

In this all-too-common scenario, management rarely gives the technology team sufficient time to come up with permanent fixes. It's a byproduct of how companies thought of technology as one-time capital investments and then left a small fraction of operational expenditure to support it. Today, we live in an SaaS world where customers expect ongoing technology improvements, and now it's up to Digital Trailblazers to budget and manage their technology investments to support it. Are you up for this challenge?

Bad Code in Modern Platforms: Still a Problem

Bad code doesn't just show up in legacy systems. It can easily appear in new code on modern platforms. Only, the stakes may be higher when bad code leads to operational issues that evolve into a business crisis.

I witness a code nightmare years later when an executive committee hires me to lead a digital transformation at a services company. They're eager to turn around a business model that collects data today only to report findings several months later. We have our work cut out for us, as every aspect of the business runs on processes and technologies requiring improvements and transformations.

But before I can move the organization into high transformational gear, there is a critical operational issue that needs addressing in their call centers.

It is a problem with several call centers that survey our clients' customers. You walk into the store, perform a transaction, and get a call from one of our agents to collect feedback on the experience. Our clients—ranging from big brands to small businesses—are all demanding, and their bonuses depend on the results. If the surveys aren't working properly, they aren't shy about letting us have it.

I inherit a set of technology and operations that definitely require improvements, but it isn't a complete disaster. The IT team manages hundreds of low-end desktops used by the agents, upgraded dialers that are the cornerstone to saving the company a ton of money, and the new enterprise survey platform that will bring the business to the digital age.

No one cares about how the technology is implemented or integrated. The executives care that they invested hundreds of thousands of dollars into it, and the surveys for our biggest clients aren't working. They care that the team can't figure out the problem. And they are furious that the client is calling our CEO and giving him an earful.

I feel like Al Pacino in the third Godfather movie when he says, "Just when I thought I was out, they pull me back in!" I'm freaking hired to transform the company, but I am now back in the trenches to solve an old-school performance problem.

I'm on the short plane ride up, thinking about what's to come. I have no idea what type of problem I am walking into because it's in a technical area where I have limited experience. I've been in organizations that have call rooms and others that perform market research surveys. This group does market research surveys with people in multiple call centers over the phone. Some of their surveys operate on a legacy proprietary application, but the failing ones run on a commercial market research platform that integrates with the dialer.

This performance problem could be a network, hardware, platform, or application issue. It might be a problem in a single call center or agent desktop that's bottlenecking the service. Maybe the hardware they sized is insufficient to support this client's larger surveys. Or perhaps the audio recordings are bottlenecking the network or storage infrastructure.

The application is given a list of people and phone numbers at the beginning of the night. It feeds the dialer these numbers and starts dialing down the list until it makes a connection. Once you pick up and say, "Hello," it routes the call to someone in the call center. You've likely received one of these calls before and may have wondered why there's a short pause between announcing yourself and hearing a voice on the other end. In this case, the attendant reads a script and asks the respondent to participate in a quick survey. If they confirm, the attendant clicks to start the survey.

What I find out is that on some occasions, the survey never appears. It's a blank screen. Sometimes it does come up after a long wait time, but the attendant has lost the call by then.

This particular survey is a big one being dialed out of several call centers simultaneously. It only has a few questions, but there's significant programming logic to it.

When I walk into the office, I can see the teams standing by whiteboards holding their daily agile standups. Even though these are surveys, they are still programmed. The output data and reporting also require coding. And even though there are many options to tag the verbal outputs to open-ended questions, the coding is largely done manually. Their legacy is in programming everything, and many scripts are copies from one market research study used as the base for the next one. It's copies and copies of code—only once the market research ends, so does its underlying code. Of course, this code isn't in version control, and code from completed surveys is never archived.

There are many opportunities to improve things here, but today I'm solely focused on figuring out why this survey, the biggest one they do for their largest customer, is failing consistently.

The leader of this team is a very rational thinker, a solid operational manager, and keeps the trains running. He knows when to ask for help and is a team player when trying to solve any form of issue, especially customer issues. He's hyperfocused on the customer because he's in a services business. Either he delivers a good experience and the results from the surveys daily, or customers are upset.

I like him and am intrigued by the challenges facing the group. He's hoping to fix the immediate problems and then move on to the greater challenges of streamlining their market research operations. He knows the group must evolve from classic market research services to digital ones. I accept the challenge and look forward to the partnership, but also warn him, "Give me a shovel and I'll start digging, but you're probably not going to like what I find."

On their new platform, this one survey has none of that spaghetti code of scripts required by their legacy platform, which is another reason everyone is angry. This new platform is there to automate their processes and bring them to the digital age of market research. It's the Rolls-Royce of market research platforms because it supports surveys collected over the phone as well as surveys completed through websites and mobile phones. The company invested a ton of money on this platform, and the payoff should come from big surveys like this one.

The failures are costing the company a lot of money.

Every night we fill the call centers and pay attendants to dial. And every night, they complete only a small fraction of the surveys. We're not getting paid for the surveys that aren't fully complete. It's a triple whammy to our financials because we take on all the costs, only a small fraction of the revenue, and we're paying a full IT team to figure out what's going wrong with the survey.

I walk into the conference room, and I know everyone there. One thing I like about this group is that they aren't intimidated by my presence. There's no feeling of, "Oh, shit, the CIO is in the room," that I sometimes get with other teams. They carry on their conversation, and it's a back-and-forth hypothesis on what's wrong.

The head of survey operations responsible for the survey thinks it's a hardware issue with the dialers. A support engineer from the vendor is on the phone, and he blames the network or possibly a hacked workstation that's flooding it with network chatter. The head of network operations reports to me and is also dialed in. He reminds everyone that the network and workstations are working fine for other surveys, so the issue must be something about this particular survey and its underlying platform. There's also a support engineer from the market research survey platform dialed in, and she wants to review all the software the development team used to integrate and move data around. That goes on the to-do list, even though the software lead is grumbling because those same integrations and scripts are components of other surveys.

I wait for an opening to chime in, and as I listen to the conversation, I think to myself, "How can I support this team? What are they missing, what questions should I ask, and where should I guide them?" It's a challenge since I am still new to the organization and know little about the architecture, so I have to reach into the fundamentals of encouraging the team while identifying improvement opportunities.

I step in at an opportune moment and say, "Lots of good theories and logic, everyone. I can see there are several moving parts to this program. There are several new platforms mixed with legacy technologies that have been in place for a long time. There's clearly something different about this survey, and we can't continue to play hot potato and hope the issue is not in our scope of responsibilities. Who can show me data on how different aspects of this system perform while the survey is running?"

There's a short pause, and it continues, and I'm getting a little scared. Surely the technologists look at performance metrics?

I finally get a response, "Leo is the best person looking at the underlying data." I look around the room to identify Leo and what he's learned from the data, but I am told he isn't in the meeting.

> When working through an operational issue and seeking root causes and remediations, make sure to have the person most knowledgeable around the operational data, alerts, and monitoring in the room or on the call. It's easy for people to chase the white rabbits and take other wrong turns, and the data should help guide teams on the optimal focus areas.

The consensus coming out of this meeting is that it's a dialer issue, but I'm not convinced. When the meeting ends, I go to visit Leo.

Leo is playing around with this new tool called Splunk. Every system administrator should have thought of creating this tool because it simplifies aggregating and querying data from multiple log files. But of course, using these tools without a strategy can be a colossal waste of time. I ask Leo, "Build me an outlier dashboard. Show me which of the four call centers are underperforming. Which agent desks are slower than the others? Which system parameters are spiking 95 percent above their means? What part of the survey are agents running when issues begin to happen?"

One week later, I am back at the office looking at the report. Leo affectionately names the report "Isaac's Dashboard," and even my name is in the URL. I laugh to myself upon seeing this, but the truth is, I hope this data-driven approach becomes ingrained in their culture and operating model without requiring my guidance.

So, I ask the team, "How are we going to test this survey offline and without impacting our client?"

It turns out there isn't an easy answer. We can test the survey, but not with the dialers. They have already tested the survey and found no issues, so the next step would have to include the dialers. The only way to do this is to staff the call centers and task them to dial the survey, but we can't experiment with a live client survey. We need to try different scenarios, tweak configurations, and even try out variants of the survey. The only way to test is to staff the call centers and dial a mock-up version of the survey. We would dial a list of people not affiliated in any way with the client and ask them a bunch of made-up questions programmed with the identical sample and survey logic used by the client.

Testing manually is a costly approach. We must pay the agents, and while this test survey is running, we wouldn't be able to run other surveys that generate revenue for the business. It's like stopping a factory floor and building fake widgets to identify quality issues.

"Set it up," is what I told them. I'd be back next week to help run the war room. In the meantime, I would have to explain this approach and the underlying costs to the executive group. I would bear this burden, and I know that I would be facing a firing squad of questions.

That's a key role for the Digital Trailblazer. Understand the problem, listen to the team's insights, ask questions, review data, debate approaches, and decide a course of action. Then go back and communicate the plan to stakeholders and provide them sufficient time and resources to address problems.

Digital Trailblazer Lessons

Navigating Tech Debt's Challenges

When you're a developer, systems engineer, or data scientist, your role is to develop and support various technologies. You make decisions on how to implement things in elegant ways. It's almost always harder to fix someone else's code than to code something new, and management rewards you for solving the problem at hand. When there are significant application performance issues, everyone wants the problem resolved and then walks away back to their daily business. As you climb the leadership ranks, the responsibility falls on you to decide which technical debt, legacy systems, and burning fires to fix, improve, or fully modernize. Digital Trailblazers with technical backgrounds may be particularly challenged because they often want the best fixes instead of temporary solutions.

And when you make it to one of these leadership positions, it's important to note that it becomes your responsibility to instrument standards and best practices. But the challenge is that teams debate them, and your smartest and fastest developers and engineers will want the freedom to self-organize and innovate with new technologies. And as a technology leader, you want them to succeed!

So, where does this end? What should technology, data, and digital leaders do differently to slow this vicious cycle of overengineering requirements, rushing development, and underfunding ongoing support and systems maintenance?

Here are five takeaways from this chapter:

1. **Focus everyone on technical simplicity when developing any kind of new system.** The best technical solutions may not come from building something new. Today more than ever, you might be able to provide good enough results through SaaS solutions. You can also develop applications on low-code platforms that provide the structure to create more capabilities with less and sometimes no code. When it's clear that you must engineer new systems, challenge business leaders to simplify requirements, and influence developers to find simple, supportable implementations. Over-engineered technology solutions developed on the latest and greatest application architectures are often the hardest to support long term.
2. **Let the data be your guide when making decisions, but also trust your instincts.** Decision-making requires balancing facts, insights from data, opinions shared by colleagues, and intuitions from past experiences. Your ability to listen to all sources and then guide teams decisively is a critical leadership skill. This skill is essential when resolving operational issues, especially as you become less hands-on with the underlying technology and less familiar with all the end-to-end business processes.
3. **Build rapport with your team by acknowledging your own mistakes and failures.** Many leaders recommend

showing humility with your team, and they also recommend using stories to help convey messages. Both practices are truly important when working with technical staff. They must know that you've been in their shoes, and from your stories they should learn your philosophies on how you tackle implementation challenges. Now it's easy to share your best practices, but this isn't always the best approach if you want others to learn, internalize, and make the lessons core to their behaviors. You didn't understand best practices only through successes. Don't be shy about sharing the hard lessons you've learned along the way, and own up to where you made mistakes.

4. **Lead teams by helping prioritize which questions need solving.** Your knee-jerk response to solving an operational, technology, or customer issue may be to get to root causes and fix the implementation. But before you go there, add some discipline to your thinking. Leaders didn't ask me to solve an ETL problem. They asked me to explain why solving it was so hard and how best to address a personnel issue. The team was collaborating to solve a customer issue, but the problem was that they weren't using data to guide their efforts. Sometimes, the question is worth solving, like how finding a way to validate the implementation changes to the market research survey solved the problem. Other times, the leader should help identify the question or problem, but parking lot any thinking and work around its solution. There's always more work to do than any organization can handle. Prioritizing is a critical leadership skill for Digital Trailblazers.
5. **Demonstrate the business and customer impacts around tech debt and legacy systems.** I don't meet many CIOs and CTOs who profess to have a complete handle on all the technical debt and full business impact of their legacy systems. It's

unlikely they have sufficient budget, business priority, or skills to address technical, data, and other forms of debt before cracks in the foundation become business crises. What's worse, the term *technical debt* is terrible to garner an executive's full attention. CFOs are used to having financial debt on the balance sheet, and COOs have more than their share of operational workarounds. Digital Trailblazers must tell the technical debt story to executives in a language they understand, like dropping a brick of paper on the desk or using a business crisis to get support for investment. And you can't go to the executives with a request to fix everything. Transforming legacy systems requires a disciplined approach to prioritize what's most impacting. Then, Digital Trailblazers must understand and implement to meet future business needs and not just upgrade systems to meet today's technology challenges. So before investing in new systems that replace existing ones, it's critical to review the problems through a customer and strategic lens. What problems are worth solving, when, how easily, and with how much investment?

■ ■ ■

If you would like more specifics on these lessons learned and best practices, please visit https://www.starcio.com/digital-trailblazer/chapter-2.

Note

1. John Reinan, "How Craigslist Killed the Newspapers' Golden Goose," *MinnPost,* Feb. 3, 2014, https://www.minnpost.com/business/2014/02/how-craigslist-killed-newspapers-golden-goose/.

Chapter 3

Ops: Wearing the CEO's Diet Coke

Today I'm thinking about Bill, one of the smartest and craziest people I know. He is a large, short man with long black hair that's balding on top. He's always sweating, loud, and often obnoxious. He loves Subway and dislikes pretentious food. Bill can drink, and he finds every good, bad, and ugly reason to take his team and people he likes for too many pours from the well. Most important, he makes people happy when they are around him. You are either Bill's friend, and he takes care of you, or you are his enemy, and he seeks to bury you for your faults, misses, or anything that he can use to show you who's boss.

He loves Disney. Loves it. He knows all the ins and outs there before there were apps and secret guides on navigating FastPasses and getting the most for your time and dollar. When necessary, I know I can always diffuse Bill's anger by bringing up Disney, and he'll switch gears to tell me all he knows. He plans my trip there, and I am grateful for his advice. He's a kid at heart but a bulldog when it comes to getting things done.

Several weeks before I met Bill, I had no choice but to say goodbye to my head of network operations. Pavel is a nice guy, and we are close, even though I had trouble making friends with the staff and my direct reports once I became their leader. For the most part, he knows how to get shit done, but he is nervous and struggles to answer questions with authority. We are a growing company, and management wants confidence in their Ops leader to keep the lights on.

Pavel is not that person.

He gets more nervous every day, and he slowly loses the trust of his colleagues. He believes everyone is looking over his shoulder and senses everyone's lack of confidence in his abilities to get the job done. He tries to address problems, but three new issues emerge for each one he puts to bed. The root causes aren't his fault, but everyone blames him for not fixing them fast enough or putting more permanent solutions in place.

And that drives him to perform a career-limiting move, something I know that he regrets.

I'm on vacation, and I manage to get away from the crazy world of startups and the insane job of being a CTO. It's heaven. My wife and I have two weeks away, with few things digitally tethering me to the office's day-to-day issues. This was pre-BlackBerry. It's not worth bringing a laptop with me for a trip to Bali, Thailand, and Hong Kong. Where would I dial into? In Chiang Mai, I visit an internet café and connect to the office email once to check in on things. But the connection is too slow, and my mailbox is overfilling. It is a futile attempt to appease my curiosity.

The lack of ubiquitous connectivity and mobile devices is a significant advantage at this time compared to today's world. Only the bigger companies and large enterprises with the most mission-critical applications have pagers with international coverage. Startup CTOs aren't carrying pagers yet, which means we aren't at the beck and call of our antsy, nerve-wracking, ambulance-chasing CEOs and boards. Because once CEOs catch wind of an operational issue that annoys them, they won't let it go. They'll bring it up at every walk by in the hallway, at every management meeting, especially when you need to update them on more pressing matters.

I return from vacation and immediately sense something is wrong when I boot up my computer.

Emails are replicating out of my account, and I'm unsure how and where they are going. The tools to trace who is behind the job and how they configured it are primitive. And I'm not a Windows or Microsoft Exchange expert. I'm a UNIX guy and can configure Linux, an Apache webserver, or a MySQL database if I have to, but Windows is entirely foreign. Regardless of my lack of expertise, when it's an inside job, it's hard to figure out what's going on, especially when a skilled network operations engineer is behind it.

I don't have the chops to trace this issue down. But Clark does, and he discovers Pavel's behind-the-scenes activities. Oddly enough, Clark and Pavel are friends, even though Clark wants to impress the boss (i.e., me, funny as that sounds) and move his career forward. I suspect Clark is conflicted with how to respond. He tells me that Pavel, our head of network operations, is behind the hack and shows me how he implemented the replication.

In the back of my mind, I can see how Pavel's nervousness brings him to do this entirely wrong act. I'm sure being away from the office for a lengthy period brought him to panic. He has no one to turn to, and the vultures are out.

I have a soft heart and want to let the incident pass, but our chief operating officer (COO) has nothing of it. She is a hardliner with zero tolerance for people the executive team feels are weak leaders, especially those who sabotage the organization. She is also new to the organization and wants to make her impression. Pavel is out, and I am looking for someone to fill his shoes.

And this isn't easy. We're growing and still have a mess of proprietary applications, server configurations, storage layouts, and network topologies. We know a system is down but have no idea how to discover the root cause of many application issues. Keeping the websites up and running isn't our most significant issue, and they are relatively stable. The hard part is keeping all the data flows running and completing data integration jobs on time.

One hiccup at 3 a.m. stops the presses, and someone must respond and recover from the issue fast enough to ensure that all the data completes processing on time. We have enough knowledge to fix the problems but have little clue how to implement robust solutions. The problems repeat themselves but with different underlying causes. One day the FTP server is down, and we're not getting files, and the next day, a network glitch stops a file transmission. If a scheduled job takes too long, its output isn't ready for the next job that's on cron with a fixed schedule. We receive a corrupt file from a customer, and the software isn't robust enough to kick it out, so the whole process comes to a halt. The web server hangs. The disk has a failure.

We Band-Aid many of these issues with load balancers, layers of scripting, overengineered monitoring, and anything to keep the process running reliably. No one wants to be on call and respond at 3 a.m. to fix these problems.

My business colleagues are growing impatient with this and other repetitive problems. They see growth, IPOs, and getting rich. In their eyes, the only thing standing in their way is system stability and performance. To make matters worse, we are hosting newspaper websites, and they expect the same operational performance on the digital side as they have in their decades-refined editorial processes, printing, and print distribution. Our customers expect five-nines of uptime even though it is highly unrealistic at that time and with our technical maturity.

I am grateful to all the people who give me advice early in my leadership career, and one of them shares the recommendation to hire lieutenants better than me. Bill is the answer. He reminds me of Ilan, our founding CTO, with his A-type personality, strong opinions, absolute resolve, and love of life. I listen to the input and hire him.

Building an Ops Team: The Good, the Bad, and the Ugly

Bill hires one of the best teams that ever reports to me, even to this day. Ken is methodical, seeks structure, and finds scalable ways of architecting solutions. Warren is a problem solver. He doesn't say much, but he is an incredible listener. He nods and finds a way to get the job done, only telling you how kludge the underlying technology is several days later and after a few beers. Yasmine is the doer and gets all the steps from A to Z done, but her real impact is being the communicator. People are comfortable around her, and they approach her before anyone else when they experience system issues or have questions.

Even before Bill, I bring in experts and outside help to work on infrastructure. There is Niles, who sells me on putting our infrastructure in a world-class colocation data center. Blake configures our networks and handles pretty much every hard infrastructure job. Delores is a master at setting up robust Oracle databases, and Patrick is the perfect account manager from our systems integrator.

But it is one thing to bring in experts to configure systems, and it is a whole other set of disciplines to manage and support them. The challenge magnifies when building custom applications, and it becomes even more critical when those applications are customer-facing. Now, add in the complexity of running an SaaS business of newspaper sites that can have highly volatile loads, and things get complicated pretty quickly.

Bill puts in the processes to manage all of the infrastructure, operations, and security. He locks down root access to the servers and requires the Ops team to perform all the code deployment procedures. No CI/CD or Infrastructure-as-Code (IaC) back then, but open source monitoring tools are plentiful, and he adds the commercial, enterprise-grade system management tools that are far more robust.

He gets his team training on all the primary technologies and develops relationships with the vendors, so he has someone to call when something goes wrong. He adds an IT service management (ITSM) tool so we have a system to track incidents and manager requests. He's always talking to the other business leaders about what's working and where there are problems, so they respect him. I don't have to get in front of him or defend this group very often because they can handle their issues on their own.

Bill does it from one root perspective that is the cornerstone of his management philosophy he promotes to his Ops team. I don't understand it, and I dislike it. I let him know that frequently, but he doesn't change, and it's this philosophy that made him successful in other network operational roles. His philosophy starts with one key principle.

Developers are fucking idiots.

He tells them that right to their faces—yes, even using the "f-bomb." He yells at them. He makes it clear that he is the boss. Put bad code on his infrastructure, and he backs it out without asking questions. He's not sitting around at 1 a.m. waiting for incompetent developers to fix their code in real time. He wants the code tested, and he leans on our quality assurance (QA) manager, Jonah, to do his job. He trusts Jonah, but he doesn't believe developers have a clue about operations. They aren't the ones waking up at 3 a.m., and they don't have to answer to management the next morning on the root cause of last night's issues and how it will never happen again.

> Companies have different tolerances for what language is appropriate in the office. But degrading people is unacceptable behavior, and in reflection, I regret not addressing it. This also was the world well before DevOps, and back then, there were frequent conflicts between Dev and Ops teams.

Bill pushes Boswell, our program manager, for plans and requirements. Sometimes he gets something that resembles a plan, but most of the time, he doesn't. Keep in mind that this is the world before agile and scrum become mainstream and tools like Jira are available. "Plans" essentially mean a mix of MS Word documents, Gantt charts, and spreadsheets. They are rarely accurate, mainly incomprehensible to development teams, and seldom up to date with the current state of the application development process.

Bill is frustrated by the developers' lack of planning and is quick to escalate his concerns to Jonah, Boswell, and me. He's livid at me if I don't hold the developers to acceptable standards, especially when his team is up all night overseeing messy deployments or resolving incidents. But Bill doesn't scream at Boswell and Jonah—at least not publicly. He sees them as teammates. They jab and poke fun at each other, but they don't throw one another under the bus. They are more likely to gang up on me when there are systemic problems.

Bill makes sure to befriend some of the better developers like Nagesh and Wes. "Nagesh is a genius," and he makes sure everyone knows it. Wes is a quiet young man who likes getting things done. I still remember the blue suit he wore in his interview, and I don't recall seeing him wear a sports jacket ever again. I go on to hire Nagesh one more time and Wes twice.

As much as Bill demeans developers and blames them constantly, he shames another group even more.

He buries vendors who aren't proactive, don't have technical acumen, are disorganized, or fail to follow through on commitments. He has no use for them, and he lets them know it. As much as he degrades developers, he further unloads his negative aggression on vendors. He makes us feel that there is nothing wrong with this behavior, and though many of us understand the approach, we're not comfortable with it.

Bill reins himself in around the business leaders, but I still try to keep him away for this reason. I don't know if he will lose it, and I am afraid his eruptions will freak out leadership. Besides, Bill really doesn't want to have anything to do with them anyway.

Despite all the technology and system management processes Bill puts in place, we still have more than our fair share of outages.

We hum along despite the recurring problems, but then, the economy changes dramatically for us and the world.

When a Strategic Transformation Collides with a Global Catastrophe

I'm not paying much attention to the economy and am more likely to know the score of last night's hockey games than where the Nasdaq closed. We hear about all the money other internet companies are raising but believe our slower and more methodical approach to building a business and partnering with *brick-and-mortar* businesses is a better strategy. When America Online and Time Warner announced their merger, it strikes a chord with our leaders and board, but life moves on. We need to grow. eBay has 12 million registered users,[1] and there is a growing fear that they are taking market share from newspapers' classified revenue streams. Craigslist job ads are only $45[2] and other ad types are free—and that rattles newspaper executives.

Our CEO and board begin reviewing strategic options to raise another financing round or other opportunities to fund our growth. We are a relatively easy business to evaluate based on our subscription revenue generated for hosting newspaper websites. But it is not easy to consider the longer-term value because the startup trade winds are starting to disrupt the industry. eBay and Craigslist are just the start, and there's also Cars.com, Monster.com, Hot Jobs, and others. You can get your news from the local newspaper website or visit Yahoo. You can buy a display ad in the newspaper starting at several thousand dollars, or you can experiment with online ads for hundreds.

So it's with this backdrop that I find myself heading to Poughkeepsie today.

One strategic option we're exploring is merging with one of our competitors. We sell one product to the largest newspapers, and they sell about a half dozen products to regional and smaller papers. We have nine newspaper companies that invested in us, while less-well-known venture capitalists still back them. We have the prestige but significantly higher operating costs in New York City, and they are frugal and scrappier, based in Troy, New York, a suburban city east of Albany.

I don't care about any of these business factors, and quite frankly, at the time, I barely understand them. What I know is that I spent the last five years of my life building a great team, an amazing product, and scalable technology. I believe it can be the backbone for any SaaS product that we build and sell to newspapers. We have a superior search engine that handles arbitrary data without schema changes. We use natural language processing to extract searchable information from the data sent to us. We launch new, fully customizable websites without adding or changing code. It is largely operational, and thanks to Bill, scalable and robust.

I'm heading up to Poughkeepsie with all this data because if we merge with this other company, our team, platform, and way of working must survive. I have architecture drawings to demonstrate our scalability. I have workflow documents showing how we launch and maintain newspaper sites without impacting our software development team from innovating and releasing new capabilities. I have spreadsheets outlining our IT assets, departmental financials, and organization structure. I brought along operational reports showing how system performance is improving. I get off at Grand Central Station with all these materials in one hand and my ego in the other.

I board the shuttle to Times Square and then switch to the 1-train to Penn Station.

It's then that I notice something peculiar. I am on the subway platform and can see a couple of trains and red signals ahead in the tunnel. The subways are backed up, and I have little time to make my Amtrak, so I'm in a bit of a panic. But the 1-train comes and gets us to Penn after a few stops in the tunnel.

As I make my way through the crowds at Penn Station to get to my track, I see out of the corner of my eye dozens of people hovering by a television. I see a building with a small fire and quickly read the caption, "Small plane crashes into the World Trade Center."

That's not good, I think to myself and pause about this news for just a few seconds, but I don't stop to watch, let alone think. I have a train to catch. I make it, and it leaves Penn Station on time.

It's the last train to leave Penn for some time to come.

I don't take this train often, preferring to carpool to many of the other merger meetings held at this secret location between our offices. So the train's emptiness isn't surprising. I am taking in the view of the Hudson River as we make our way north.

Suddenly, the train comes to a screeching halt about forty minutes into the hour-long ride. Five, ten, then fifteen minutes go by, and there are no announcements. I take out my brick of a cell phone to call one of my colleagues to let him know that I might be late. But there's no signal.

I look around, and a few rows back, I see a man coated in white dust, and his face, clothes, and bag are all chalky. He looks like he crawled through a construction site. He has a radio and is listening attentively. I'm not one who regularly reaches out to strangers, but I ask him, "What's going on?"

He tells me, "I was there on the ground when the plane hit. I'm covered in it and knew this is bad and decided to get out. The news reports that the tower fell."

It takes moments for this to sink in. The instinctive mind that wants to respond without thinking isn't working. There's nothing in my hippocampus that registers what this man is telling me. All I can muster is a self-reflection, a wait, a pause. If this were today, I would instantly understand what he was telling me. But this is before terrorist attacks and mass shootings made regular headlines in the United States.

He senses my inability to comprehend, so he repeats himself. "The tower fell," he said a second time.

I instantly feel nauseous and, a few seconds later, sick to my stomach. "The tower fell," I hear the man say a third time.

Pictures come to my mind of a 100-floor building toppling over. Which way did it fall? Is it in the harbor? Oh, no, wait, did it fall forward into the middle of Manhattan? Terrible thoughts now creep into my mind.

Our office is in lower Manhattan, three blocks south of Canal Street. Would the Tower reach that far? Is half of Manhattan ablaze? My wife Michele works in Union Square on 12th Street. Surely the impact didn't extend all the way to her. But wait, our office is on Canal, but our data center is further south on Broadway at the Nasdaq building. We chose it for its proximity to the office and its security. Was that gone?

My head continues to think in circular questions, and I lose track of time until the train begins to move again. I still can't put this all together, and I still want to believe that none of it is true. But I can't think beyond my direct impacts, and my mind doesn't let me think beyond my immediate circumstances.

I'm on a train to Poughkeepsie to sell the benefits of our team, practices, and platform. One of the World Trade Center towers is gone, and I can't reach my team, but they are all in proximity. I have no idea what's left. I can't think past the data center being down and losing everything. My mind is blocked from thinking about the people. Our people. Our team. People in the tower. People nearby the tower.

My imagination doesn't go into the unimaginable until the train starts going. We arrive at our destination forty minutes later. I take a cab to the hotel where we're meeting. I walk into the hotel and see a TV on at the bar. As I approach the screen, the second tower falls in front of my eyes.

I confess it's hard to remember much more about this day. I was at the bar for a while watching the news unfold. No one else from my company or the one we were merging with show up, and I am there alone at the bar, thinking about who is alive and what parts of my life may now be shattered. I see the footage of the buildings coming straight down instead of toppling over Manhattan, as I originally feared. I think about my wife Michele and believe she is fine even though I can't reach her on her cell. I have an uncle in the building and think of him.

The surprising thing about this day is that despite the horrific catastrophe, some things do return back to normal faster than you might have ever anticipated. Cell phone coverage returns in the afternoon, though it is hard to make a connection. I reach Bill and find out the team is starting to check in on Yahoo Messenger. Our email server is still in our office without power, but as people turn on their laptops, Messenger logs them in, and the app shows them as available. They haven't accounted for everyone yet. The data center is up. Bill tells me to find my way home.

The Amtrak south runs again that evening, and I board it with a heavy heart. Forty-five minutes later, I step off the train in Yonkers and see the cloud of smoke spewing from lower Manhattan. I feel cold, depressed, and angry as I walk on the platform toward the exit.

Michele is at the end of the platform waiting there for me. We hug for a long time before heading back to our apartment and then sit there for days watching the news unfold.

Chaotic World, Chaotic Leadership, and Its Organizational Impact

In early 2002, we complete the merger, and the heat turns up to prove to our new board and merged leadership team that our technology is scalable. During the merger talks, I sell the technology, the team, and our processes as solid, scalable, and reliable. We compete with our New York City sophistication against the more manual-intensive practices we inherit from the Albany-area company that merges with us.

Mergers are awful. It requires you to beat your chest so hard that buyers believe you are a master of your domain and that they're acquiring a technical masterpiece and not a lemon. During the merger talks, I put on my sales hat and demonstrate the best aspects of our people, processes, and technology. I don't fabricate, but I highlight the good and gloss over the everyday speed bumps. It is survival, and it is pride. And we believe we can build, fix, and integrate anything.

> I will discuss different types of transformations later in the book, but for now, I want you to recognize two different types. A merger is a strategic "fork in the road" transformation where the board decides to pivot and combine two businesses, their operations, and their culture into a single entity. 9/11 is a tragedy above all else, but it also represents an externally driven transformation propelled by greater forces outside of the business's control. In these transformations, leaders must pivot their business models and adjust priorities while helping employees adapt to a new normal. In either transformation, leaders must make smart, quick, and prudent decisions, or the chaos trickles down to everyone in the company, as you will soon see.

During the merger talks, we discuss how to combine the strengths of both businesses to create a force multiplier that drives our growth and hopefully, transformation in the newspaper industry. We sell to medium and large newspapers, while they are stronger selling to smaller regional ones. We have world-class infrastructure and processes. They are lean and highly responsive to customer needs. We have a platform that scales and can be used to build new products. They are faster than us and buy and develop their way to a portfolio of products.

The natural question is, how are we going to put the two platforms together? How are we merging infrastructure, development platforms, development cycles, teams, people, and office locations?

When the business leaders fail to convince the combined boards on a growth strategy, we focus on finding a synergistic one. And once again, all eyes fall on me, the CTO, to determine how we might rationalize two technology organizations and platforms into one, go-forward, scalable, and integrated SaaS operation.

We try to find common ground at the platform and application level. We know it doesn't make sense to invest in Java and Microsoft development platforms or Oracle and Microsoft SQL Server databases. We want customers to buy multiple products and end users to have an integrated experience.

But in the end, merging multiple SaaS products into a single platform built on common technologies isn't easy.

Here's an example. We build Oracle databases on Sun servers, storage area networks, and storage clustering. The team configures the architecture for high availability to failover servers, storage, and networks, and the infrastructure doesn't require much daily maintenance. Since most of the product's queries are hitting the AltaVista search engine, the load on the databases is manageable and relatively predictable.

They are running Microsoft SQL Server on a bunch of servers. To enable redundancy and failover, they replicate the data from a master database into a child database. Database replication is a fairly standard process, but in their case, the replication and storage fail occasionally. By occasionally, I mean several times a month. And the database isn't just tables and data; it's code, and a lot of it is stored procedures and triggers. We never audit how much code uses SQL 92 standards and to what extent they leverage Microsoft proprietary features. Meanwhile, we both struggle to keep data flows humming along without hiccups.

As you can see, merging databases isn't a slam dunk, and the application level is even harder. You can't combine J2EE, Microsoft ASP, and ColdFusion without a ton of code rewriting.

Combining these platforms is hard, expensive, slow, and would derail us from our primary survival mission in the post-bubble, post-9/11 realities.

Instead, we concentrate on synergies in IT operations and data centers. Bill is in the spotlight to help consolidate network operations, data centers, networks, and platforms as much as possible. He has to cross-train people from both companies on each other's infrastructure and applications. This consolidation isn't easy given the disparity in platform, practices, and culture.

Bill starts by focusing on the things we have in common. We must be more reliable and more efficient. We don't want to get screamed at for outages, and we have enough people in IT to make managing a 24/7 operation humane. It is just a matter of getting two teams to adopt a common mindset and operate as one organization with a mission.

And this is exactly Bill's approach for finding common ground with everyone on his team. They come from different cultures and platforms but have common objectives of keeping systems running, avoiding the wrath of business leaders, and sleeping at night.

But the work of combining cultures and ways of working isn't easy, and Bill needs an outlet for his emotions. He ups his game on blaming and beating up vendors. It is an easy out for his anger and aggression. He goes after all the vendors, big and small, without care. And he is loud about it.

Today we are in the New York City office during a blockbuster episode. Our primary data center is down, and our vendor is taking its time to resolve a network issue. Sadly, this is becoming more common as many IT vendors have no choice but to cut staff after the dot-com bubble burst.

So here is Bill on the phone with the data center's network operation center and getting nowhere. It is a classic battle over whose end of the network is faulting, and the argument breaks down over who misconfigured their router and which team triggered the latency.

Our CEO walks into Bill's office in the middle of the debate.

The geniuses of our board that put these two companies together haven't agreed on a post-merger business strategy and neglect to budget sufficient funds to help merge the companies. But their biggest misstep is to keep both CEOs in place as co-CEOs. It's frustrating because the company cultures are shadows of these two men, and while they more or less behave well together in public, their philosophies and strategies are quite different. It leads to long periods of indecision.

> The board leaving two CEOs in charge after a merger is a kick-the-can down the road move and a punt from making a critical leadership decision at a crucial time. I'll be sharing more about leadership decision-making in a later chapter, but for now, I want to point out another example of a place where delaying decisions can have long-term consequences.

But one thing they do decide is that IT should report to the CEO of the Albany company. He carries more of the operational responsibilities while the CEO from my company focuses on sales and marketing. So here he is, coming into Bill's office for the first time, sucking down a Diet Coke at ten in the morning and watching Bill deal with a major outage.

Bill's going back and forth from being a nice guy—your friend you'd grab a beer with—to a hard-nosed, get under your skin, demanding tough-guy who exposes vendors' shortcomings and finds ways to get what he wants.

"Ping our gateway. You see it, right?" he asks.

"Yes, we get a response, but we're still seeing packet loss," the NOC manager replies. "And we reverted all changes back to configurations we had in place a week ago. We've been at this for a few hours, and we need to change shifts here."

Bill replies, "I see. Where are you guys located?"

Bill gives me a look. I know something is up his sleeve, and that sense of danger starts building in my gut. Where is Bill going with this?

"We're in Troy, New York," came the response.

"Oh, yeah?" Bill replies. "Where are your offices in Troy?"

"We're in the Troy office park," comes the reply.

And here is Bill's response. "I see. Do me a favor and look out your window. You see that flag across the green that says PowerOne Media?" He pauses. "Good," he said. "Now listen, you know us as AdOne, but we recently merged with another company, and we rebranded as PowerOne Media. I'm in the offices across the park from you."

There is another pause. And then Bill said.

"And if you don't stay at your fucking desks and help us fix this issue, I'm going to come over there and fucking kill you."

My mind goes into rewind. What did Bill just say?

But the CEO has a more immediate response, and I wear the Diet Coke that he spits up all over me for the rest of the day.

Digital Trailblazer Lessons

Controlling Emotions and Managing Risks

Tragically, Bill passed away soon after. I got the call from his wife one Saturday morning, and then I shared the news with the CEO and the team. I handled it terribly and wished I had done more for his family. I had no experience and no training to manage the loss with greater empathy. We knew Bill wasn't in the greatest health, so we weren't completely surprised. But Bill and I spoke daily and often on the weekend, shifting from work, technology, management, personal matters, travel, and life. I miss Bill dearly to this day.

Here are some lessons and takeaways I hope you'll take from this chapter:

1. **Be human and empathetic, but control your emotions.** While leadership requires that you articulate a vision and demands that you hold teams accountable for results, it also requires you to show positivity and be motivating. Your teams need to see signs that you listen to their needs and care for their well-being. Also, you'll have a hard time influencing others outside of your department if they don't see you as both a leader and a credible, honest, and thoughtful person. If you're not sure how strong your emotional intelligence is, consider taking a test to identify your strengths and weaknesses.

Part of being human and a leader is controlling your emotions. It's fine to show restrained anger when applied to the right issues, but it's absolutely not acceptable to be hostile to people, including vendors. Let people know when you're disappointed with the results or a team's performance and follow it up with a discussion on where to make changes or drive improvements.

Most important, don't be afraid to be vulnerable and share personal struggles, disappointments, misfortunes, and tragedies. Everyone in your office faces these, and they are even more reluctant to open up and share them if you don't.

2. **Develop communication strategies for all severity levels.** Most IT organizations have their definitions of incident severity levels and, ideally, service level objectives. But I find a minority has well-defined communication strategies for who gets informed by type and severity issue and what information is expected in the communications. Remarkably, even fewer define communication protocols to announce changes, including application deployments.

   Digital IT teams must make communications a point of strength and not a weakness. Most digital teams driving transformation programs overload themselves with too many parallel initiatives that create dependencies between teams. Managing through conflicting priorities, direction changes, and complex inter-team dependencies can be stressful for teams and their leaders. In addition, digital teams pressure themselves to release changes frequently, which can be a good thing if customer feedback helps drive future priorities and requirements. But it's also risky and often leads to unstable IT applications. Strong communications can help teams manage these speed bumps.

Your communications plan should include strategic tools such as sharing vision statements, scheduling town halls to announce major strategic or priority changes, or requiring easy-to-read weekly updates written by team leaders. Tactically, digital organizations are good at picking tools but should create communication protocols. For example, what tool and communication should teams use to resolve interdependencies, communicate changes, or propose a best practice?

Lastly, when teams focus on communications, it helps them plan for the worst unknown risks. We didn't expect 9/11 or plan for our email servers to go down, but we thought Yahoo Messenger was a good communications tool as long as everyone was committed to using it. Many years later, when Hurricane Sandy hit the northeast and we lost power to one of our central offices, a strong communication protocol enabled us to react quickly to this issue.

3. **The best technology doesn't ensure high reliability.** IT leaders make many investments to ensure the high reliability of the infrastructure. We put in multiple cloud zones, data centers, redundant servers, load balancers, data snapshots, and other disaster recovery practices. IT operations teams add responsive monitoring that detects issues and automates responses. Having a strong incident response process is key to ensure that when problems arise and incident response teams are alerted, they have a defined process to review and address the issue. But equally important is to accept that the unexpected will happen and services will go down.

   While many IT teams focus on keeping databases, applications, APIs, and services at high reliability, many underestimate the engineering required to have robust data integration jobs. Today, access to accurate and updated information is business critical, and IT leaders need to select tools that enable fault-tolerant data processes.

4. **Protect the team and partner with colleagues.** One of the most crucial leadership jobs is to empower teams to be successful. Most leaders also know their job is to protect teams from distractions or from being under fire for one reason or another. We all have the mental picture of the major league baseball manager running from the dugout to argue a call with the umpire and protect the batter from doing this and possibly being thrown out of the game. And even though hockey teams may have a fourth-line goon, the whole team steps in when their competitor makes a dirty play against a star player. In all sports, great teams know that winning starts by playing a great defensive game.

   Digital Trailblazers understand that protecting the team starts well before they are in trouble or under fire. Bill made clear his team's priorities and challenged those who made the team's objectives harder to fulfill. To ensure goodwill, he partnered with his colleagues, cracked jokes, took people out for drinks, and championed developers to implement things the right way. When Bill's team ran into trouble, they were far less likely to get thrown under the bus. There was a layer of trust and camaraderie already established.

5. **Take real breaks away from operations.** It's very easy to get burned out in IT leadership, and I've been there several times. You cobble together solutions and address issues, but before anyone truly has time to celebrate, business leaders are off to a new set of priorities and issues to address. In IT, we know we are truly never *done* as there is always ongoing support. Double that down in digital, where implementation starts with experiments and proofs of concept,

and the best ones evolve to production applications with continuous release cycles.

■ ■ ■

Digital Trailblazers must spend time away from it all to relieve the stress and enable new lines of thinking. That means truly disconnecting.

If you take anything away from this chapter, I hope it's a renewed, healthy outlook on work and life.

If you would like more specifics on these lessons learned and best practices, please visit https://www.starcio.com/digital-trailblazer/chapter-3.

I wrote this chapter before the COVID-19 pandemic, and I was able to think more clearly through this catastrophe thanks to lessons learned from crises, including 9/11, Bill's passing, and Hurricane Sandy. I didn't change much in this chapter to preserve memories without a pandemic filter applied to it.

Notes

1. Carol Tice, "Amazon and eBay Crowd into Each Other's Turf," *Puget Sound Business Journal,* Jan. 5, 2003, https://www.bizjournals.com/seattle/stories/2003/01/06/story3.html.
2. Katharine Mieszkowski, "Are You On Craig's List?," *Fast Company,* Nov. 30, 2000, https://www.fastcompany.com/56496/are-you-craigs-list.

Chapter 4

Product Management and Architecture: Trials and Triumphs

It's fair to say that I've worked with some challenging product owners.

Or, more precisely, I'll just say that some product managers can be unrealistic, and some, dare I say, can just be unreasonable, pompous, arrogant, and self-serving.

And then some are true collaborative geniuses. These maestros win over stakeholders to buy into visions and customer value propositions without getting sucked into appeasing everyone's wish lists. And they know enough about the architecture, technology, and data to ask agile teams smart questions without getting under their skin.

But the reality is, unfortunately, that some product leaders lack a sufficient understanding of how technologies work, what processes make development teams successful, or even the simplest things like treating developers nicely.

The requests they make in their requirements are often outlandish. The timelines are insane. The expectations are that everything should just work like their favorite websites developed by unicorn consumer startups. The belief is that developers must replicate a web designer's work of art with pixel-perfect precision. Like it's Picasso's design even though it's gone through dozens of stakeholders and hundreds of revisions that convert a work of art into a messy, confusing canvas.

Seriously, it's really easy to get developers on your side. Compliment a developer and show interest in what they are working on, and they're yours like puppy dogs. But some product owners just ask, and ask for some more, all without giving any form of thanks or acknowledgment. How foolish and shortsighted is it when product owners beat up their development teams?

But here's the reality technologists know and have the treads on their back to prove it. When something goes wrong and the business wants someone to blame, the most challenging product managers pummel the technologists.

And maybe it is the developer's fault that there are delayed releases, outages, security issues, defects, clunky user experiences, mounting technical debt, poorly documented applications, duct tape integrations, shoddily architected databases, code without unit tests, manual builds, and error-prone deployments. Perhaps it's the development team's fault when their software releases require patches, emergency break fixes, or hotfixes—whatever your organization calls them.

Or maybe it's product management's fault for overpromising and pushing every stakeholder's whim downhill into the development backlog. Perhaps it's their fault for saying yes to everyone and then blaming the technology department for missing deadlines, scope, or quality. It doesn't take a rocket scientist to know that a team of five developers can't deliver fifty features in three months. But go ahead, say yes to everyone, and then blame the development team when you get called out. That's a surefire sign of a poor product manager.

> Hold on, hold on, you might be saying, let's not fault anyone. We use retrospectives to improve collaboration on agile teams, and in DevOps, we ask groups to perform blameless postmortems. But here, I share the frequent rift between product owners and development teams and a common sentiment—which is what retrospectives and blameless postmortems try to address.

I have to confess that I am an internet veteran who started work on web applications in the mid-1990s. That was before the Agile Manifesto,[1] the DevOps movement, user experience (UX) best practices, and sophisticated agile and Kanban tools. So, while I worked with product managers, there was no role or job description of the agile product owner as we know it today. Some product managers were old school and spent their time developing and managing large requirements documents. Others just came to us with their ideas and requests. It didn't matter too much because we didn't have a significant legacy of technical debt to maneuver around.

And the technical expectations were low. Back then, you had a server that passed a request off to an application, and then it returned HTML back to the browser. There was no JavaScript, and there wasn't even CSS. We were most concerned about the quality of search results, basic design principles, and page performance. Delightful user experiences, large-scale scalability factors, advanced analytics, and best security practices were not the top considerations.

Quite frankly, some of the product managers I worked with in those early days of the internet were super-talented and excelled at building products. Some lead product management functions today at large software powerhouses, while others run their own businesses. They "got it." They understood the role of product management, operating a swivel chair in the middle of everything.

On one side of the chair, some existing customers want things to work better. On the other hand, business function leaders from sales, marketing, and operations want to grow revenue and become more efficient. Then there's the list of customers who say they won't buy the product until it has all these bells and whistles—at least that's what the salespeople say. Then there is the CEO. Yes, the CEO comes in with today's big idea and stacks it on the pile of pots in the sink.

But great product managers don't dish it out. They don't just take everyone's orders and throw them into the kitchen. The restaurant only serves so many tables, and if everyone orders at the same time, the kitchen backs up, and it delays customer service. The restaurant has a menu with options to address customers' interests and dietary restrictions, and many won't let patrons design their own dishes. In well-run restaurants, the front-of-the-house staff knows how to work with the back-of-the-house crew. They know how to ask for special requests when they are genuinely needed. They're skilled at thanking people. They know how to share constructive criticism when people need to learn from mistakes and failures.

Other product managers really have no clue. Instead of listening to customers and markets, they sit in their offices dreaming big and writing novel-long requirements documents. When business leaders ask for everything, they demonstrate how well they capture requirements and how slow technology teams respond. They attend agile sprint reviews so they can cover their asses or better communicate status to leadership. Technical debt is not their problem. Fixing defects and operational issues are the must-eat vegetables on the side of the product owner's perfectly well-seasoned steak. The development teams should address them on top of everything else they prioritize.

I suspect these product managers are on alternative career paths today. But organizations are so poor at understanding product management, it's likely some of these poor performers are still doing the same things, just with different companies and teams.

So, let me share with you some of my stories working with product managers, architects, UX designers, agile teams, stakeholders, and executives in taking customer-facing products and employee experiences from ideas to successful realities. Everyone in this group has responsibilities for innovation, instituting best practices, and delivering business outcomes. But they come to the collaboration table from different disciplines, often with conflicting implementation objectives. Being a Digital Trailblazer requires finding the right balance across each discipline's best practices, prioritizing the optimal levers to pull, and pivoting the plan when necessary. The balance to turn pie-in-the-sky ideas to great experiences developed on scalable architectures isn't easy to orchestrate. I've had my share of challenges, mistakes, and lessons learned along the way.

What to Do When Asked for a Roadmap

Things were crazy in the heyday of the internet's startup, but when the internet bubble burst in 2001, companies had more time to develop web applications with higher quality. In the twenty years since then, more companies have invested in developing web applications, but there remains a lack of knowledge among business leaders on how to work with technologists.

One day, I am sitting in my office trying to get some quiet work done. It's a school holiday, and I have the fortune of bringing my son to work with me. Ronan is six years old with a mind of his own. It's the early days of iPads, but pre-iPhones, and he is showing signs that he may grow into an innovator and great engineer.

He takes apart everything.

We never have a television remote with a back cover. Every remote-control car he has is in pieces through his version of quality assurance testing. I forget how many DVD players are in shambles from his tinkering. Everything to him is a science project, and he experiments with taking things apart and seeing what's inside. He rarely puts them all back together.

But that day, he is in my office with my iPad and in his own personal heaven. He never runs out of things to do, bouncing from one application to another. If he gets tired of playing a game, he can put on YouTube. My wife and I are afraid of having our kids wear headphones, so my biggest issue is reminding him to keep the volume low. People drop in to say hi, and I have to prod him to look up and respond.

Meanwhile, I am reviewing my team's plans and application architectures. We are in the early stages of building a new platform for an SaaS product. Of course, we *never* call it SaaS. It's a faux pas to say that an information media company is a data, analytics, or God forbid, a tech company. It boggles my mind that company executives don't want to admit technology's importance to their business. To many, it is heresy to suggest that we should operate like a tech company. Never mind that a media company is worth maybe twice its revenue, while any technology company, let alone one with proprietary business data, can easily fetch a tenfold revenue multiple.

I ponder this while reviewing the architecture plans. The corporate CIO requires business unit CIOs like me to work with the enterprise architects who report into a central IT organization. Unfortunately, these architects are two steps to the right of having any accountabilities to the business, and they have very little responsibility for making engineering teams successful. They all have experience with enterprise systems, but from what I can tell, none have any experience with web, SaaS, or customer-facing technologies. Yet, they come up with the most beautiful and elaborate architectural drawings. In PowerPoint. Everything is neatly depicted in rows of capability with one line of integration up and down the stack. Their presentations should have been titled, "Build this, and all will be great."

There's more fiction in an architectural drawing delivered via PowerPoint than the best web designs concocted in Adobe Illustrator. And anyone who has ever been hands-on with any platform, system, or proprietary application knows too many architectures defined by ivory tower enterprise architects are complete fabrications. They look good. They make executives feel like they are buying and building something achievable and straightforward.

But in reality, these drawings, fabricated in the La-La Land of some "expert's" office, are complete bullshit.

But it's my job to review this PowerPoint. I must see what to support and where to dig in and challenge.

Sorry, but I must digress. As I write this now, almost ten years later, I'm sitting on a plane. The guy sitting next to me is staring at a PowerPoint slide, "Lambda style data lakes." I'd love to look over and see more details because the slide looks like a small urban sprawl of boxes, cylinders, channels, and other shapes representing hundreds of components. I'm willing to bet it will never get developed.

I see the luggage tag on his laptop case, and he works for one of the Big Six consulting companies. They make a fortune selling PowerPoints and spreadsheets to executives who want a plan wrapped up in a big-name consulting company ribbon. They'll deliver it with a seven- or eight-figure pricetag, a multiyear timeline, and their proposal to lead transformation.

Ten years later, some things haven't changed, and there are smarter, faster, safer, and more innovative ways to transform an organization's technology architecture.

So, I am sitting in the office with one eye on these crazy architecture PowerPoints and another on my son watching YouTube videos when I hear a knock at the door.

It's Johnathan, the new product manager who now has full responsibility for the product that's in early planning. Nice guy. Experienced, which is somewhat refreshing, and he's coming to see me early in his learning process. That's a good sign since I didn't get to interview him and have no idea whether he is overly opinionated and arrogant or a collaborative and a well-rounded product executive.

After some smalltalk, he looks up at me, notebook on the desk, pen in hand, and goes straight to his primary question.

"What's your roadmap, Isaac?"

A roadmap? I am with the company for less than two months, and he is with the company for less than two weeks. What the hell is he looking for in a roadmap?

I'm pretty sure that's not how I respond to him, but instead of following up with any details, he repeats the question with more words. "What's your roadmap of where you want to take the product? What releases do you have planned?"

My kneejerk response that I say inside my head is, "Hey, buddy, that's your fucking job, isn't it? You come up with an unrealistic roadmap. You sell it to the executives. You promise the world to customers and make great friends with the salespeople with your grand visions. My job is to take your work of fiction and make it close to reality. And somehow do this in record time, with a team that has historically struggled with execution, and then also ensure that the application is reliable and secure."

But the real problem is, I don't have a roadmap yet, and I don't even have releases. I am just getting the team to understand basic agile practices. How to run a sprint, what meetings we need, how we should use agile backlog tools, how to properly run a standup, how to get process improvement from retrospectives, what commitment means, how to get users' stories officially done at the end of the sprint, and how to run a sprint review. The basics. The teams aren't ready to define software releases, let alone roadmaps.

Had I told Johnathan just that, I probably would have gotten him to walk away. Instead, I give him all the details and never answer his question. Maybe if I share some of the technical issues with him, he'll go away?

I answer, "Our databases are an urban sprawl of tables, integrations, and the most complex queries you've ever seen. Our search interface is six-screens long because the last product manager wanted to ensure that all search capabilities were available to every user type. Never mind that it takes over 10 seconds to render this page. We're not using any of the latest web 2.0 user interfaces, so customers are sitting there watching entire pages refresh after making a couple of clicks. And then there are all these other analytics capabilities we sell to customers, but today they are engineered in Microsoft Access databases and shipped to customers on CDs."

He just sits and stares for a few seconds. I celebrate in my mind, "Yes! I overwhelmed him! He has nowhere to go and can't think of a follow-up question!" But after all my ramblings and a brief pause, he repeats his question.

"Isaac, I get it. But you must have a sense of where you are leading teams. You must have a semblance of a roadmap in your mind, right?"

This banter going back and forth is getting tiring, but not for my son. He just keeps hearing roadmap, roadmap, roadmap.

He figures he'll help his dad out, just like raking leaves in the backyard. While Johnathan and I are going back and forth, and without either of us noticing or paying attention to him, Ronan goes to the whiteboard and starts drawing.

And after the fourth time Jonathan asks for a roadmap, Ronan announces that he has an answer. "Daddy, here's your roadmap." (See Figure 4.1.)

Ronan draws a swirling set of roads curving around, overlapping, connecting, and separating. It is a mess of roadways on a map. At six, he is just listening and developing solutions. It is fantastic, and I am proud of his simple, though obviously nonfunctional resolution.

I look over at Johnathan, who is embarrassed and insulted, though through no real fault of my own.

But the genius is that the roadmap he drew is the best response for today. We have no sense of direction, which as a senior product

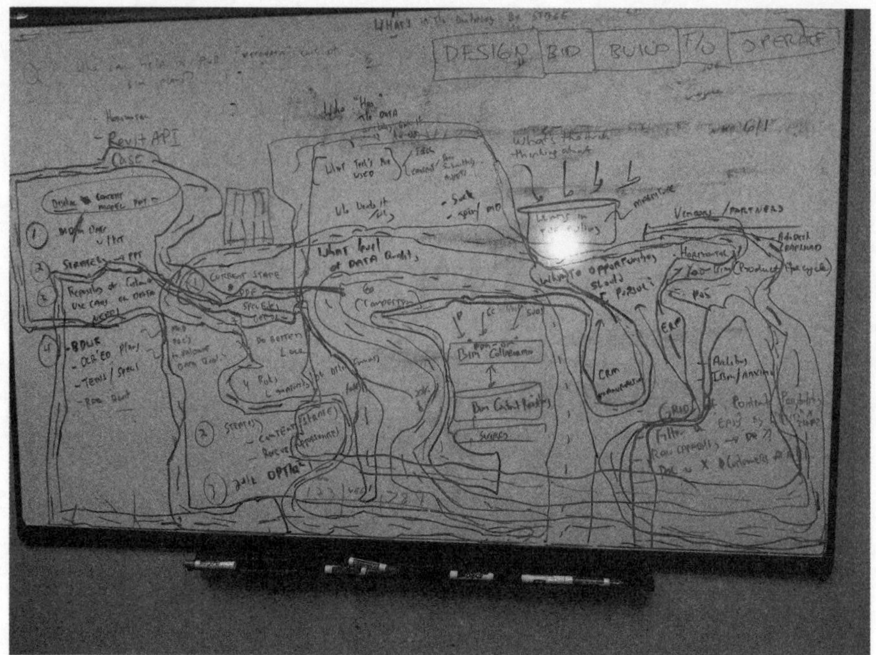

Figure 4.1 Ronan's Roadmap Stayed on My Whiteboard for Months

manager is Johnathan's job to learn and share with the team. We have no architecture, but we know some of the problems that need addressing. We are still developing our agile processes and are not ready to plan and execute releases. We are a mess and need to straighten things out before forecasting, documenting, or communicating a roadmap.

But that question and requests for roadmaps keep coming to me in other means and forms.

When the Product Roadmap and Architecture Require a Hard Pivot

A few weeks earlier, I was working with another product manager. Charles spent six months working with the technology team on getting a new business intelligence platform approved at our enterprise. Getting this approval was no easy feat because the platform they wanted required an exception from enterprise standards.

If you don't know what that means, let me explain. The enterprise architects, the corporate CIO, and everyone and anyone in an operational role will make your life insanely difficult for asking for new technology. Never mind, there are no financial incentives to use their standards. They haven't developed plans, training, or best practices to help business units succeed in applying the selected technologies. Standards are largely elaborate PowerPoints or slide decks that communicate why the central IT group chose the platform, and the architects who develop these decks are rarely hands-on enough to test or prototype with the technologies.

But Charles somehow got past all the blockades and obstacles. IT installed his business intelligence platform in the data center (another miracle that I should point out because back then, it took months to get IT ops to install new infrastructure). He has a corporate sanctioned team from a service provider working on it. They are even using agile methodologies and are on their fourth sprint of application development.

It's my first week at the organization, and the CEO pulls me into his office. "Isaac, before you do your assessment of the technology team or start thinking about developing a plan, I need you to go check out this analytics product that's in development. The team working on it says the product will go live in August, and I'm hoping that it will be a big win for the organization."

I start thinking about the timeline and making some back-of-the-envelope calculations in my head. It is May. The team is sprinting, but they still need time to test the application, validate performance, and meet security requirements. I expect the team to be largely done with product development and coding to hit the August deadline. The main functionality should be demonstrable, and they ought to be planning user acceptance testing, performance testing, and security reviews. It's with these expectations that I meet Charles and the development team for a demo and review of the implementation.

I watch the demo with growing fears. It ends in under five minutes, and my jaw drops, the mic is on the ground, and I am screaming inside my head, "Oh, no, this is a shit-show."

I am appalled at what the product looks like and where they are in its development.

Imagine you have a contractor upgrading your vacation home only a couple of months before you plan to visit over the summer. Only the house is in shambles, and everything they install is done with shoddy materials and lacking any craftsmanship.

When you look at a business intelligence (BI) tool, you expect some decent-looking, easy-to-use charts and graphs. I hope to see stacked bar charts, some versions of pie charts, trends, and some usable data grids. But that's not what I see at all, and I think an early version of Lotus 1-2-3 has more inspiring data visualizations.

These charts are primitive line graphs, and a few places on a web page are labeled as "dashboards." There is no navigation or user experience, so I'm not sure anyone but the brightest subject matter experts with a strong understanding of the data can do much with the tool. There are no indicators on what questions and problems end users can ask and answer using the "dashboards."

This isn't a product ready to launch in a couple of months. It is not an MVP, and it's barely a prototype.

Charles has a blank stare through the demo. I feel like I'm at the poker table with a pro who is staring me down, knowing that I have to make the next move. He wants my reaction and does a good job guarding his own. I don't know him at all and can't tell what he's thinking. Does Charles think the team will close the gap and finish the product on time? Or is he also disappointed with the results?

I formulate a calculated response to what I see and ask, "Charles, can we review the design and some of the requirements?"

I might as well start at the top. In addition to selecting the technology, the team spent a significant amount of time and investment with a web design agency to construct a user experience and site design. It is pixel perfect. I don't know enough about the customers, business, or underlying data, but the design certainly looks like a finished product.

So what accounts for the difference between the design and what the team produced? This isn't my first time seeing a significant gap between a product manager's expectations and the team's delivery. I've made an art and science of closing the differences, but I still need to learn more details.

I'm new to analytics and business intelligence tools. I've seen their output in the form of dashboards and reports but spent little time learning about their construction.

Now that I've seen the product and the requirements, it's time to understand the technology better. I look over at the team and ask, "Can I see the platform and the code?"

They look perplexed, and that takes me by surprise as I don't think this is an unusual or outlandish request. They're doing agile and having demos during their sprint reviews, right? Or maybe they're just a little taken back by this new CIO coming in and asking to look at code.

The developers tell me it takes about thirty minutes to set up the demo, so I pass the time chatting with Theresa, the development team's program manager.

I never had program managers with responsibilities on agile projects before, so I am intrigued. Theresa runs the standups with the offshore development team. They have one analyst with them, but the rest of the team is in India. Their standups last about forty-five minutes (red alert signals going off in my head) and sometimes as long as an hour and a half.

"Is that normal?" she asks.

Well, no, that's not normal at all, but I let it slide. The team is running month-long sprints. Did I hear that right: Month-long sprints working on a new product with new technology? I find this highly unusual, but I hold back judgment.

The demo starts, and the developer shows me the BI tool and the development environment. Quite frankly, the whole demo isn't memorable at all except for one key point that stays with me for a long time after the event.

The developer shows me the code, and there's nothing spectacular about it. It reminds me of the old computer language Logo where you issue instructions on what to draw, except the one he's showing me is for a bar chart. Set the axis, add the data, design the bars, format text, and other configurations. He's walking me through this and scrolling through lines and lines of code. Maybe a couple of hundred lines of code to produce what? A single chart?

I'm hoping some rapid development tool generates the code, but the developer tells me that coding is done by hand using a text editor.

Oh, crap. And now I am having an *oh-shit* moment and start adding things up. How many charts does this dashboard require, and how many dashboards are necessary for the product launch? And how many lines of code are needed to generate it? And how many iterations, improvements, and technical debt does that create?

It slowly becomes apparent what's wrong here.

I have a product design that could be a Picasso, and on the otherhand, I have hundreds of lines of code that generate charts that look like vintage MS-DOS. It's being engineered halfway around the world in India through an agile process that, other than using the terms *standups* and *sprints*, bears little resemblance to the actual scrum process. And to make matters even worse, the program manager has limited agile experience, and she's been reporting that the program has a "green" health state for the last few months.

It's then I realize that they don't really know how bad this is. In fact, this business team didn't select the service provider or sign up to manage the project using agile methodologies. It's handed down to them from "corporate" citing best practices—which I had a hand in creating, by the way—that new products and technologies are an ideal beachhead for teams to learn agile development practices.

Only no one is coaching them on agile or the use of the technology. Not the technology vendor, not the service provider, and unfortunately not the corporation.

I hold back my thoughts and judgments until meeting with the CEO the next day when I break the news. "Adam, there's no way this product is launching in August, and that's not even the bad news."

He's looking at me like he's trying to figure out my next words. Like what could be worse than being off on their deadline.

I continue, "I'm pretty sure the team is working with the wrong platform. And yes, I know they spent nearly six months convincing corporate that they needed this one."

I say this with the mental picture of lines and lines of code scrolling by and the mental image of what the product looks like today. There's no way he's seen the product. I've demoed other products to him before, and he definitely knows what a polished business application looks like when it's a couple of months away from launch.

He looks at me. "Isaac, let me get this straight. The team works for months on selecting a platform and signs off on a design that looks great. They get an experienced team, run a project for several months, and report a 'green' status. Now, you visit the team for a day and are telling me that this is all bull?"

I pause for a minute and think. There's no easy way to put it. "Yes, Adam, that's exactly what I'm telling you."

He thinks for a few seconds while his ego comes down from the stratosphere. Adam is also new to this organization and is looking for quick wins, but not for himself. He has nothing to prove given his success at completing several significant business turnarounds. No, this is needed for the organization to get its confidence back—to demonstrate they can do something new and different. He needs this win to buoy their belief that they can innovate with technology, and with that, ideally bring in new customers and revenue.

Adam looks over at me and says, "Okay, Isaac. How do we fix it?"

And inside, I think to myself, "Fuck." I know better than to show up at the CEO's office with a problem but without a plan or a solution. I have nothing formulated as the next steps, let alone a plan. I'm so proud of myself for dissecting the issues in such short order that I hurried to his office without thinking about the next steps and what I will need to develop a plan.

More important, I have no idea what I need from him and the organization. What are the changes that are going to get this product back on track? These are things that you can't shoot from the hip. Even if you get it right, a good CEO will see right through you. You're bluffing at the poker table with a mediocre hand at best, and now you need some cards to fall your way.

I take a deep breath and reply, "We have to take a few steps back and review the vision behind this product. I saw how the existing product is delivered and have a basic understanding of its value. I saw a new design that looks great on paper but may not be feasible to implement in a reasonable amount of time or with a team that is still learning the customer needs, data, and technology."

Alarm bells go off in my head. I'm losing him, I think to myself. I have to bring this back to earth. "The developers are following the whims of one product manager who knows the business and customer needs well. The rest of the team doesn't, and they're just trying to get the technology to do what the design requires. We need to pull up and make sure the team understands the product vision, and we have to help the product manager better understand how to pursue a minimal viable product."

> Notice, I don't use the acronym MVP when speaking to a CEO.

I'm watching Adam's expressions now, and I know he's beginning to understand. He's seen this before. But I go on because this isn't just a product management issue. "Then, the team is following agile ceremonies, but they aren't applying the practices in a way that solves problems. They need coaching, and I will step up to get this started. It's through this dialog we'll also review the underlying technologies and course-correct if necessary."

Have I covered everything? I trace through all the issues to decide what's relevant for the CEO to hear. Yes, there is one more, so I continue. "I'll also have to look at how we're defining projects and reporting on status. There's no way this project should have been labeled green for the last four weeks. There are plenty of signs indicating that this project is, at best, yellow and probably red. We can't have people sugarcoating status or afraid to report problems."

Adam gives me his okay. It's his way of saying that he got it and wants me to come back with something more substantive.

When You Pivot a Major Initiative, Step In and Help the Teams to Transition

This story doesn't end here. I have to get this team to change their mindset and practices quickly. I start with the basic agile ceremonies and help Theresa adjust the forty-five-minute "stand-up" to a properly run meeting lasting no more than fifteen minutes. We spend a ton of time documenting the product manager's vision, reviewing how customers use the legacy product, and defining some of the aspirations of the new product. We help the team understand how to write agile user stories and leave requirements documents as an artifact of the past.

But that is the easy part. The next step is separating the vision from the user experience and design, which was created in a vacuum absent of any realities of what it would require to engineer the underlying solution.

I pull the whole team together—Charles, Theresa, the engineers, the general manager of the business, and the head of sales for this product. I try to help the team understand. I start by sharing an honest assessment of where the product is and looking around the room to confirm where there is buy-in. There are questions and some challenges that we work through, but I halt any suggestion of blame on one person's part.

I try to explain to the team and the business leaders in terms they understand. We work in the construction industry, and I draw some analogies and differences between architecting buildings and engineering experiences with data and technology.

"The challenges we see in the product and implementation are not a product management matter or a technology one. It isn't happening because of corporate standards and requirements. Don't blame the service provider or suggest the issues lie in India. We have a collective problem in how everyone is working as a team.

"On the one hand, you can't have the architect designing your new kitchen without an engineer there to provide feedback on the construction. Otherwise, you might end up with a design that requires upgrading foundations and takes too long or is too costly to construct. On the other hand, you don't want the engineers ripping floors and walls apart until they better understand what the new experience requires.

"Now some gotchas can happen in construction that can throw a curveball to a plan. Maybe an exposed beam is rotting and needs reinforcements. Perhaps the customer sees a new cabinet being installed and has a change of heart on her selections. In commercial construction, both situations require the owner, architect, and engineer to agree to pivot and adjust their priorities."

I continue, relating the problem at hand to the construction analogy.

"In application development and technology projects, the number of unknowns is far greater. We work with a mix of familiar technologies, legacy ones, and new ones where we're trying to innovate. Just like in a construction renovation project, we might find technical debt, the equivalent of a rotting beam that needs fixing. We're equally likely to find that our customers better understand what they need as they see and use the product.

"It's for these reasons that we can't fully lock in the customer experience before and work completely independent from the engineering teams. Similarly, this team can't architect and select technologies without prototyping some of the underlying use cases.

"The designer and the engineering team must work together, iteratively, while building up confidence that the design and underlying technologies meet customer needs. And when we finish an iteration, we need to demo it in front of some users to get feedback. Are we on the right course? Is this showing the data you need to help drive decisions? Are we using the right terminology?"

Over the next several weeks, my leadership team and I work with this group to start afresh. We get agile fully in place with two-week sprints. We then break down the essence of the product to a vision, high-level epics, and then a handful of priority features.

We also start working with a different BI tool. Technology teams can't select platforms solely on their alignment to an exhaustive laundry list of current and future state capabilities. The selection process should include a better understanding of required skills and how the team wants to work. Checking all the feature boxes but requiring significant learning, skills, and programming to configure is not optimal for teams that want to build and test quickly. Time to value is a critical design criterion for digital platforms and seeking technologies that provide self-service capabilities to business users has significant advantages. Especially in data and analytics tools, where the subject matter expertise is with the business and the best tools are easy to learn and adopt.

But selecting nimble, self-serving tools comes with trade-offs that require significant and repetitive dialog with business leaders. Some are still stuck with the 1990s notion that technology teams and platforms must fully align with business requirements—in other words, the business selects technologies, and IT implements them.

Screw that. It's dead wrong, and this misstep buries many IT organizations with hard-to-use legacy systems that are complex to integrate and support. Business leaders must articulate the vision, customers, value propositions, business opportunities, and constraints and then partner with technologists on solutions. And when I say technologists, that often means architects, developers, engineers, data scientists, security specialists, and others versed in the problems and applicable technologies.

And sometimes it takes a blow-up moment to get everyone to understand it. That moment happens with this team about two months later.

How to Create a Blow-Up Moment

The team accepts the new technology and is sprinting with the product owners. But I am watching the demos and getting wary of what I am seeing.

Charles is still trying to make the team match a specific workflow that he has in mind—a way of navigating the application that works for him as an expert, but not necessarily one that would work with customers. The dev team implements the workflow in the BI platform, but the performance is poor, and the experience is lackluster. The team hasn't learned the platform's best capabilities and how to design optimal experiences. Instead, they are trying to make the technology work against its best practices.

So even though they are operating in sprints, they aren't collaborating or learning together. What's worse, they aren't bringing all their stakeholders to their demos and getting broader feedback to make adjustments.

I could let this go on if I want, and the team will probably get a working product this way. But it will be subpar and unlikely to resonate with customers.

So I fix this on the grand stage.

Our CEO Adam and the whole management team visit this group for a full day of meetings, and I schedule a time slot on the agenda to do a demo. Charles would demo what the team is working on, but I fear a ho-hum reaction. The product is better than where it was two months earlier, but it isn't going to wow or impress anyone.

And I know how this will go down. No matter how much I try to get business and technology teams to collaborate, business leaders are more likely to blame the technology team when projects aren't going exactly as planned.

I can see how this will play out. A big room. All the executives there, and the demo is less than perfect. The executive group is still new, and we're not operating as a team yet. They know I drove the changes, and I have a couple of supporters in the room, but I'm still new to the rest of them. So when the discussion goes south, the darts will flow in my direction.

Time for a preemptive strike. Anticipating this, I have an alternative demo in my back pocket that a friend of mine helped create in case things went south.

He's an expert on the BI platform, and I know the technology can do more than how the team currently uses it. I know it can look better, function better, and perform better. Sometimes a team just needs a bit of help to get started, and sometimes they need a little bit of a shock.

My friend reviews the data and the application and comes up with several alternative experiences that are more visual and vibrant. They use clickable charts instead of drop-down filters, which should be easier for our customers to use. These dashboards show purpose and focus on specific questions and problems. And they're fast.

I share them with Charles and the team, but it's a lot to absorb. It's like looking at three completely different kitchen designs, knowing they are all functional kitchens. But which one will the customer want? Which is easier to use and sell? We need additional time to research these options, but I inform Charles that I may elect to share these screens with the executive group to get their feedback.

Awkward Blow-Up Moments Often Lead to Innovative Solutions

Charles does his demo at the meeting, and I read the room. It's the first time the executives have really spent time on this product, and I see a group of blank faces. They are watching a demo of a sophisticated B2B product designed for a customer segment that many of them don't know very well.

But Charles has his own stakeholders he works with on the product. They are highly knowledgeable and work with customers daily. Some of them are also experts with the underlying data and perform ad hoc analysis on it regularly.

No one in the room is shy. The experts start asking Charles questions, and he does his best to answer them. Can it break down the data with customized dimensions? Can we add columns on the fly and implement nested sorts? Can we develop custom searches to define the views?

More questions are voiced, and Charles doesn't know all the answers. He lets the group know. "I'm not sure if the technology can do what you're asking." That works the first and second time, but by the third time, I definitely see a drop in everyone's confidence.

And as expected, now everyone's eyes are focused on me. I see the pitchforks and torches, and they're about to scream, "Burn the CIO!" They're thinking: He chose the technology platform and brought agile here. He works with the corporate IT groups.

At that moment, I went for it. I didn't have anything to lose at this point. The group needs to see what the technology and the team are capable of implementing. When you walk into the car showroom, there's always more than one model on the floor. And when you're at the poker table, always leave yourself outs, and in this case, the alternative design is my big bet.

I display the alternative designs and begin talking through what they're seeing, but I'm not an expert on the data and the use cases. Instead, I just let the visuals do the talking. The dashboard has a map and some stacked bar charts to help users navigate to answers. It looks a lot better than the screen of drop-down filters that Charles demoed earlier.

But we have detractors in the room who have high expectations. A demo to them implies a finished product. Charles hasn't invited them to the agile demos, so they aren't used to seeing a work-in-progress application. They aren't versed in providing constructive feedback.

The executives are getting wary. This is supposed to be a team-building meeting, not one that creates new frictions. I can see the

CEO is ready to cut off the conversation, and he has no problem killing dead-end projects. I've seen him do it before.

But while this is going on, the head of the product's sales has stepped up to the screen. He's looking at the map and the bar charts. He's not your average salesperson; he's more like a sales consultant as he helps customers leverage our analytics products to grow their businesses. And he's more than a consultant because he's a stakeholder to our agile development practices and provides feedback on what customers need and around the user experience. He knows the dashboards must demonstrate the breadth of data and the value of the analytics, but also be easy to use.

It's at that moment that he turns around to everyone and announces, "Folks, this is exactly what we need."

And over the next few years, this team builds three analytics products, adds customers, and grows revenue. The products turn around the business, and this is one of the legendary moments that truly aligns the team.

Digital Trailblazer Lessons

Leading Innovation and Developing Products

I filled this chapter with hard lessons learned about product management, architecture, teams, culture, leadership, and agile practices. Developing consensus around innovations, technology platforms, and feature roadmaps is difficult—no, it's nearly impossible—and that's a reality Digital Trailblazers must navigate. Waiting for everyone to agree on a direction is stagnation, and transformation leaders must steer the culture toward experimentation and real-time learning rather than perfection and utopian harmony.

Here are key leadership lessons to take away from this chapter:

1. **Align on the product vision because roadmaps are rarely straight-line journeys.** Organizations often try to pack too much into their business cases—resulting in lengthy presentations that may look impressive in the boardroom but are too complex for implementation teams. It's important to align everyone on the product vision before detailing the user persona, journey maps, values streams, and functional requirements.

   Start by creating a single-page vision statement that clearly outlines how your product will benefit customers and stakeholders. It's easier to secure a shared understanding from a single-page vision document than from a seemingly endless scroll of business artifacts. My company's vision statement is available for free at https://www.starcio.com/digital-trailblazer/vision-statement.

   Remember, the road to great products and experiences is never a straight line. It's easy to get lost in the details. And along the way, the product documentation will likely evolve through ongoing feedback and experimentation. When you have a single-page vision statement that you can continuously point to as your north star, you'll be better positioned to keep your teams and business stakeholders focused.

2. **Start with basic agile and scrum fundamentals when establishing new teams or course-correcting struggling ones.** When teams aren't working well together, it is not easy for them to accomplish their goals. There's a sizable gap between textbook agile and scrum processes compared to how people in groups interpret agile principles, mindset, and culture. So, when I hear a team is doing agile but missing goals, I start digging into their process. For new teams, I always begin by reviewing their scrum ceremonies, even if

there are standards, tools, or expert coaches in place. Once the team has basic practices instituted, I review how well they use agile approaches to solve planning challenges and execution problems. All too often, teams go through the scrum ceremonies without understanding how to apply them to solve their issues, opportunities, obstacles, and conflicts. This isn't an overnight improvement, and the transition from practicing agile to agile mindsets takes time, best practice guides, and coaching.

3. **Begin agile continuous planning immediately after defining the vision and agreeing to pursue a new idea.** It's a misconception that agile practices begin the moment the development team kicks off its first sprint. It actually must begin sooner—from the point when a leader transforms an idea into a vision. Agile planning should start at the exact moment when someone begins working on the idea with little detail, like a row in a spreadsheet or database record identifying the business need or opportunity. That may seem premature but starting early sets up the entire product development process for success.

   Too many organizations miss this critical step. As a result, key team members miss out on the opportunity to add their input. Once the business need or opportunity is identified, agile processes should be adopted to ensure speed to market and deliver sustainable solutions.

   This means the product owner must iterate on the vision statement with the full team. The designer must iterate on their understanding of personas and user needs, and they must partner with engineers to gather their ideas and best practices. Architects must prototype with engineers using different technologies and implementation approaches, formulating success criteria that helps everyone align on an execution strategy. When product owners implement continuous agile planning from the get-go, they are setting off on a stronger course.

4. **Promote team culture by listening, reserving judgment, asking questions, managing conflict, and just being nice.** You're probably nodding your head around this lesson as people largely have the right intentions when working in teams. But as pressure mounts to fulfill requirements, address quality standards, meet stakeholder expectations, and hit looming deadlines, we all lose our cultural compass at some point.

   We forget to do the little things like thanking people for their best efforts. We pass judgment too quickly without realizing we might be offending someone's hard work and best intentions. We're offended by questions as if someone is challenging our expertise, knowledge, or integrity. Asking questions is the required theater to build a shared understanding and secure "business-IT alignment" or just alignment in general.

   One of the key differences between great teams and average ones is how they create and manage conflict. Teams that can learn how to step on each other's toes without hurting anyone are more likely to learn from each other, handle stressful moments, have fun, and create a culture that more people are excited to be a part of. Because these teams are open to challenging each other and debating solutions, they are more likely to challenge legacy practices, innovate collaboratively, and deliver robust solutions. When I showed the alternate BI dashboards to the leadership group, I hoped my colleagues would understand my intent and goal to bring a great product to market.

It also means that these teams are more likely to avoid the hot-potato culture—an environment where people avoid taking on new challenges and responsibilities. When there's a gap in ownership, people on these teams step in to fill it, knowing their colleagues will respect their judgments. For example, let's say your QA engineer is unexpectedly out the week of a major release. Who should step in and review the performance, security, and functionality tests for any major issues? On great teams, you'll find several people willing to step up and fill the gap.

5. **Answer the question before steaming through jargon-filled details, and have some ideas on the next steps.** The single hardest thing engineers, product managers, and data scientists must master when progressing to leadership roles is answering questions top-down without brain dumping all the underlying details. If the person asking the question wants details, they'll let you know what information they're interested in. While you must operate in the weeds, don't lose your audience in the swamp before providing answers to their fears and aspirations. And don't make the mistake of not thinking a couple of steps ahead on where to go next. Getting it wrong is okay and should be strived for, especially if it brings forth a dialog. If you are in the weeds and don't have answers on where to go next, then you truly are lost.

   So how should you adjust your approach to answering questions when your engineering, science, or business training often leads you straight into the details and problem solving? Part of the answer is coming into a discussion prepared. When I met the CEO around the product launch delays, I had a pretty good idea of what I wanted to say, but unfortunately, I made a serious mistake of presenting the problem without being prepared to discuss the next steps or solutions.

Then when you are asked a question, don't allow your voice to run faster than your mind. Develop your active listening skills by pausing, thinking, and making sure you understand the question's intent. Get to the answer in your mind, and then you're ready to articulate it to your audience. Active listening, top-down thinking, and succinctly answering questions are key leadership skills, especially when managing up to your bosses or trying to influence colleagues.

It was impossible for me to present product management and innovation without touching on agile practices, ways of working, and culture. And if you read my first book, *Driving Digital*, you know that I believe agile is fundamental to leading transformation. In the next chapter, I share some of the stories and lessons learned in developing agile teams and challenging an enterprise's waterfall practices.

If you would like more specifics on these lessons learned and best practices, please visit https://www.starcio.com/digital-trailblazer/chapter-4.

Note

1. "Manifesto for Agile Software Development," 2001, agilemanifesto.org. https://agilemanifesto.org/.

Chapter 5

"That's Not Agile": Defining Your Organization's Agile Way of Working

Matthew talks a mile a minute. I'm sitting in a room interviewing for an IT leadership role, and he's just going on about NoSQL technologies, user experiences built on top of social networks, and getting the perfect office environment to practice agile. What's more, our interview includes a couple of agile coaches, and I can't tell if he's been working with them for a while or if they're also interviewing for roles. The coaches keep steering the conversation toward scrum best practices, democratizing the development process, empowering engineers, and achieving a zen of collaboration.

What's clear is that they're sizing me up based on my reactions. So be it. I can play this game, and they're putting me through all the common agile team problem scenarios.

"How do you handle a team with a developer that's not finishing their stories?"

"What's the best way to handle product owners who ask the team to overcommit?"

"What should the team do to improve their velocity?"

To nail this interview, I have to strike a balance between listening and sharing my approaches without overwhelming them with expertise that may come across as arrogance. Plus, these guys sound like they have their shit together, although, almost to a fault. It's as if they plan to develop an agile religion inside the company.

I've run agile teams without coaches and without all this jargon around culture, mindset, or striving for happy teams. Until then, as a startup CTO, agile was a means to get to an end. It was a way to guide development teams that were never told the complete requirements, and if they were, the business requirements documents were too long for anyone to digest. And the requirements changed all the time anyway. Can you imagine scanning version seven of a twenty-page requirements document before Microsoft Word had the track-changes feature? Plus, we had to deploy features to users just to see what worked.

We were naturally aiming for lean software development lifecycles and low overhead so we could push features frequently. We had plenty of automation in UNIX scripts and open source sysadmin apps, but they were kludged together without standard ways of orchestrating end-to-end processes. Back then, we met daily, but we didn't call those meetings stand-ups. We raised the issues that might prevent us from completing a feature on schedule but didn't have scrum masters or formal agile tools to record these issues as blocks. We constantly talked about improving our processes, our code, and our ways of working with our business leaders, but we didn't call it a retrospective meeting. It was, well, just an obvious way to get work done.

I pass the interview, and one month later, I start my new role as the vice president of technology for this business.

It's only then that I realize how freaking clueless I was about agile.

My teams and experience to that point had all been with startups and relatively small development organizations. When the IT team was big, it was because we had gotten that way through acquiring new businesses and had teams working on independent applications in different locations. In other words, I had only worked with a whole bunch of small agile teams that didn't need to collaborate, share best practices, or engineer their way through dependencies.

In my previous roles, our employees and contractors simply had to learn our development process. There wasn't a legacy waterfall mindset for anyone to latch onto as a sacred institutional cow. Yes, there was significant technical debt, but we didn't have to worry about integrating with legacy enterprise systems. Our applications were in data centers, but we managed them and convinced our system administrators to make changes and deployments when required. We tested because it was the right thing to do to ensure quality, not because there was a brand at risk or a compliance issue if we deployed shitty code.

I'm one month into this new job at an eighty-year-old enterprise, and the leaders want to develop their own proprietary customer-facing web applications. I think it's crazy that they want to operate like a software startup, and I tell them as much, but they insist they need to develop an innovative way of interfacing with customers. It's before "digital transformation" is a popular buzzword, and most companies think of technology as a build-versus-buy decision. And back then, most large enterprises were buying technology—not building personalized customer experiences or overly tailoring workflows—because it was expensive and difficult to plan, develop, and maintain custom code.

How did I get here? Why did I pivot from startup glory and secluded environments to a messy, political, and sometimes backward enterprise role?

Bringing Agile Startup Cultures to a Large Enterprise

I loved startup life. Every day brought new challenges, and it required all of us to wear many hats and evolve our ways of working. One day I am sitting behind a screen debugging code, and the next day I am meeting customers and potential business partners. I even met the younger Elon Musk when he was at Zip2 and seeking partnerships with other media startups. I reached my fix at growing startups with mostly so-so wins. Financially, I did fine and had some exits, but I never achieved sit-on-the-beach, cash-in-and-done success.

I often think about one of my favorite opening movie scenes in *Rounders*, where Matt Damon's character is driving a truck, making deliveries to convenience stores. He opens the movie saying, "You don't hear much about guys who take their shot and miss, but I'll tell you what happens to 'em. They end up humping crappy jobs on graveyard shifts, trying to figure out how they came up short."

This isn't me exactly. I definitely feel as though I've taken my shot, and this isn't a crappy job by any stretch of the imagination. But it is a job with new rules and ways of getting things done that are foreign to me. They hire me to bring a startup technology capability to this enterprise that, somewhere in their executive wisdom, decides it needs technology and data to be a core competency. They want me to get them there. Here's what I'm walking into.

Matthew leads a small group on this new customer-facing web application, a cross between a curated content management system and a social network. It's July, and they're starting to prototype the technology architecture, user experiences, and data sources that will play important roles in the product's architecture. The team they've appointed to work on this app includes a few contract developers from one company helping with the development and a second consulting group coaching the team on agile and scrum. They are also working with several employees from the department, though not enough, and I plan to bring more onto this team so that they learn agile and the new technologies.

This small team is collocated in one corner of our office space. To foster collaboration, they proactively open up the enclosed area by removing the cubicle dividers, a feat that gets me a visit from the head of facilities for several infractions. The team's fishing around for agile tools, but they're using note cards and boards for now. We don't have a product owner yet, so Matthew is wearing a few hats, playing a part-time innovator, agile coach, technical lead, architect, product owner, and technical recruiter.

It takes me time to understand Matthew's vision fully, but to this day, he is one of the smartest and most innovative people I've known.

The good news I see in my first month is this team is highly motivated and is proactively finding ways to identify talent, hire experts, prototype technologies, and kick off agile practices. The bad news is that I also see their upcoming institutional impediments, and it's going to be on me to bulldoze through them.

It's a job I'm not sure I know or understand. Actually, I'm freaking clueless about how to get things done in an enterprise. At startups, I was the one creating the standards and formal practices; here, they thrust them on me with little explanation as to why they exist, what's required, and when.

And sure, we had our share of politics and organizational dysfunctions in my startups. Which board member came up with the brilliant idea of keeping two CEOs as co-CEOs after a merger "of equals"? Who thought it was smart to run television commercials weeks after launching a website on new technology platforms? What venture capitalist believed it was wise to participate in an angel round and then demand monthly financial updates from the founders?

In the end, these were all just bad decisions that I either worked around or bulldozed if I had enough will and muscle to take them on.

Here and now in an enterprise, the impediments I'm seeing are indoctrinated behaviors and corporate guidelines. I'm here to guide this agile development team to be fast and nimble, but with no formalities and planning practices, which I will guide them on. But these agile ways of working and startup mindsets are on a collision course with the enterprise's rigid business processes, slow decision-making functions, highly formalized financial management rules, and strict technology standards. These aren't archaic, bureaucratic, or politically driven practices, but they are too slow and structured at a time when the business I work for requires faster decision-making and execution. I have no experience successfully melding a startup mindset with these enterprise standards, and I don't want to be labeled a maverick by working around them.

The primary issue is timing. The business leaders tell me that the funding approved for this project is just for a small pilot. We must make a business case for the entire investment.

Well, what goes into making this business case, I think to myself? I find myself navigating through layers of corporate technology functions and meeting their leaders to figure it out. Because I don't have time to read through reams of outdated documentation buried in a half dozen SharePoint sites, let alone the other requirements no one bothered to document.

Here's what I learn. You must present in front of two committees: one to get approval on the architecture and a second to review the business model, project plan, and financial returns. These committees meet monthly, and there's a series of ceremonies to complete even before getting on their agendas.

Okay, so I must come up with a bunch of convincing PowerPoints. How hard can that be? I can do that.

The more difficult issue is timing. The business leaders want a working prototype by the end of the year. The deadline is strategic because it's the best way to start building momentum within the business behind the program and to ensure funding will continue into the next year.

I start running a schedule in my head. I don't know when the executive committee finalizes budgets, but I estimate no later than November. I guess it will take at least four months to build a functioning prototype, which means we must be hardcore coding by no later than August. But it's already July, so the earliest we can get through all these committees is also in August. And that means we must develop all the materials, get on their agendas, and pass their investment criteria, otherwise we won't have signoff on the funding for the people and technology we need.

We have nothing to show at these meetings. There's no project plan, no financials, no architecture, and barely a team. But what we do have is a small group practicing agile, so I have little doubt they'll be able to build the prototype in time. What troubles me is wondering how we'll complete all these materials and estimate a multimonth plan before the first committee meeting.

It's then that I also realize we don't have a technology architecture defined. All we have is a bunch of half-developed diagrams and several technology vendor proposals that haven't been thoroughly reviewed. While the developers have some new technologies installed on their desktops so they can code, none of it is installed in the data center yet. From what I understand, that alone is a process that often takes months, and we can't even make that request until we get through all these committees. And these committees want to see a fully baked plan showing how we'll take the upfront investment and turn it into profit, specifically a profit with a defined internal rate of return that exceeds corporate guidelines.

Holy crap, this really is an agile bus that's picking up speed and about to collide into a slow-moving enterprise freight train.

I go with my gut. No, we aren't going to sidestep these procedures even though my leadership team suggests it. I challenge the status quo by presenting an agile program, and it isn't anything like these committees have seen before. I share an architecture that's only a development environment and one that we plan to experiment and iterate on and improve. Because that's all we have right now, and we don't have a test, prod, and disaster recovery environment proposed even though it's required. We need to use the prototype period to iterate on the architecture. Imagine that?

No, I'm not presenting a Gantt chart with a fixed timeline and deliverable. We're starting with two-week sprints, and we'll have a working prototype with a handful of essential functions that make up an MVP. The financials show an investment without any returns. Our key performance indicators are designed to prove the architecture, demonstrate we can succeed with agile in an enterprise, and deliver a working prototype business leaders deem a successful MVP.

I concede that once we achieve these goals, we'll come back to the committees with an update and forward-looking plan. It's a concession I loathe because it means I'll have to prepare and go through this charade again, but there isn't a way around it.

I'm on vacation the week the final committee is meeting and elect to fly back for the day to deliver the presentation. I just can't see them greenlighting a controversial project with a new vice president presenting remotely.

I walk in with my colleagues, including Jerry, the head of the digital strategy, and Josh, our controller. Having the controller there is a requirement but bringing the business leader is my idea. Committee members are sitting around a U-shaped table in an enormous conference room on one of the top floors in this iconic New York City skyscraper. There isn't Zoom, and the conference room doesn't even have screens in it—just a single speakerphone in the center. I'm damn happy I went with my gut and decided to fly in for this meeting.

This presentation is ten slides. We're on slide three when the door opens, and an older gentleman wearing a blue suit walks in. He sits in a row of chairs on the left side behind the committee members. I don't know him. For that matter, I don't know most of the people in the room, but I can tell they all take notice of him coming into the meeting.

Despite the bureaucracy and archaic process, it's efficient, and the presentation must be completed in twenty minutes so that they can tackle several of these in each session.

We finish delivering the presentation, and I look around the room. I see the corporate CIO and the head of enterprise architecture looking at each other and sharing a couple of nods. The corporate controller flips through the pages in front of her and looks up like she's about to say something, but her eyes veer toward the man in the blue suit, and she backs down. There are no questions, no comments, and no reactions. They thank us for the presentation, we exit the room, and I think to myself, "Wait, what the hell just happened?"

Later that day, I hear the committee accepted our proposal with a few inconsequential follow-ups. I also learn that the man in the blue suit was the president of our segment, an executive-level position reporting to the CEO who oversees several information and media businesses. He's a well-respected right-hand lieutenant to the CEO, and it's entirely out of the ordinary for him or anyone at that executive level to show up at one of these committee meetings.

It always helps to have a rabbi in your corner.

> To this day, I don't know exactly why he came, but I suspect it was because the company was *Businessweek,* a favorite business of McGraw Hill's CEO, Terry McGraw. It was a business everyone wanted to succeed in, despite all the digital tradewinds blowing against it. It was 2007 and bringing agile, NoSQL, and developing customer experiences based on social networking capabilities were all relatively new, especially at an enterprise. People and leaders need mentors, and controversial transformation programs sometimes need them too. That's the notion of a rabbi in this context, someone who is very well-respected who looks after your well-being despite the obstacles.

Not One Agile: Adapting an Agile Way of Working

And now we must pull it off. Develop a large-scale customer-facing application on new technology with a scrum process. I'm back on home ice—a hockey phrase—with obstacles and challenges that all seem surmountable. We have a smart, collocated team, working well together and finding their way through blocks. We aren't far enough along for the detractors to emerge, but I know they'll come. But today, I feel good about where this program stands and what we need to do to succeed.

I return from lunch and walk the hall toward my office, past a conference room with a door slightly open, and hear someone say it.

"That's not agile."

Today is the first time I hear this phrase, but it comes up over and over again throughout my career as a CIO. These days, it often comes up when I lead workshops and agile center of excellence programs as StarCIO's CEO. It's tiring, but it's also something I must address when someone raises it.

Sometimes the person is really saying, "No way I'm doing that." Other times, it's a chest-beating, "I know agile, and I want to control the agile way of working around here." Sometimes, there's a less forward meaning like, "I'm a certified scrum master and have certification . . .," which can be a polite way of saying that they never learned what I'm sharing at one of their training sessions.

I'm instantly frustrated because I know I may have a heckler to deal with inside the group. Or maybe it's someone who needs help understanding the differences between agile ceremonies and agile ways of working. Then my initial anger subsides, and the cool, experienced Isaac takes over and realizes that he must slow down.

Getting people "on board" with agile methodologies means they must understand the "why" even more than the "what" around the roles, practices, ceremonies, and target outcomes. When people understand the "why," it drives agile ways of working, agile cultures, and agile mindsets.

After getting through our approvals, we go straight back to work on developing the application but also on formalizing our agile way of working. By then, we have a small team of developers cranking out code and have a tool to track the user story backlog. We also hire a product manager to assume the product owner role, and we're trying to get him off old-school thinking around writing long-form requirement documents.

It's early days in our development process when I am walking down the halls and hear that first "that's not agile." I peek into the room to see who uttered those words, and they came from one of the agile coaches working with Matthew and the team.

The phrase irks me, but I decide to let it go and let the team work it out. I turn the corner to head toward my office when I hear the product owner raising his voice and sounding frustrated. His exact words are, "You guys can go do your agile thing and convert my requirements documents to user stories."

And now, I feel compelled to inject myself into how Matthew, the coach, and the team want to run agile. The team's success depends on introducing some of my experiences into the discussion, and I want them to look beyond some of the idealized agile principles. We are still operating in a large enterprise that has some reasonable requirements. Plus, I know I need to have strong collaboration and partnership between the business and the development team to establish an agile culture. That means the team must make some adjustments to the out-of-the-box scrum.

I invite myself into the meeting, which isn't out of the ordinary, at least for our agile meetings, because we institute an open-door policy for brainstorming sessions like this one as well as our sprint reviews.

Brainstorming sessions are for problem-solving. We schedule two of them weekly, and there's often a battle on what's on the agenda. Sometimes it can be an implementation issue, like figuring out how to modify a schema to support a new business requirement. Other times, they are strategic, and we whiteboard different user experiences, realign people on agile teams, or break down complex requirements. Brainstorming sessions have a format for running them, and there's a requirement to invite a small and diverse group to participate in them.

When I walk into this brainstorming session, I can see that estimating and planning the next sprints of user stories is on the agenda. Our product owner, technical lead, agile coaches, and Matthew are in attendance. I listen to the debate for a while, and I hear the plight in the product owner's voice. He's happy to know what the team commits to at the start of the sprint but has no idea what comes afterward. He prioritizes the next features on the backlog, but they're not broken down by the team or estimated. He wants some visibility so that he can manage stakeholder expectations.

But the coach responds again, "That's not agile," and wants the team to have more flexibility at the start of every sprint. The technical lead is concerned about the added time required to break down and estimate more features. Matthew seeks a compromise, where the team analyzes one feature for the product owner, but not more. I think he sides with the agile coaches but wants to resolve the conflict and figures a token analysis isn't going to take the agile team off course.

I wait until I hear everyone's opinion before chiming in. We're in a brainstorming session, which means they start with problem statements, require a presentation of data and facts, provide time for everyone's opinions, lead to collaborative debate, and end with decisions. Now that I've stepped in, they expect me to contribute, and the team knows that I'm not shy about providing an answer.

How far to plan agile backlogs is a crucial decision for agile teams. I sense it at the time, and resolving it becomes a seed I nurture for the next decade working with other organizations adopting agile methodologies.

But today, after acknowledging everyone's opinions and thanking them for open dialog, I get straight to the point with how we need to move forward. Here's what I tell Matthew, the coaches, and the agile development team:

"I need everyone to think about planning their backlog beyond the next sprint. The business teams need some visibility over what may come after we finish the current sprint and what work we're planning for the next ones. Yes, I know that there are no guarantees, and we are likely to adjust priorities and requirements based on customer feedback, but there's a dialog we need to have with stakeholders before we can write the next set of stories.

"In this sprint, we must schedule these conversations about work that may not be developed for another couple of sprints. We're going to need to review and discuss what we're planning and get your understanding of how the features we're considering break down with some early estimates."

I think the coach almost fell out of his chair. It was then he said one last time, "That's not agile."

Now estimating was not a revolutionary request. James Grenning introduced planning poker back in 2002,[1] and Mike Cohn published his book on agile estimation[2] and planning in 2005. Truth be told, I didn't know about the book or planning poker and was just following my instincts, so I explain both what and why we needed to expand our notion of planning beyond the next sprint.

Let me explain the jargon for those of you new to agile and scrum. Agile estimating is a process where teams quantify the complexity and effort to fully implement an agile user story—a single, small, atomic improvement to an application, a dashboard, or whatever the team is developing. Agile user stories must deliver value to a customer, and a best practice is to write requirements with pass/fail acceptance criteria. Many teams estimate in story points, an artificial metric, and often use the Fibonacci sequence to indicate easy-to-implement improvements (one-point stories) and others that are more complex, need more team collaboration, or require significant implementation effort (13- or 21-one-point stories). Agreeing on the number of story points is part art and part science, and planning poker is one popularized approach to help teams agree on the estimate. But it's an approach I don't advocate in StarCIO Agile Center of Excellence (COE) programs because it gamifies instead of creating a dialog around solutions and implementation options.

The coach explains his objection to agile estimation and planning multi-sprint backlogs. "Agile is about giving the product owner the ability to prioritize every sprint and learn from feedback when the team demos at the sprint review. Why should we plan sprints ahead if we reprioritize the work anyway? And why would we estimate when the product owner should prioritize on business value and impact to end users?"

These are good questions, and I have spent the better part of my career answering them for many teams. The programs I offer at StarCIO help organizations adopt planning and estimation practices that I've been using at different companies for well over a decade.

My favorite objections come from groups that have tried to adopt the Scaled Agile Framework (SAFe)[3] but struggled or failed. SAFe, a system for implementing agile practices at scale, is a rigorous process for establishing scrum standards across a large development organization. By large, I mean thousands of people, although I'm sure that SAFe practitioners suggest that it works in smaller organizations. I'm sure it can, but at what cost to implement all the framework's rigor?

SAFe advocates a process called Program Increment (PI)[4] planning where organizations break for a sprint, called the Innovation and Planning Iteration,[5] to do an increment of planning, which is typically between eight and twelve weeks[6] in duration. This practice often includes gathering for a few days so that teams coordinate their plans and resolve dependencies.

Now that doesn't sound very agile to me. Trying to gather the best minds to flesh out all the nuances in a plan and then go back to their offices over the next several months to execute on it? That sounds, well, very waterfall to me.

I explain to the coach, as I've done many times since then, "Agile teams must be continuously planning. Every sprint, you deliver an improvement to the product, and you should also be updating the plan. To do this with an organization full of stakeholders requires the product owner and technical lead to plan several sprints ahead of the team's work. The team must partner with the product owner by helping them understand different solutions, break down features into stories, and provide estimates. These estimates help product owners better decide what to prioritize and when to reduce scope, especially when their requirements drive technical complexities.

"Only the estimating process must be efficient, and the product owner needs to understand how to use this information. I can't have product owners haggling over story points even though I know that will happen. The point is to get the right engagement with customers, end users, and stakeholders so that we work on the right things."

I take a slug of coffee and continue.

"Now, in a startup, maybe all the development and planning can happen within the two-week sprint. They're working on new technology with very talented engineers. They can process feedback quickly because they only have a few customers using their products in the early days. They don't have legacy technology and likely have minimal technical debt to work around. They're going to figure out how to operationalize their product later. Some may underinvest in compliance, security, and supportability of their application. That may fit their risk profile, but it doesn't work for organizations with customers, brand reputations, and applications with high usage from day one.

"In this world, we'll need more time to plan to bring in the right mix of designers, engineers, architects, information security, and other experts who might weigh in on the acceptance criteria of a user story or recommend aspects of its implementation. We'll also want stakeholders to see the designs, experiences, and workflows. The last thing we want is to start coding on something only to find out that key users of the system have diverse, better, or alternative ideas that the team never heard or considered."

To this day, I give variants of this monologue during workshops and keynotes. Agile's Manifesto[7] provides starting principles and practices for teams to adopt. It's a loose set of guidelines that companies need to define and improve as part of *their* agile cultures, *their* agile ways of working, and what it means to have an agile mindset.

The Agile Manifesto, signed by seventeen renowned technologists, established four values and twelve principles in agile software development. It introduced foundations such as customer satisfaction, working software, self-organizing teams, and continuous delivery but was not prescriptive to how organizations should interpret or implement them. Today, because people come into teams with different agile experiences and understand distinctive agile frameworks, it's important for Digital Trailblazers to define and evolve what an agile way of working means in their organization.

Sometimes self-organizing teams need me to come in as the heavy enforcer. They want to self-organize on a practice required by their team, only there may be contention around the methodologies, with their bosses, or with the team's product managers. Suppose the team starts hearing, "That's not agile," but is trying to implement a process that makes sense for their circumstances. In that case, that's where Digital Trailblazers must step in and facilitate an agile way of working discussion.

Prioritizing Technical Debt—Because They Are Business Issues

Many years later, one of my teams is working with a product owner who slams feature after feature down their throats. They're in a race to gain adoption of a new product, and the product owner is trying to get more salespeople to push his product. He is in that Catch-22 where the salespeople are pushing back: "If I don't have this widget, then I can't sell the product." Eventually, the company CEO steps in and calls bullshit on this behavior. When it reaches the level where it's an excuse for poor sales performance, then you must call in the really big guns.

But until then, my team escalates a problem to me that this drive for features is creating. This team is accumulating technical debt like teenagers who are maxing out their credit cards. The product is developed on new technology and went from prototype to proof of concept to pilot and then beta in record time. Since then, they've been adding and changing things to meet product needs. Only the work is getting harder, slower, and more error prone.

I get into the weeds to better understand the issue. As a leader, you must do this, especially when you're about to define a standard way of working. People will ask why and push back. Others will escalate their concerns to their sponsors, and you'll have to defend your decisions.

I assess the code, the testing, and the deployment processes the team is currently using. I also review the features the product owner is prioritizing. When I go to discuss my thinking with him, I listen first. Why did he prioritize the features? Who's the customer or persona they're targeting? What problem or opportunity does this capability address?

It's unfair because he doesn't know what I'm after, and I'm trying to determine whether I buy into his priorities. Sell me that the features you need are customer needs and business priorities. Convince me that you listen to the team's recommendations on the implementation, including sequencing the work, addressing defects, implementing reliability improvements, and reducing technical debt.

I then ask questions to see if he understands some of the technical issues. The good news is he does. The problem is, he just doesn't care enough and believes the team should work these technical issues out on their own as they work through his priorities.

And that's where the red flag goes up. I don't say it, but that's clearly not agile. He could have debated the importance or priority with me, but instead, he suggests the team should work on technical issues in addition and separate from his priorities. And quite frankly, I don't buy into his plan.

I decide this team should dedicate 30 percent of their commitments to address technical debt. I rationalize the number based on how software companies, before the days of SaaS when they charged license and support fees, invoiced 20 percent of the license as a yearly maintenance fee. If software companies need 20 percent for support and maintenance, then surely, we as a non-tech company can't be as efficient, so I asked for 30 percent.

Months later, I write the blog post, how to get the product owner to pay for technical debt.[8] It's a signature piece and a foundation of the agile programs I guide organizations on today.

Why Agile? It Connects Transformation Strategy to Execution

This also isn't the only time I confront product owners who don't share enough information with their team. Teams need to understand *why* a priority is important to customers. What is the *value* that's being addressed? What's the pain point? What are the alternatives end users are taking to work around the issue? Most importantly, teams must understand and believe why the product owner prioritizes a particular feature over the others.

Agile requires trust and shared understanding. I expect the product owner shares this information with the team. It's more than an expectation; it's a requirement for success.

It's also not easy, and it is time-consuming.

I truly believe product managers and owners have the hardest job in rolling out applications that delight customers and transform the organization. They experience huge demands on their time to talk to customers, stakeholders, and industry experts. To understand how the product is performing, they must consider market research, expert feedback, and many different reports from different systems. They must articulate the strategy and ensure they translate to precise business requirements—the *who*, *what*, and *why*—without overly defining the *how*, which should largely be left to the team to explain and defend.

By the time some product owners are ready to engage the development team on a product, a release, or a feature, they may be burned out from the time-consuming top-down communications. Some product owners feel the time pressure to start the development process, and some are lazy. Others don't see the value in sharing the depth of information with their development teams. They'll say, "They have their stories, they have the acceptance criteria, and I prioritized the backlog. What else do they need?"

When this happens, I'm the one who's saying, "That's not agile," but again, to myself, because the team must learn key agile principles, especially around knowledge sharing. The product manager or owner is missing how important it is to share context, rationale, and data with their teams. Trust is built by bringing agile teams on the journey and allowing them to ask questions and gather their input. This dialog needs to happen well before product managers firm up requirements—it should be a collaborative process with the agile team technical and quality leads.

In instances when I don't see the dialog, information sharing, and collaboration happening, I'm left no choice but to specify the operating principles and best practices. Much the same way, I want the IT operations team to share data on how a product is performing in production. I also want product management to share data on how the product is working with customers. I don't want this rehearsed, and I ask these leaders to open tools or build dashboards that share the underlying data—no slides and no spreadsheets. By showing teammates how to access the underlying data, eventually, they will self-service answers to their own questions.

Here's how I explain the operating principle to agile teams: "Let's pull up from our preconceived notions of a feature as only an end user capability. If what I am delivering can be expressed as a customer and business benefit, then it's a feature. It means features can include operational business needs, quality improvements, and compliance requirements. Security, performance, or reliability needs that improve customer experiences or reduce risks are features. Anyone can propose features to the product owner but should express them from a customer need, articulate a business value, and where possible, bring data to back up the proposal. Then, I expect the product owner to lead the discussion and finalize a balanced feature prioritization, accounting for growth, competitiveness, end user experiences, risks, costs, and other factors."

By taking this approach with the data, I'm empowering product managers to partner with appropriate stakeholders and share the most relevant information. The operating principle is that before you prioritize features—everything from product features and operational business needs to security needs and compliance issues—key partners should be able to see relevant data to understand the customer benefit and business value. That's not to say that the data will be conclusive or perfect in articulating their story. The operating principle forces the story to get told, and whatever data are available to be shared. Now that's agile.

Here's the thing. No one ever fully understands the first time I explain these concepts. You can conceptually understand agile concepts in a class or workshop, but it's not until you step into the process and adopt specific roles that you feel the experience. That's when teams truly begin to understand agile, and that's when many become evangelists. I explain the *why* behind the practice and basic details but share many of the mechanics during the implementation. I answer as many questions as I can and try to find who's willing to trust me. I start with them and sometimes leave others behind. They'll catch up.

Digital Trailblazer Lessons

Driving Agile Practices, Culture, and Mindset

Is agile a process in your organization, or is it underlying your company and organization's culture? Is the scope of your practices on delivery, or are you also planning and strategizing with agile methods and mindsets? Is agile only limited to your IT department and teammates, or are data scientists, product managers, marketing, finance, and operations participating in agile teams?

I hope you come away from this chapter asking these questions and pondering how to evolve the scope and depth of how to lead agile in your organizations.

Of all the areas I focus on as a leader, I use agile as the backbone for driving organizational change, experimentation, innovation, and process improvement. Digital Trailblazers take an active role in shaping their organization's agile ways of working.

Here are key leadership lessons to take away from this chapter:

1. **Drive transformation by emphasizing the *why* and coach on the *how* and *what*.** While this lesson should apply to almost everything you do to move your business, organization, and team forward, it's critically important to drive agile practices and culture. So much of agile focuses on the ritual and tools of implementing scrum or Kanban, and even my

programs from StarCIO emphasize process rigor. But people only adopt *what* you are trying to accomplish when they fully understand and embrace the *why*. To bring everyone along, they must understand from the beginning *why* it's important for the organization, *why* their participation is vital, and *why* you're prioritizing agile methodologies. Bringing the *why* to life takes effort and responsibility, especially when your teammates suggest alternative ways to accomplish your goals with an approach different from *what* you are trying to convince them to do. It will likely require repeatedly emphasizing *why* before everyone truly understands. That's why it's so important to have lieutenants who echo the message. Even more critical is that you eat your own dogfood. No one will buy into *why* a change is important if they don't see you embracing *what* you ask them to do.

I also suggest coaching people and teams on process and culture transformation. Coaching specifically means repeating the message (i.e., the *why* and *what*) with multiple people, done in the context of the work they're doing. That's the best way to get meaningful adoption.

2. **Align with your organization's principles and requirements before changing the culture.** If you're working in a startup, you likely have a relatively clean slate on establishing your organization's culture and practices. Your greatest challenge is hiring people who embrace your values and have diverse thinking and experiences. You want them to challenge your thinking with new ideas but also embrace your organization's core principles.

   That's a lot harder in non-startup organizations with established norms, cultural principles, and required practices. If you try bulldozing agile principles, practices, and culture into your organization without stating it from the existing context, you'll be labeled a maverick. You may achieve success in pockets that are willing to work outside of the organization's requirements, but you'll never get the support and backing to scale it. Institute agile practices in waves of participation because you'll lose new entrants if you break principles and rules too early.

3. **Develop a shared understanding of product owner, stakeholder, and agile team responsibilities.** In agile, there should be a healthy tension between the product owner and the team. Empower agile teams to commit to the work they accept for a sprint, and the product owner must trust that the team works to their full capacity. But that doesn't stop many product owners from asking and often demanding that more get done. They'll challenge estimates, push the team to increase velocity, and add to scope because their goals and responsibilities often demand it. In response, some agile teams will inflate their estimates, commit to less, or use other slow-down tactics. Some agile teams will also demonize product managers and owners, especially if the product teams report to a different organizational leader. It might help agile teams bond when they find a common scapegoat to blame for their stress, but it doesn't alleviate the underlying problem.

   Digital Trailblazers teach teammate empathy. It's time-consuming to get product owners to understand the technical steps to build quality deliverables. It's equally challenging to get agile teams to see all the business pressures and stakeholder demands the product owners face every time they say "no" or "later" to a legitimate business need. When these tensions escalate to agile leaders, drive empathy by helping everyone sit in each other's shoes.

4. **Show me the data before selling me your ideas.** I start all of my keynotes with a mix of data, charts, and data-driven insights. I select legitimate sources and hope these facts bring a data-driven context to my audience before sharing any big ideas. I do this at board meetings and workshops as well, and it's the first principle I emphasize with stakeholders trying to influence the priority and substance of an agile backlog. This data-driven approach, or operating principle, can infuriate some people because it adds work and discipline to their demands. My answer to this objection is, "Exactly."

   If you have a great idea for a feature, identify data that can help give you insights on whether customers will seek this capability from your product. If you must address technical debt before working on that feature, show some data illustrating why this is a critical undertaking. You don't need comprehensive data that demonstrates causality. Rather, you're seeking evidence to set the context of the request and help discern its priority versus other business needs. In other words, if you don't have any data to back up your story, it's nothing more than an invalidated idea.

5. **Reduce technical debt by making it everyone's responsibility.** If we all agree that innovation, customer experience, and operational efficiencies are primary business objectives, then technical debt is the friction that slows down and can even halt our ability to plan, deliver, and experiment. In fact, it's not just technical debt that can inhibit progress. Most organizations also have built up debt in operations, data, compliance, security, and other areas. The problem is bigger than fixing these issues or getting priority, budget, and skills to make adequate investments to reduce debt. No. The bigger

problem facing organizations is when there isn't holistic responsibility taken for the underlying product and operation. Believe me, I don't like to have to resort to edicts, and it's very hard to sell the *why* behind them or create empathy for those impacted. But I can analyze and share the data when backlogs are tracked by the type of prioritized work. I'll use that as the basis of my operating principle when teams underinvest in addressing debt. When that happens, they often fall victim when they can afford it the least, and the debt progresses into legacy systems or recurring operational incidents.

■ ■ ■

If you would like more specifics on these lessons learned and best practices, please visit https://www.starcio.com/digital-trailblazer/chapter-5.

Notes

1. "Wingman Software | Planning Poker—The Original Paper," 2021, Wingman-Sw.com, https://wingman-sw.com/articles/planning-poker.
2. Mike Cohn, 2005, *Agile Estimating and Planning*. Pearson India.
3. Moira Alexander, "What Is SAFe? The Scaled Agile Framework Explained," CIO.com, Feb. 9, 2021, https://www.cio.com/article/220569/what-is-safe-the-scaled-agile-framework-explained.html.
4. "PI Planning," Scaled Agile Framework, https://www.scaledagileframework.com/pi-planning/.
5. "Innovation and Planning Iteration," Scaled Agile Framework, https://www.scaledagileframework.com/innovation-and-planning-iteration/.
6. "Program Increment," Scaled Agile Framework, https://www.scaledagileframework.com/program-increment/.
7. "Manifesto for Agile Software Development," agilemanifesto.org, https://agilemanifesto.org/.
8. Isaac Sacolick, "How to Get an Agile Product Owner to Pay for Technical Debt," Social, Agile, and Transformation, https://blogs.starcio.com/2015/08/get-agile-product-owner-to-pay-technical-debt.html.

Chapter 6

Transforming Experiences with a Global Perspective

"Here's how we survive the fourteen-hour flight to Mumbai. We arrive at the airport early, check-in, and go straight to the international lounge. We enjoy a light dinner with two adult beverages. For me, that's two glasses of wine, either Chardonnay or Pinot Noir, depending on what's for dinner. Our flight is at 7 p.m., and we should be in the air enjoying our first in-air drinks 30 minutes later. Enjoy two more beverages and some water to hydrate yourself. Then, prepare to knock out for as long as possible."

I'm getting ready for my third trip to India in as many years, and I am slowly becoming one of my company's expert guides. I share this advice with Eleanor, my business colleague who is joining me. It's her first time traveling there, and she is understandably nervous. In fact, her partner paid me a visit several weeks earlier to check me out and ensure I would be a strong guard and a trusted guide for this trip. We plan to visit the cities of Mumbai, Chennai, and Kolkata, where our teams and business colleagues work and live. We want to thank them for their work, see their progress firsthand, share upcoming priorities, and listen to their ideas. They are members of our extended team, and we hope they feel our genuine interest in getting to know them personally.

After Mumbai, we will bounce through Delhi and drive the long five hours on the "old road" to Agra to see the Taj Mahal. Of course, we won't be doing the driving ourselves. We'll have a chauffeur from one of the service providers. Driving in India is not for the faint of heart, even with GPS apps providing directions. I promise Eleanor we will see the beautiful, the ugly, the happy, the depressingly sad, but mostly the friendliest people she will ever meet.

But first, we must survive this flight.

I explain to Eleanor what to expect on our long fourteen-hour flight from Newark, New Jersey: "We take off in the evening, and we spend the night flying over the Atlantic Ocean. Because we are flying against the sun, we have a shortened day as we fly over most of Europe. When we get to somewhere around Turkey, the flight veers south over Iran, Afghanistan, Pakistan, and then over to India. By then, it's nighttime again, and we land in the very early morning hours in India. We'll check into our hotel at 3 a.m., and then we'll want to get up early to do some sightseeing. So we need to get a good rest during the flight."

We follow my dining recommendations at the lounge, and I opt for two glasses of Chardonnay with a bland chicken dinner, still better than anything we would get on the plane. I pass on the desserts as I don't need to feel bloated or get a sugar high right now. We hear the announcement for boarding, head over to the gate, and take our seats at the very front of the business class section.

I take note of my surroundings. My previous trips to India were on modernized Boeing 747s with fully reclining pods. Their service was what you would expect: pleasant but direct to the point. I prefer taking the flight to Heathrow Airport and then switching to a direct flight to my Indian destination. But things aren't as lovely on this trip where I am taking a long direct flight to Mumbai. The cabin is dark, and the flight attendants are cold. It's amazing how easy it is to pick up the crew's mindset, their focus on getting to our seats, and their determination to get luggage stowed away. No smiles or questions about our well-being.

The flight takes off on time, and we have our first beverage. I know Eleanor well as a business colleague, but we haven't spent much time together outside of the office until this point.

We first met several years earlier and worked together at another company. I was the CIO, and she led consumer marketing. My priorities were to innovate in our consumer-facing business areas, and Eleanor and I didn't cross paths very often. But I was always seeking new areas where technology could provide value, which often included underserved parts of the business where tools, integration, or analytics could unearth hidden opportunities.

I share one of those hidden opportunities in the next chapter around data. Marketing is the front door to growth, and their responsibilities are partly creative but very technology and data driven. When seeking areas to transform the business, marketing is a prime place to get started.

Eleanor was full of ideas and always saw possibilities one or two leaps beyond where they were operating. Her teams were encouraged to experiment to see what worked. She challenged her staff to come to her with their ideas and championed those with merit. No slackers allowed, and she expected them to execute. If someone let her down, she explained why in direct and stern ways. She sought out technology solutions and tried to understand their benefits, but she didn't get into the weeds on how things worked inside. She expected the technology to work as described. When we missed a detail, her words were just as stern to me, the CIO, as they would be to anyone she managed. If my team was late on a deliverable or disappointed her with the results, then I knew she'd call it out. I can hear her now: "What do you mean, the data integration isn't working as expected?"

The second round of drinks arrives, and we don't waste any time finishing them. We both play with the television screen to see what movies are available. I have a glass of water. Drifting. Drifting. And I am out.

But I am having one of those weak nights of sleep. Waking, turning, falling back to sleep for a bit, and waking again, but never getting up. I keep trying to get into a deeper sleep, but the more I try, the more I feel my mind racing and thinking about the past.

I remember previous trips to India, like one trip where I watched the film *Slumdog Millionaire* on the flight from London to Kolkata. That first day, I visit Dakshineswar Kali Temple in Kolkata, just outside the city. My driver can't get close enough to the temple and suggests I walk about a quarter-mile to the entrance. He tells me I have to leave my shoes at the front of the temple. I recall scenes from the movie I had watched only hours earlier of kids sifting through shoes left by the side of temples. They were looking for the pairs in the best shape and selling them for a few rupees to pay for a meal. I leave my shoes in the car and make my way to the temple barefoot.

I learn a lot from that experience. It is Sunday, so the temple has thousands of people visiting and bringing flowers as offerings.

The temple was built in 1855 by Rani Rashmoni, a philanthropist and a devotee of Kali, a Hindu goddess, the destroyer of evil forces, and Mother of the Universe. Twelve shrines are dedicated to Shiva, one of the supreme beings who creates, protects, and transforms the universe. As a foreigner to India and Hinduism, I know very little about the meaning behind all the symbols and rituals. However, it is easy to comprehend the importance of the temple to all the families visiting that Sunday, not only for its spiritual significance but also one of history, architecture, and national pride.

But it's the crowds I remember most. Families. Children. Merchants on the side of the road selling flowers. Fryers, grills, and stovetops selling wonderfully delightful snacks that I would never try because of the fear of getting sick—but trust me, I am adventurous at the local restaurants. Hundreds of shoes lined up outside. Rows of parked motorcycles and drivers standing by their rickshaws waiting to take people home.

This isn't my first experience with the enormous crowds in India. I remember my very first trip and my first day in Chennai. After arriving at 3 a.m. at the hotel on a Sunday, my driver and guide pick me up and take me to the Mahabalipuram temples, a collection of seventh and eighth century CE temples and a World Heritage Site that's about forty miles south of the city. What I remember most about this day is how it ends. After a light and early dinner, I am not quite ready to return to the bland walls of the hotel. My guide has already turned in for the night, so I am left with a driver who barely speaks English, and I convey to him that I want to go where people from Chennai go on a Sunday night.

He takes me to the beach. In Chennai, it's too hot and the sun too strong for people to spend their day there. But the beach is the equivalent of a national park to locals, and thousands of people are there with their families burning fires, eating, playing soccer, and just hanging out. My driver turns onto the local road alongside the beach, and we start the sluggish drive. We're on a road one lane in width but with two ways of traffic. It's slow, and we're frequently stopping and taking sharp pivots. Cars and trucks are parked five-deep on both sides of this road. The front vehicles are mainly motorcycles and mopeds, but the ones in the back are small trucks, many with people sitting on their roofs, making a sport out of guiding cars around each other. Driving in our white Mercedes through this maze makes for quite a spectacle. In the worst jams, we face several vehicles and must maneuver around them. It feels like we're moving at a snail's pace, and with every car passing, I am getting a little more claustrophobic.

There are no exits.

The cars keep coming, the motorcycles squeaking by, and the trucks on either side feel as though they're narrowing in on us as people yell down from the rooftops. We pass thousands of people this way. I am beginning to feel the jetlag and the alcohol from dinner. The smoke from the bonfires is starting to irritate my acute asthma. When I see the break and our chance to exit, I tell the driver to take it. I'm done.

But the biggest crowd I experience in India is at the International Kolkata Book Fair. Can you imagine a book fair that attracts what seems like tens of thousands of attendees? I can't, so after a day of touring with my colleagues, I decide to be adventurous. I leave the walled hotel with its security guards in front and join the light crowds walking toward the fair's entrance. The street is under construction, with a new bypass being built above the main road. It is dusty, dirty, and loud, but I make it to the entrance while tracking my steps so I would know how to get back.

The fair is on a site that Westerners might mistake for a construction site. Publishers and book resellers operate booths in outdoor stalls and inside larger buildings. I shouldn't be surprised, but I still am when I see the McGraw Hill booth. Even though I am a CIO in a McGraw Hill information and media business, and the enterprise is on its way to becoming a financial powerhouse, its heritage is in the global publishing and education business. I thumb through books there with some pride. I buy a cookbook for myself and the book *Barbie: I Can Be a Computer Engineer* for my daughter.

I step out of the building, and it's now dark outside. It's getting late, and I better find my way back to the hotel. The crowds are growing, and there are relatively few lights outdoors. A thick blanket of smoke and soot hangs in the air from the food vendors cooking with burning wood. I am finding it difficult to breathe and afraid my asthma may kick in. It's at that point that I recall only seeing one entry and exit to this fair, and the crowd is noticeably larger now that it's Sunday night. I'm feeling scared, and worst-case scenario headlines flood my mind. I imagine the headline, "Mob scene kills hundreds, two Americans dead"—one of those stories that only receives a short mention in the Western newspapers. I retrace my steps. I'm out of the fair. Back to the hotel. Back to my room.

When I return to New York from this trip, I receive a visit from the company's head of security. "Don't ever do that again," he sternly warns me. Several years earlier, during the terrorist attacks in Mumbai, he oversaw the evacuation of several employees staying at the Taj Mahal Palace Hotel.

My dream is slowly becoming a nightmare, and I finally wake in my seat to the sounds of clanking in the airplane kitchen.

I don't want to wake up. I am sure I was only out for 30 minutes, and that the flight attendants are either preparing or, in the best case, cleaning up from the dinner meal. My window shade is still open, and I see the darkness outside and the dimmed lights in the cabin. I can't fall back asleep.

My next instinctive reaction is to turn on the television and review the flight map. Hopefully, we are mostly across the ocean, and I would get to see the sunrise and set across Europe.

The screen illuminates, and I see the plane's icon. We are flying over Pakistan and about ninety minutes from Mumbai. I was out for almost twelve hours.

It is then that I finally look over at Eleanor, expecting her to still be asleep. But she is wide awake and gives me a stare, a vision I have burned in my memory to this day, that speaks to me.

"I'm going to kill you."

She never fell asleep. She was awake for the entire fourteen-hour flight. She followed all my recommendations, but the formula didn't work for her. She's not blaming me but is upset about the outcome. It's a lesson for me because wine knocks me out, and I should have found out what approach works for her to provide better guidance.

Why Visit India

My first experience working with development teams in India was almost ten years before this trip.

I am the CTO at a startup and working on Wall Street in New York City. After the dot-com bubble burst in 2001, we move out of our inspiring office space in Tribeca, with its floor-to-ceiling windows and access to some of the best restaurants in the city, into this fortified, locked-down, dreary space on Broad Street. I swear, my walk to work feels cloudy every morning as I pass the barricades, bomb-sniffing dogs, and the metal detectors that are now a post–9/11 staple in this part of the city. The one highlight of the space is a backdoor entrance to the Starbucks on Broad and Beaver Streets. This Starbucks is a local gathering point where I network and hold vendor meetings. It is too complicated getting visitors through security, and besides, our office of twenty people shares a single conference room.

It's at the Starbucks where I meet Hesam. His IT outsourcing and services company is tiny at the time, especially if you compare it to some of the large and established Indian outsourcing companies. He is friendly, passionate, and inquisitive, and I trust him almost immediately. We don't discuss dollars for developers. Rather, we speak about solutions and how complementing an in-house development team with his talent could accelerate the development of new products.

The meeting isn't remarkable or important until about two months later when a new CEO takes over our company. It is going to be my second meeting with the CEO this week, and I am reasonably sure I know why he wants to meet again.

Several months earlier, we acquired another SaaS company out in the Midwestern United States. I was on the team that evaluated the business and gave the green light for the acquisition from a technical due diligence perspective. Our customers wanted more from the platform, and there was a backlog of prospects ready to sign up for it.

They had a substantial intellectual property that backed the application, which made up for some shortcomings in the UX. Of course, this was in the early 2000s and well before great UX was considered a business differentiator.

What is essential is having a reliable, high-performance, and scalable platform. I love their technology stack—it's ahead of its time. Their stack operates entirely on open source software, running on Red Hat Linux with MySQL databases and Perl web applications. They have successfully built a knowledge graph on a product then called Tuple Spaces from IBM, a predecessor to the graph databases that are more prevalent today. They use the open source search engine Lucene, while the business I founded was paying Digital Equipment (DEC) tens of thousands of dollars per year in maintenance fees for a search engine. They run on commoditized, low-cost Dell servers and figured out how to automate system installation and configuration. At the same time, my platforms run on expensive hardware from Sun and DEC with clustering software from Veritas, a high-end storage area network, and Cisco load balancers.

Yet, with all that engineering and automation, their systems are unreliable and difficult to manage. Customers complain about frequent outages and delays loading in content. Their software deployments require almost the entire tech team to jump on a multi-hour midnight bridge call as they resolve issues and make last-second code changes. The application is over a million lines of tangled Perl code, and even the super-talented recruits from a well-known university struggle to make code changes that don't break things. While the application is highly configurable, allowing us to launch new clients without code changes, the configurations still take a long time and require significant knowledge to set up for each client.

So, when the new CEO comes to see me, he has two questions. First, he tests me to see if I am aware of the issues. I am. Check. Second, he asks if I have a plan to address them. I tell him I have some ideas but need time to formulate them, especially because they will require investment outside the existing budget. I also alert him to challenges I foresee to achieving scalability. While we might be able to find some fixes to address the application's reliability, a longer-term and riskier investment will be required to achieve the desired scalability.

He gives me two weeks to structure a plan, and I am glad to have told him we would need added investments to scale this business's product and technology.

I return with a two-phased plan.

First, we must introduce high-end load balancers that have built-in in-memory caching. All of their web pages compute dynamically, even though the underlying data doesn't change often. Their most trafficked pages don't have much personalized content, so we can safely serve pages from the cache without impeding the user experience. It's a move that would relieve some of the traffic hitting the servers and enable us to respond to customer traffic even when the databases or web servers aren't responding. More important, I am using these load balancers and caching to buy time for phase two of my plan.

The second phase of my plan is a bigger pill to swallow because it requires a rewrite of most of the application. I determine that supporting and innovating off one million lines of intertangled Perl code modules is not sustainable. I have support from the application's development team to rewrite it in enterprise Java and move it to an open source application server. The business leaders are also excited because the rewrite gives them a new opportunity to fix broken areas of the user experience.

So, yes, I spend much of my time with this development team learning their ideas and incorporating them into the architecture and details of the plan. It's a sizable application, and we need some upfront groundwork on how we want to transform the customer experiences, workflows, and data models while improving the reliability and scalability of the platform. But what I don't tell them upfront is that the development program includes bringing Hesam and his team from India to help rewrite the application. There is no way the development team can do a full code rewrite in a reasonable amount of time while maintaining the existing application. Even if time weren't a factor, skill is. They have little expertise in programming Java and managing a new type of application server. We need outside help, and Hesam is willing to do it at a very reasonable cost.

The plan to bring in Indian development teams didn't sit well with this team at all, though they don't protest right away. At first, they keep quiet (at least to me anyway). But slowly, over time, they escalate concerns and issues to the leaders they trust.

"The code is terrible, and there are too many defects."

"The early morning calls are problematic."

"The team in India doesn't speak English well, and the phone quality is awful."

And so on.

I can't tell you how this story ends because I exit the company before the project is completed. But it leaves a scar that I remember for the rest of my career. My intentions mean well, my strategy is sound, and my approach made technical and fiscal sense. But I totally underestimate how much ongoing effort is required to get a team of engineers to accept, be on board, and embrace a technical partnership with non-Americans living halfway around the world. I don't understand detractors who might never accept a different way of working. I don't know how to support our Indian partners to enable everyone to succeed while still managing their team as a vendor with a defined scope of work, timeline, and budget.

But I don't give up making a global partnership work for everyone. Several years later, when I become a CIO, my teams and I pioneer ways to positively partner with our Indian-based teams. We are no longer client versus vendor. We are one team, with one mission, sharing identical KPIs.

This approach is a far cry from how many enterprises work with service providers. Enterprises typically submit requests for proposals (RFPs) to multiple service providers, review the responses, and select a winner. For the most part, they manage these teams as vendors, expecting them to deliver on time, on budget, and in scope. Even when some of these contracts accept an agile development process, leaders elect to manage the process from a distance.

I take a very different approach. Our agile teams are a mix of employees and consultants from the service provider, and we define roles and responsibilities clearly upfront. For example, if you are a business analyst, technical lead, or delivery lead, you have consistent obligations regardless of what organization or location you report into.

My trips to India are one-third based on meeting with my teams. I answer questions and explain to the group, in person, our collective goals for the upcoming year. Our service provider manages the operations here with different networks, desktops, and seating arrangements than we have back home, and I want to help our teammates here address any issues with their work environment. I observe their ways of working, where people sit, what equipment they are using, how they interact with each other, how they run agile standups, and how well they practice other agile disciplines. I share my insights to develop trust and then ask for candid feedback. I learn what slows things down and their perspective of the communications issues with my teams back in the United States. They want to innovate just like any other developer desires. They hope for clear requirements and the empowerment to commit to what they can get done in an agile sprint. They need to earn a reasonable salary, get honest feedback, and receive acknowledgment when performing well. They intend to go home to their families at a reasonable time.

In these respects, our contract developers in India are just like any other developer who aspires to do good work and achieve a reasonable work–life balance.

I look for talent just like I do back home, but it's harder remembering everyone's name and the correct pronunciation. Abhishek, Amit, Ananth, Angshuman, Anirban, Ankur, Arun, Avik, Avisek, Chayan, Debarshi, Devadoss, Dhirendra, Faisal, Ganesh, Ganeshan, Geetha, Gobinathan, Heather, Indranil, Jayashree, Jebastine, Jeyakumar, Jimmy, KK, Koushik, Manoj, Muthu, Neha, Nilay Nitin, Pankaj, Partha, Praveen, Raja, Ramesh, Sameer, Sandeep, Shilpa, Shovan, Somnath, Soumadeep, Srinath, Subodh, Subrata, Sudarshan, Sudipta, Uma, Umashankar, Venky, and many others are all friends now. I remember coming back one trip and going straight to one of my directors, "Find out who was wearing the orange shirt when I visited. He's amazing and should come stateside for a while to work with us."

I also look for their innovations and ideas and always schedule at least a half-day with my partners to hear their views on providing added value or new capabilities. They range from the very practical to the absurd, but they all made us think blue sky and contemplate new opportunities.

The world is a big place with lots of opportunities. If you confine your business processes and innovation to people you can hire and only work in your offices, you leave behind vast opportunities.

Digital Trailblazer Lessons

Transforming Experiences

I have always been a fan of traveling and seeing the world. It brings new perspectives, which drives leaders to be both empathetic and promote diverse thinking. But hiring global teams is not easy for everyone in an organization, some of whom may see outsourcing as exporting jobs. Others prefer solving problems on their own and without outside help.

The world is too competitive, too fast, and too complex today. It doesn't matter if you're a 1,400-person startup, a 100-year-old company that continues to survive because of a low risk of digital disruption, or a large global enterprise. Failing to look beyond your walls for talent, expertise, innovation, and efficiencies is a recipe for falling behind. And organizations that fall behind are at risk of being disrupted by competitors who take advantage of global partnering opportunities.

Digital Trailblazers should first develop their global mindsets by traveling, meeting people, trying new foods, learning a language, experiencing a country's art, listening to international music, watching foreign films, or other ways to appreciate other people's culture, religion, and ways of living. From there, it requires managing through real-world experiences to learn how to structure global teams and improve collaboration. Limiting your trailblazing to only familiar grounds limits the business opportunities and innovation you can bring to your organization.

My stories on forming global collaborations are a backdrop to the full lifecycle of finding partners, building experiences, selecting technologies, and managing ongoing operations. Here are several takeaways for Digital Trailblazers:

1. **Understand customer experience by reviewing the pain points and desires.** As technologists, we focus more on the functionality, performance, and security of our implementations. Even for product managers, recognizing the qualities of delightful customer experiences (CXs) that drive buying,

customer retention, and loyalty is a bit distant. But think about how positive experiences influence your purchasing decisions. In the example I share about my fourteen-hour flight to Mumbai, getting me there safely and comfortably is the functionality, but the cabin's appearance and attentiveness of the flight stewards are part of the experience. Understanding CX and UX is not an easy skill, and Digital Trailblazers should elicit the help of specialists and apply design thinking practices when brainstorming new products or modernizing applications.

2. **Partner with marketers on where technology, analytics, and hyperautomation can improve results.** In my example, I sought a collaborative relationship with Eleanor and found a great partner in exploring where and how to leverage technology to drive subscriptions and leads. If you wait for a marketer to define a business requirement or a business case, then chances are they will have already selected a solution. Maybe they even started implementing it on their own. If you want to define the architecture, platforms, and integration, you need to be partnering with marketers from the start before they know the problem or opportunity.
3. **Promote global team collaboration by helping colleagues learn the culture and foster personal relationships.** My mistakes and learnings drove me to this conclusion. I failed to see how bringing "outsiders" to the Midwest would be difficult for the employees to accept. I believed they would partner on the implementation because we agreed on the technology approach and architecture. I should have invested more time with the in-house team to help them build understanding and develop relationships with their global partners.

   My trips to India have always been a way to build a higher level of understanding and trust between my partners and my employees. Once personal relationships are in place, then innovation, productivity, and quality can come to fruition. A true partnership begins to form when there's an open, two-way dialog around ideas. Global partnerships should be a goal of Digital Trailblazers, but this, like digital transformation, is a journey.

4. **Target supportable platforms because cutting-edge technology may cost you.** If you want to work on the latest and greatest technologies, then consider working at a startup, technology business, lab, or other company where they have the talent and practices to support these innovations. The MySQL database and Lucene search engine of two decades ago are equivalent to today's popular open source technologies, newest public cloud services, and bleeding-edge startup platforms. But many companies investing in customer experiences, software applications, big data, and analytics need business impact more than cutting-edge technology innovation. They require solutions that can be developed and supported by the talent, technology, and management practices that are realistic for their size, budget, and organizational complexities. Most companies that try to emulate Google, Apple, or Netflix will fail. I'm not saying picking emerging technology is a bad idea, but Digital Trailblazers select them strategically and where there are overwhelming benefits.
5. **Know the operational issues—and be clear about costs and risks.** As you move up in the organizational ranks and have more responsibilities, you'll end up owning a more significant share of the operational risks, issues, and other technical debt. When the CEO or other business leaders ask about them, you better understand more than underlying technical issues. As a leader, you must also be aware of the impact on

customers, sales, and operations, as well as other business considerations. Don't be afraid to buy time if you need it to formulate solutions and plans, but come back with answers by the agreed-upon deadline. Planning for perfect answers is not a viable approach to address ongoing operational risks.

■ ■ ■

If you would like more specifics on these lessons learned and best practices, please visit https://www.starcio.com/digital-trailblazer/chapter-6. I've also shared more photos from my travels to India and other locations.

Chapter 7

Buried in Bad Data

"You will never get businesspeople to leave their spreadsheets behind and adopt your business intelligence tools. You are leading everyone here astray by suggesting that companies should stop using Excel."

In fact, that's not what I said at all, as I look to my left to see who is speaking up during my presentation.

I'm angered and frustrated standing in the middle of the u-shaped conference room, looking for reactions from the thirty IT leaders attending my session on becoming a data-driven organization. We're at a SINC conference for IT leaders in Scottsdale, Arizona. It's perfect blue-sky weather outside, and I want to make sure my audience finds value in the time they're spending indoors with me.

So, I repeat myself to him and everyone in the room. I have a lot of patience, and as a leader, you'll often have to repeat the message from different vantage points and hope the reframing helps people understand the "why" on your perspectives.

"I don't tell anyone to give up spreadsheets," I say calmly, and continue. "Used within boundaries, they are extremely effective tools, especially when reviewing new, smaller data sources. The problem is that no one tells people the guidelines, and one simple spreadsheet slowly becomes an operational forecasting machine that's updated weekly with formulas that are never validated. Then one day something goes wrong. An error is found. Or the spreadsheet has become such a monster that it's taking too long to process the data. Or some new data is dropped in and the spreadsheet can't easily accommodate it. Or the person running it leaves the company. Then what do you do?

"My point is that there are better tools, and part of our mission as IT leaders is not just buying and deploying them, it's illustrating where to use them and demonstrating best practices for how people should use them."

I see some nodding heads and continue.

"And whenever there are new tools, there are legacy ways of working that need to be challenged. Why would I want the analyst to continue manually updating their spreadsheet if they can build a more useful dashboard that connects to live data? They'll only get there if they take a step away from what they're doing today. That requires finding examples where new ways of working drive business impact. It means nurturing people in the organization on how to use the new tools, providing them with data best practices and governance. You need to identify which leaders are willing to challenge the status quo and catalyze them. Leaders must confront what tools, practices, and behaviors should be left behind, like using spreadsheets as Swiss Army knives."

I don't even have to tell the group about the security and privacy concerns of organizations that copy and share data willy-nilly in spreadsheets. IT leaders love soapboxing how this technology or that poor process (never mind, the complete lack of process) creates security issues. It's a license for some of them to say "no" to something and move on. For some IT leaders, those were the good old days, when IT fortressed the status quo by finding a security or compliance concern to block change and progress.

But I rarely go there because I want to move IT leaders away from blurting out a knee-jerk "no" to new technology requests. My goal is to get them to say, "Yes, but." As in, "Yes, you can have access to the data, but I have to mask these personal identifiable information (PII) fields that you probably don't need. Yes, I can give you access to the data source, but you need to secure analyst permission from the data owner."

I've been giving this same speech throughout my whole career to open the minds of IT leaders. I want them to see what's possible with self-service data and analytics tools. That way, when they see analysts in their companies with overengineered spreadsheets, they have the courage to challenge sacred cow technologies. I am hoping they shift from the command-and-control mindset that steers them to "no," and challenge them to enable more people in their business to access, implement, and leverage technology and data. I am helping them see the benefits of citizen data science coupled with a proactive data governance program.

Occasionally I'll get pushback like from people like this. It's unusual, but this isn't the first or last time I've been challenged during one of my talks or workshops. It's good to be challenged, even when it's coming from another consultant who just wants to be contrarian to steal the spotlight. But in the back of my mind, what I'm really feeling right now is, "Who the fuck *is* this guy?" and how do I not let him distract the other leaders in the room from broadening their perspectives?

Over the years, I've learned some hard lessons and fought some challenging battles around data practices and tools. Admittedly, I haven't worked with the largest data sets nor the most experienced data scientists. I've only worked with a subset of the latest and greatest big data platforms. I fight the small data fights because that's where businesspeople have the most exposure to data. Win these small battles, and you open the organization to tap into their bigger data opportunities.

The biggest challenges often come from the finance department. Their tools have been antiquated for decades, and they have many years of practice pulling data from the ERP, wrangling it with other data sources, and then making it all presentable. Financial analysts see the world in rows and columns, and they usually don't believe the results unless they've had a hand in programming the formulas themselves.

Much worse is that many financial analysts aren't motivated to change. They see the writing on the wall and are thinking, "If IT automates my financial spreadsheets, then why will they need me around?"

But here's the thing—my primary mission isn't just to automate. Automation is a byproduct of democratizing the data so a larger group of people can access it and self-serve answers to their own questions. Why should I have to go to a financial analyst to see how the IT department is spending against our budget? It should be a dashboard that I can look at any time I want. I should be able to give my lieutenants access to that data so they make fiscally responsible decisions.

I also want to enable real-time data for decision-making and not settle for stale week- or month-old data or reports. And the data need to be accurate with procedures to measure and improve data quality. You can't easily move to reliable, real-time data processing when there's a human in the middle muddling data from multiple sources via spreadsheets.

Automation is a means to this end, but it's not the primary mission. If I lead with automation, it'll scare off the team I'm partnering with to help when instead it should liberate them. In most cases, the analysts are freed to spend more time exploring new areas of data once I help automate their data integrations, transformations, deduping, normalizing, blending, joining, cleansing, and mastering. But they won't see that opportunity upfront. At first, all they see is the writing on the wall that Isaac plans to automate their job. I once heard one financial analyst say to his colleague, "He's the executive who goes to India, so watch out."

The truth is that financial models are full of exceptions and workarounds. There's so much bad data buried in corporate systems that analysts are forced to program their spreadsheets to accommodate data quality shortcomings. This in turn is hard to model even with all the right data integration, data quality, and master data management technologies. The financial analysts will bury your agile data team with all this complexity, and in some cases, they'll do it with a smile. When they get a working prototype, they'll easily find the use cases where the model or automations don't work or the data visualizations aren't yielding the correct results.

If you find yourself here, you're in the death spiral of subject matter expert challenges. You might have three swings of the bat to address issues and make improvements. But that's it. Remember, the finance department reports to the CFO, and they're not that interested in seeing agile improvements. To them, iterations are wasteful—at least until you get them to adopt an agile mindset. They're thinking to themselves, "Why didn't they capture the requirements and implement the technology correctly the first time?"

As one of my best mentors told me repetitively: "You can't push a rope uphill."

But sometimes, I must learn from my own mistakes. Let me explain.

Avoid Bulldozing Institutional Hills as Your First Transformation

It's the end of the company's fiscal year when I attend its advisory meeting. It's the first time I meet the group, and I sense the enthusiasm in the room around my arrival. The executive team wants better technology and needs to launch new products, and they hire me to make recommendations and lead aspects of the implementation.

The meeting isn't anything special, and the group is happy with its financial results. Great news, I think to myself, because many of my most successful roles involve both digital transformations and turnarounds. They're transformations in that the organization needs to rebuild its customer experiences, products, services, and operations to compete in a digital world. But they were also turnarounds because the organizations were already losing market share and revenues were declining. When a transformation and turnaround are happening at the same time, it's a double whammy—sort of like running a marathon with a painful, injured leg, hoping to complete the race without risking further damage. It becomes a triple whammy when the culture is slow, full of detractors, and seeks perfection over experimentation. When I assess companies and their leadership teams, I'm sniffing out whether they need digital transformations, a turnaround, and what types of cultural transformations.

They often need all three, but for now, I'm just happy to see that I may have some financial runway to run the transformation here.

Only several weeks later, when I return to the office, the executives' enthusiasm has turned to somberness. It turns out their forecasts were wrong, and it wasn't a good year after all.

"Wait, what?" is all I can think to myself. It's not unusual to have inaccurate forecasts in the first, second, and sometimes even the third quarter. But by the end of the fiscal year, you expect most businesses to know where things stand within a couple of points depending on how last-minute, end-of-year sales come in. But this forecast misses by a lot more, and this team needs to dive into the root causes.

I sense an opportunity to fix a data and a business process problem. I step up to help and figure that, at minimum, I'll get a better view of how the organization operates.

It doesn't take long to get a high-level view of the problem. Forecasting is always a messy cocktail that requires moving data between customer relationship management (CRMs), ERPs, and other operational systems, and that's what I find here. The sales team isn't using the CRM with any discipline—aka governance—so leadership can't make accurate forecasts of the current state of the pipeline. The financial quote-to-cash processes aren't uniform, and since this is a services company, there's an added element of when and how much to invoice compared to what salespeople record in the CRM. None of the data are centralized or integrated, unless you call a financial analyst's spreadsheet a reasonable data warehousing solution. Most leaders wouldn't, but they rarely dive into how data goes from workflow to system to forecast. You can end up with bad data, misguided insights, and inaccurate forecasts simply with one bad formula, one copy-and-paste error, or some other undocumented assumption.

The problem here, and with many companies that I advise, is that this is far more than a forecasting and data issue. It's an opportunity to insert more rigor in their business processes, which requires executing a high-level formula many CIOs and chief data officers (CDOs) know. The components of this formula include creating sales process disciplines that are implemented in the CRM. It requires streamlining the order-to-cash processes and automating invoicing. It means using ETLs to move data between systems, centralizing all this data in a warehouse, and then adding a self-service business intelligence tool so that the sales, finance, marketing, and other teams can generate reports useful for their decision-making needs.

Piece of cake, right? It is until you add in all the human elements of changing the sales process, the financial team's tools, and executive decision-making methods all in one shot. These problems are data issues wrapped around several business process issues. Solving them demands leaders agree on a way of working and create a structure to business processes. It requires people in multiple departments, roles, and seniority to shed outdated technologies, redefine manual processes, and replace them with citizen data science and data governance best practices.

But the hardest element of data-driven transformations is realigning executives who don't recognize that letting anyone do anything they want using whatever tools they know creates risks, inefficiencies, frustration, and sometimes chaos. In many situations, I am stepping into a sales-driven process connected to hearty leadership bonuses. These processes often encourage selling anything to anyone and transition to ad hoc fulfillment processes.

This is a big-boulder problem and one that requires top-down buy-in before instituting bottom-up changes. If the CEO, head of sales, and the CFO aren't on board, then you're pushing a rope uphill, and your data-driven transformation needs to start elsewhere.

I've made many mistakes trying to move this boulder. When leaders aren't truly on board, instead of guiding a transformation, you're actually pushing a rope called "change" uphill. You don't want to challenge the status quo without leadership support when the big sharks are in the water hunting for next year's bonus.

So, let me give you a better place to start a data-driven transformation. It's called the marketing department.

> I'm often asked where transformation leaders should start their organization's data-driven journey. My first example of challenging spreadsheet use and transitioning to self-service data visualizations is a great start because it's a tactical transformation where you can target specific early adopters. In the next example, you'll see that play out in the marketing department, where you'll again meet Eleanor, the marketing executive whom I traveled to India with. But trying to change an organization's process and tools tied to compensation? That's pushing a rope uphill and not an ideal starting point for transformation.

How to Find Early Data-Driven Partners in the Marketing Department

I love the marketing department because its objectives are often full of opportunities. Their teams are already versed in experimentation practices, and they most often have a test-new-things mindset. Their jobs are to try many experiments, sunset the ones that aren't working, and scale the ones that generate the desired results. There's usually some acceptance that not all their experiments will yield fruitful results.

Guess how they make these decisions? Yes, marketing is a creative process and requires experience and intuition into customer buying behaviors, but guess what grounds marketers in making faster decisions or delivering personalized experiences? Bingo, give that leader a Starbucks card. It's data and analytics. Only it's not that simple.

Marketers use data and analytics in many facets of their work, including when deciding what market segments to target, which campaigns to run, which messages to use, and which keywords to buy. They're often eager to collaborate with a technology partner willing to say "yes and" to their ideas and requests. They also need support because there's a lot of noise out there.

As of this writing, there are over 8,000 different tools that a marketing team can use to automate campaigns and analyze results. Scott Brinker, known as the godfather of marketing technology, publishes a landscape supergraphic[1] of all the various tools yearly, and it's grown from 150 back in 2011.

With all of these tools at the marketer's disposal, your CMO can become mired in choices. Her teams are trying to figure out what tools to select and how to get the most from them. Your marketing colleagues must decide what experiments to run, how to interpret the results, and how to join the data from multiple technologies to create a 360-degree view of customers and prospects. Along the way, they must also dedupe data, cleanse addresses, scrub emails, and figure out company hierarchies.

Newsflash. The marketing team is not doing all that in Salesforce or any other CRM, no matter how well the salesperson claims their CRM is a one-stop-shop for all things marketing and sales.

Whenever I deliver my data and analytics keynote at IT conferences, I ask attendees to raise their hands if they work with their marketing departments on data, analytics, and machine learning. It's only in the last year that the number of raised hands is approximately 10 percent of the people in the room. It used to be only a few slowly raising hands.

> I'm always shocked by this result, even though I see a few more leaders raising their hands these days. Seriously, how are IT, digital, and data leaders truly transforming the business without partnering with their CMOs who have the charter to grow brand, business, and market share? I discuss transformation in Chapter 10, but if yours only targets operational efficiencies, it doesn't fully qualify as a digital transformation.

Marketing is ripe for collaboration with the technology, digital, and data functions. Marketing needs technology help. They need a ton of data help. They have a budget to spend, and, most importantly, their objective is to *grow* business, not just find ways to cut costs.

When you're looking for a strategic business partner to experiment and collaborate with, try identifying a team in the marketing department that could benefit from your technology expertise. Just make sure that you've done your business homework and are approaching the conversation already having a basic understanding of marketing's goals and priorities. Ultimately, you can use these collaborations to build champions for the transformative work your team is taking on.

I'm about a year into my job as CIO when Alice comes to me with her small data problem. She's had roles in corporate reporting, and our CMO Eleanor hires her to make sense of all the different marketing campaigns they are running. Alice comes to my office, and my son's roadmap is still on the whiteboard.

"We're buying keywords across three platforms and placing ads in several magazines," she explains. "We run surveys and award the top businesses, which gives us a powerful lens over who may be prospects for our products. But a lot of our work includes buying marketing lists and providing leads to the inside sales team, only they push back when they miss their quotas and claim we've given them unqualified opportunities."

I try to picture what this well-oiled machine looks like and ask Alice if she'll share with me how this works today.

"Can I bring in Donna to show you?" she asks.

Five minutes later, Alice returns with Donna, an early-career marketing analyst, who opens her laptop and starts showing me how she's doing her work today. "I get lists from three providers and merge them into three sheets in this Excel. I then have to merge them into one, but that's not easy because all we have are names and email addresses with spelling errors and other idiosyncrasies."

Donna shows me a gargantuan formula that helps merge the list and walks me through several of its components. I am impressed because she has an organized problem-solving approach like a coder, but she's a marketer, and I wonder if she's had any computer science training. I ask her to tell me about her background, and I learn she studied anthropology in college and interned with our company the previous summer. This is her first job out of college.

Donna goes on to show me the websites where she downloads data as well as the data she pulls in from our CRM web analytics data, user registration data, and her other data wrangling efforts. It's then that I notice her spreadsheet has about thirty worksheet tabs at the bottom.

Holy cow, this anthropology major really has a developer's mindset. At that moment, I recognize the paradigm shift when IT offers governed self-service business intelligence tools and practices throughout the organization. It can spur citizen data science within our walls. Donna may not be a trained data scientist or software developer. However, she's a digital native who grew up immersed in technology and is not intimidated to learn new tools independently. While she has the skills to work in IT, seeing her work in marketing is actually more powerful because she can apply her data skills to their daily challenges and transform how the department operates as an insider. She's on her way to becoming a Digital Trailblazer.

I ask Donna and Alice to partner with me on a data-driven journey. Their eyes light up when I show them the Tableau dashboards we are working on for customers. They see the utility and the ease of use, but more importantly, they buy into a different way of working. Instead of Donna becoming a one-person data hub for the marketing department, they will empower all their colleagues by creating a center of excellence focused on becoming data driven. Instead of creating manual work in spreadsheets, they can prioritize questions, develop dashboards, and roll out tools to their colleagues. I agree to mentor them and partner them with a data warehousing consultant who would join, cleanse, and develop a data warehouse.

Alice thanks me profusely as she leaves my office. She wasn't expecting this much support from the CIO!

At that point, I'm ready to approach our CMO. I now better understand marketing's goals, have seen their challenges firsthand, and I know how I will help their cause. I must talk to Eleanor now because I need her to buy into the vision and approach.

When recruiting citizen data scientists, here are some things you should be looking for:

- Are they open to sharing what they're working on with someone outside of their department?
- Do they appear to be learning on the job through experimentation (e.g., try something, measure the impact, adjust)?
- Are they inquisitive and ask questions that can lead to actionable answers?
- Do they try, ask for help when needed, and are they ready to learn the best practices on implementations?
- Can they create a pivot table in a spreadsheet, or are they well-versed in using business intelligence tools like Tableau?

Democratizing Data Exposes Data Quality Issues and Backbones Transformation

Identifying citizen data scientists, deploying self-service data visualization tools, and enabling data access is only part of the equation in transforming to a data-driven organization. You hope that empowering people with data and analytics leads to operational and culture changes, but this often requires leaders to spark the transformation. Then, democratizing data exposes many underlying data quality issues, and transformation leaders must leverage this feedback to drive proactive data governance programs.

So let me share with you three stories that touch on the challenges around transforming behaviors and addressing data quality.

The year is 2008, and I'm working at *Businessweek* magazine. Businessweek.com represents a growing percentage of the overall revenue, but the majority comes from the magazine's print ads. We have no idea how long we can continue selling expensive print ads, which can cost tens to hundreds of thousands of dollars. From my experience working with newspapers, the answer is not long enough. We need to grow website and mobile traffic quickly and then figure out how to grow digital revenue from these digital channels.

The problem is that to get more traffic, we also need to create more content. People only go to a handful of websites regularly, and the rest of the traffic comes from people searching Google, finding interesting articles in their Facebook news stream, or clicking links from other articles. Having more content optimized for search is like having more fishing lures in different areas of the lake. Hopefully, those lures catch the people's attention with their diverse interests, and we're able to reel them into the website.

Once they land on the article, we have the second challenge of helping them click on a second article.

To make all this happen, we must change how the editorial team sees their jobs. The editor has almost full autonomy in the magazine on topics to pursue, whether an article is newsworthy, and how to best illustrate it.

Surprising as it may sound, content for the website works in similar ways even though the audience and medium are completely different. As CIO, I support the content management systems (CMS) where writers submit articles and a list of related article links into a publishing workflow. Once approved for publishing, the section editor decides where and how to represent the piece on their channel page. We have channel pages for technology, small business, markets, and other topics.

If we succeed in getting editorial to produce more content, we will have to get them to change how they're spending their time. Jerry, the head of digital strategy who joined me in the executive presentations about our architectures, understands the problem right away. He asks me how we can use technology to replace some of the manual steps editors perform today when updating website content.

Brian heads the digital editorial team. He's open to new ways of doing things if he believes in the change, but to get others on board, he needs a solid story to sell to his staff. Telling editorial to do something different from their own beliefs is incredibly challenging. They're wickedly smart, dedicated, opinionated, and sometimes stubborn people. At *Businessweek*, I learn to admire how they come up with new angles to pursue stories, their process for finding sources, and their integrity to tell the story accurately.

Jerry agrees with the editorial team's charter, but that doesn't always mean the editor knows what readers want best. Yes, they've mastered representing the reader's interests in the magazine, but that publishing cycle is relatively slow, even for a weekly magazine. People either subscribed or they didn't. They bought the magazine from the newsstand or they didn't. It's difficult to capture whether a print article received due attention because there's no real way to measure what people read in print.

But that's totally different on our website, where we can use web analytics to see what readers are engaging with. By generating interest in one article, we can drive ongoing readership. To do this, we need to publish more articles online that meet our standards for high integrity while luring a wide swath of readers into a subject area.

Jerry realizes he'll need data to sway editorial minds. There's no way he can go to Brian, who leads digital content, with just ideas on adjusting long-standing editorial policies and beliefs.

So Jerry organizes an experiment with Brian's permission. It's a simple A/B test where we sometimes show articles with the related content selected by the article's author or the editor. Other times, we use an algorithm to choose the related article links based on keywords, reader interest, and analytics on what people are clicking.

Sometime later, we gather to review the results of this experiment. To this day, the image of Brian's reaction remains burned in memory. He's looking at the results on paper that show the machine outperforms editorial. He stares at it for a while, and I can tell he's thinking through all the implications of machines challenging their hard-earned institutional knowledge. It's a scene right out of the movie *Moneyball*, and he is in dismay, but not in denial.

But Jerry's not done sharing the findings. The second insight comes from analyzing the channel pages that the editorial team sweats over daily. Who gets the lead spot? What articles, and in what order? They have the web analytics metrics from the previous days, weeks, and months to see what readers click on. They know which stories demonstrate editorial excellence better than others. They also know they need to share the spotlight between different writers.

But there's one key metric they aren't looking at regularly. It turns out that a highly significant percentage of the traffic to these pages isn't coming from readers. It's coming from Google and other search bots indexing the site. The data show us that most people arrive from search, land on an article, and, hopefully, find another article to read. That's why related articles are critically important, and even a small percentage of improvements can drive increased readership. But other readers come to the homepage, hopefully see an article of interest, and go directly to the page to read it.

The number of people affiliating themselves with a channel and going to these pages is quite small. Meaninglessly small. It's important to have these pages for the bots, but not for people. The implications are that the time the editorial staff spends in the content management system ordering and presenting content on these web pages is, well, not the best use of their time.

It's a pivotal meeting to how we change Businessweek.com. We bring in user experience designers, heavily leverage web analytics, interview subscribers, and leverage agile methods to drive significant changes to the site. By the time we finish the more important parts of the upgrades, there's almost no manual work to manage content on the site. Articles are entered and approved. A small news team decides which articles are newsworthy and slots them in for the home page. The content areas of Businessweek.com are automated with rules and machine learning that we develop with the editorial and sales leaders.

> **When you need to change policies, belief systems, and significant parts of ingrained operational practices, you best lead the discussion with data. Don't spell out all the insights as you want people to realize them independently. As a transformation leader, sit back and wait for this to happen, and when it does, make sure the insights lead to actions.**

Several years later, I am in a situation where a group absolutely needs new data technologies to scale their product. This story is about the products we developed with Charles, the product manager whose dashboards I challenged in Chapter 4, which ultimately led to the launch of several analytics products. The story doesn't end there because the products' successes required us to reengineer their workflows and data platforms. Their version of duct tape architectures includes an early version of Oracle keyword searching, a Microsoft Access database, and a bunch of manual steps to connect the two. The database stores these long, multi-line queries, and Oracle executes the search as a nightly batch job.

Charles knows this jalopy is well beyond its time and usefulness. Oracle Text was developed generations before the days of Google, and the query dialect is archaic. What's worse is that these are searching multi-page documents, and there's significant, complex logic in the queries to find word proximities.

We are loading 70,000 document folders yearly, with each folder storing up to dozens of documents. Our goal is to search for 30,000 entities, about three times more than what we are doing in the legacy system. To do this, we need higher grade tools and capabilities so that our subject matter experts can hire others to grow and maintain the dictionaries and taxonomies.

Here's the thing that you probably won't realize until you take on one of these projects and believe you see the light at the end of the tunnel. I find there are two types of stakeholders when working on upgrading data technologies.

The first group just assumes the upgrade works better than its predecessor. They don't get involved in reviewing and comparing the output of the new systems compared to the older ones. They don't want to test the new system before it goes live to make sure it works as expected. When you ask for their help, they walk away from the responsibility.

Some will call it a QA responsibility, and there's truth to that assertion. QA should be validating data pipelines and performing A/B testing wherever it's possible. But there are some areas that QA can't be expected to reasonably test, especially with natural language processing tools applied to industry-specific documentation. For example, let's say we compare the results of multiple tools that scan an architect's building specification and they produce different results. How is QA supposed to know which one is the correct specification for a building exterior without knowing how design architects write specifications? They would have to build up as much subject matter expertise as our business sponsors to realize this answer. Often, that's not feasible given time constraints.

So no assistance is an issue because it's hard to know when the new system is sufficiently accurate.

But trying to compare accuracy also has its pitfalls, and this second group aims for causal proof that the new system outperforms its predecessor. That's not easy to prove when the results are subjective or when each algorithm has its areas of strengths and weaknesses.

In this case, our product owner is well aware of accuracy because the product and business model require it. If we say the building exterior is red, it better be red because the accuracy of this information is the business value of the product offering. He defines a sample set of tagged documents and puts them through the legacy system as a control. We then put it through the new system, call it a machine learning algorithm, and perform a comparison.

When working with machine learning algorithms parsing and interpreting documents, getting accuracy this way is not a trivial undertaking. When the algorithm is wrong, is it because of the data quality, the choice of algorithm, algorithm configuration, features selected, or a human error? When you tweak the algorithm and get a new output, now you have two comparisons to do: one against the original baseline and possibly a second against the previous run. Is it better? Where is it worse? How do you *explain* why it's working better, and under what conditions is it worse?

> Explainable AI, MLOps, and ModelOps are disciplines tied to machine learning model accuracy and maintenance. They all require business leaders to define quality and accuracy metrics based on how the models are used to drive business outcomes.

You might think this issue only comes up with machine learning algorithms but finding and agreeing on algorithm accuracy is a much broader issue.

Years later, I'm working with the nonprofit Charity Navigator (charitynavigator.org) on their rating systems. They rate charities based on their financials, accountability, transparency, and impact. Charity Navigator started as an industry watchdog, but over the last several years, they've become a go-to source when trying to find reputable charities in causes that might interest you. Are you concerned about impacting the environment, people's health, the arts, or animals? Are you looking to assist people affected by COVID-19 or a natural disaster? Charity Navigator helps you identify trustworthy charities that match your goals. President Obama[2] and Secretary Clinton[3] have tweeted Charity Navigator's blog posts during times of need. The Gates Foundation is a donor.[4]

When I join, their challenge is expanding the scope of their ratings. More charities, more data sources, and a wider breadth of ratings, including rating the charity's impact on their constituents.

The problem is they are using a system that could not scale to do any of those things. Moreover, just replacing and upgrading the system to better technology isn't good enough. To scale and handle the rating of more charities means developing a process that requires less manual review and input from the rating analysts. And to enable new and evolving ratings, it needs data lineage and data quality capabilities. So when the analysts tweak or add to the rating methodology, which charity ratings are impacted? And how do you define whether the change is a *good* one?

Loads of other data science questions come up during this journey. For example, Charity Navigator has criteria to determine a charity's eligibility for rating through its methodology. Some criteria evaluate whether the charity is large enough and has been in business long enough to be rated fairly. There are hard and weak dependencies between the rating calculations and eligibility rules, and the data science on their methodologies requires ongoing improvements. So, how and where should Charity Navigator expand its eligibility criteria and rate more charities?

And how do you drive transformation at a $4 million charity organization[5] with a small team? You can't just throw advanced big data tools like Apache Spark and expect them to have the data science expertise to select and operationalize optimal algorithms.

As intriguing as all these questions are, the basic ones hold us back for months. We build a new system that processes the current ratings. New data comes in, it goes through an extract, transform, load platform, and out comes a rating. In this new process, very few places require a person to review the rating. One place that requires review is the cause and type of charity, and we use some basic natural language processing algorithm to help with this assignment. It works well for some cause types like animal charities but is less accurate in others like human services, so we ask an analyst to finalize the assignments.

But our progress is slowed down from even more basic quality issues. The calculations are documented on their website,[6] and they are relatively straightforward to implement. That is, until you get into boundary conditions, rounding differences, and sequencing the business logic.

We run some comparisons between our new process and the legacy one. For example, the legacy system might calculate that a charity has a 2.31 percent growth, and the new system comes out with 2.37 percent. In aggregate, 85 percent of charities come out with near-identical scores, but 15 percent are off by as much as 10 percent. Are these defects worth pursuing or insignificant rounding errors?

That's not easy to answer. What looks like a rounding error can influence a donor's decision on whether and how much to contribute.

But the more important challenge is gaining analyst confidence in the new system and way of working. This isn't just replacing an old system with a new one. It's a transformation in their entire operating model, and that takes time for everyone to learn new tools, challenge results, adjust to new processes, and grow to new responsibilities.

Today, Charity Navigator's new ways of working, systems, and advanced methodologies help them rate over 195,000 charities with their new Encompass Ratings[7] that include beacons on impact and leadership. Now that's significant progress and a worthy journey.

Sometimes it is worth moving boulders, but it requires teamwork, and it's never easy.

Digital Trailblazer Lessons

Leading Data-Driven Organizations

Over the next decade, organizations chasing the new oil of data, analytics, machine learning, and artificial intelligence must pursue these questions: What's a rounding error, and how much accuracy is required? What data quality issues need improvements? Where are there biases in the training data? Is the machine giving us valid results? Where is human intervention necessary and valuable? When should we improve the algorithm? When we make a change, is it *better*?

Most importantly, how can we expand the number of employees asking questions, analyzing data, formulating insights, and presenting data-driven decision recommendations?

When archeologists dig and find fossils, we learn more about our past and our future. There's a disciplined process to review and share the findings, but there's always room for people to develop their own correlations and insights.

And that's what we seek with data. More people interpreting data for themselves. More insights. More significant correlations. More people asking questions and seeking answers backed by valid data and algorithms. More debate on results and insights.

Here are some lessons learned from this chapter:

1. **Understand how company culture and norms impact data quality initiatives.** You can learn a lot about a company's culture by understanding how it defines quality in its products, operations, forecasting, and decision-making. And underneath these business definitions of excellence is an underlying requirement—or at least an expectation—around data quality. Sometimes this gets expressed in service levels, for example, expecting that data for financial reporting is available by 8 a.m. You may hear leaders state that they don't trust the data, are frustrated with duplicate CRM records, or are confused when different data sources show conflicting information. Until a proactive data governance program[8] gets instituted with data owners assigned with tools, processes, and data quality metrics, many of these data quality issues are escalated to IT to fix.

   Measured or not, expectations around data quality become ingrained in business processes and then culture, especially when people perceive that it's their job to review and manipulate data manually. That's why upgrading data processing systems or *automating* them becomes a significant transformation management battleground. What was once a back-office IT process now comes front and center, and you're not just improving technology, you're changing the company's business process and possibly challenging its mission and culture. It's one reason to target data processing changes as a transformation because you're not just putting in a new set of data pipes and infrastructure.

2. **Focus on meaningful problems because data journeys can be long and complicated.** The first question you must ask about a new data challenge is whether it's worth the

investment to solve it. If the sponsor asks a question and builds a dashboard to seek answers, then how does she make it actionable? And what is that worth? Most organizations have their analytics, machine learning, data visualization, and data integration wish lists. And then there's the second list that must be factored into any discussion around data strategy and priorities, and it's a list that no one wants to talk about: DataOps, data governance, data debt, data policies, data security, and data privacy. Just like in technology, organizations have more data-related problems and opportunities than they have people available to solve them. So before you embark on a data journey, make sure there's an articulation of business impact made long before you take too many implementation steps.

3. **Seek easy onramps and avoid selling automation.** You probably read about advanced companies that have departments of Ph.D. data scientists, the latest big data technologies, and have their public relations firm sharing their latest and greatest machine learning successes. Those organizations are the outliers. Most companies are somewhere in their journeys to become smarter and faster organizations. While it's critical to prioritize meaningful problems, I also seek out the ones with easy onramps. That doesn't mean the problem is easy to solve! It more often implies that I have a collaborative business partner and an open-minded agile data team ready to work iteratively through the challenge.

   The stated business priorities might include scaling a process, making it more efficient, or adding new capabilities. But I've learned my lesson and avoid labeling the solutions as *automation*. Some expect automation to deliver near-perfect quality, and they'll use this to roadblock progress. They'll reason it out with their colleagues and neglect to mention all the expensive-to-implement exception use cases. Sure, you can handle these as data quality exceptions and pass them to a data steward to manage, but then it's not automated in their minds. Remember, data processing is part of the culture. State expectations upfront and avoid setting them too high when naming initiatives or labeling solutions.

4. **Pick appropriate data technologies aligned to a future way of working.** I only mention a handful of technologies in this chapter, but I don't want you to believe that the underlying technology isn't important. In fact, it's critically important to select technologies that not only solve the business challenges but also fit the structure, governance, and skills of the organization. I didn't mention many technologies because I've implemented different solutions and stacks in every example I shared in this chapter. There are many data technologies to develop dashboards, move data from point A to point B, improve data quality, create data catalogs, enable master data management, or simplify machine learning. Platforms may offer similar *capabilities* but target different people, experiences, productivity, and quality. The best approaches in selecting data technologies require partnering with experts, running several proofs of concepts, and validating that platforms meet performance and compliance requirements.
5. **Invite experts and colleagues to contribute to your data-driven journey.** Data and analytics projects rarely materialize on their own. If you want to find the opportunities and business challenges, you need to step into the weeds and find them.

It's critically important to get out of the office and learn from peers, but learning is a two-way street. Even if you're highly introverted, you should seek out ways to share what you know. The feedback will make you a stronger leader.

You don't become a leader by getting a promotion. You must take the first steps in the journey on your own, make some mistakes, and figure out a leadership style that works for you. And you must bring people along in the journey, so leadership is not just what works for you. You have to adjust to your audience, mission, culture, and goals. And what worked for you last time around may not work this time. You'll always be stepping out of your comfort zone. Get used to it.

■ ■ ■

If you would like more specifics on these lessons learned and best practices, please visit https://www.starcio.com/digital-trailblazer/chapter-7.

Notes

1. "Marketing Technology Landscape Supergraphic (2020): Martech 5000 — Really 8,000, but Who's Counting?" Chief Marketing Technologist, https://chiefmartec.com/2020/04/marketing-technology-landscape-2020-martech-5000/.
2. Barack Obama (@BarackObama), "The best part of my job was meeting people like this—ready to make a selfless act in a time of need. Many Americans are already making deep sacrifices to keep our communities healthy, but if you're able to, consider helping those hit the hardest." Twitter, March 19, 2020, https://twitter.com/BarackObama/status/1240660590600892417.
3. Hillary Clinton (@Hillary Clinton), "I'm thinking today of our fellow Americans affected by the earthquakes in Puerto Rico. Many families

have been left without power and water. If you can, support an organization providing disaster relief here: charitynavigator.org." Twitter, Jan. 7, 2020, https://twitter.com/HillaryClinton/status/1214607714627796992.

4. "Committed Grants | Bill & Melinda Gates Foundation," 2021, Bill & Melinda Gates Foundation, https://www.gatesfoundation.org/about/committed-grants?q=charity%20navigator.
5. "Charity Navigator—Rating for Charity Navigator," 2021, charitynavigator.org, https://www.charitynavigator.org/ein/134148824.
6. "Charity Navigator's Methodology: Charity Navigator," 2021, Charity Navigator, https://www.charitynavigator.org/index.cfm?bay=content.view&cpid=5593.
7. Charity Navigator Encompass Rating System: Charity Navigator," 2021, Charity Navigator, https://www.charitynavigator.org/index.cfm?bay=content.view&cpid=8077.
8. Isaac Sacolick, "What Is Proactive Data Governance," Social, Agile, and Transformation, https://blogs.starcio.com/2020/03/proactive-data-governance.html.

Chapter 8

Transformative Culture, Empathetic Teams, Diverse Leaders

Today I'm sitting across from my teen daughter, Pietra, in our attic, locked down because of COVID-19. She gets through her daily studies on Google Classroom and then shifts to virtual classes on art and dance. She's incredibly creative and builds wonderful multi-story mansions, dynamic amusement parks, and enchanting underwater castles in Minecraft, her favorite game where she can easily express her imaginative ideas. I'm happy for this intellectual distraction, and it's certainly better than some of the digital sugar streamed at her on TikTok and YouTube. I try to get her interested in coding, but she hasn't shown interest yet. Growing up a digital native, and with her imagination and originality, I wonder what opportunities she'll pursue and whether this evolving world of digital experiences will someday lead her to take on a job that hasn't even been invented yet.

I'm reminded of a situation two years ago when my cousin asked me to come to Queens, New York, for her school's career day. I was there to talk about technology job opportunities, and these high schoolers were not shy with their questions. "You're a chief, right, a CIO—how much money do you make?" came from one student, while the next asked, "Should I even bother learning Java, and should I develop my apps in React or Angular?" But my favorite question came from a girl who was intrigued by my writing and speaking.

She showed me her scrapbook, and it was clear she was talented at drawing figures and elaborate fantasy scenes. She asked me, "I know becoming an artist isn't easy, so how can I prepare myself for roles in technology?"

There are incredible technology roles and opportunities for her and my daughter. Today, employers might be looking for full-stack developers, cloud engineers, and data scientists, but many other important technology opportunities are in demand. Companies need more creative people to collaborate, innovate, and develop simple and delightful customer experiences. There are opportunities to build the next generation of video games, create industrial AR/VR experiences, and architect sustainable smart buildings.

Yes, I want creative people on my teams from diverse backgrounds and with different skills and interests. And there are many reasons why crafting high emotional intelligence (EQ), diverse teams is important for the Digital Trailblazer who wants to innovate and deliver business outcomes.

Only 25 percent of the computing workforce are women, with only 3 percent African American women and 2 percent Hispanic women, according to the National Center for Women & Information Technology.[1] Only 18 percent of women make it up the ladder to become CIO.

And here's one reason why diversity is essential for innovating and creating high-performance teams:

> Companies with above-average diversity produced a greater proportion of revenue from innovation (45 percent of total) than companies with below-average diversity (26 percent). This 19 percent innovation-related advantage translated into overall better financial performance.[2]

Learning Team Building and Culture Without a Playbook

There's more research, writing, courses, and best practices today on the importance of developing collaborative, diverse teams and transformative cultures. But when I assumed my first CTO role back in the 1990s, I didn't know much about these important subjects. I was more concerned about filling gaps in my technical knowledge, hiring super-skilled developers, and defining our best practices. It didn't take long for me to realize that part of the role required me to influence the team's attitude, norms, and behaviors. I had a startup founder's title, too, so I was also setting an example for our company culture. No one told me this, and at that time, there weren't dozens of books from Silicon Valley spelling out the importance of organizational culture or how to implement it well in growing startups.

I made it my business to get to know the team as a group and as individuals. Many times, that meant going out to bars and having beers, and working near Chinatown gave us other unique options to explore and be adventurous. Steamed pork leek dumplings. Salt and pepper baked squid. Vietnamese pork chops. They were all favorites of our CTO, Ilan, and he paved the way for our adventures in Chinatown.

I used to tell people that our office was on the great divide of culinary greatness. From our offices on Franklin Street and Broadway, we can walk east into Chinatown for an amazing lunch for less than ten dollars a person. Or we can head west into Tribeca's growing culinary scene. I loved a late breakfast at Bubby's and lunch at Walkers. There was a Thai place on Varick near Canal Street that I thirst for whenever I think about curries unscathed by attempts to appease the bland American palate. Our night trips were up to the East Village where we hoarded sushi at Iso, drank to the hardcore beats at a basement sake lounge called Decibel, and then went across the street to Veselka to carb up in an attempt to avoid next-day hangovers. You can still visit Decibel and Veselka, and I highly recommend them.

When we started as a group, there were just four of us coding hard and sometimes partying harder. With every round of funding, the group grew a little bigger, and we tried to keep a work-hard, eat-well startup culture going. We didn't have room for a foosball table in the office, but we did have a Sony PlayStation and spent countless hours playing hockey on it. As the company got bigger, we eventually had enough space to add a ping pong table.

Food, drink, and games. Is that what startup culture is all about? It was certainly fun, but our culture needed to be defined differently as the team grew.

When I assumed the CTO role, there was already a counterculture forming at the company that heralded MBAs from fancy schools wearing expensive shirts. Our team wasn't focused on selling new business or developing the marketing plans that made us look bigger on paper than we were generating revenues. Our colleagues thanked us only occasionally. IT is often a thankless job, and to keep up morale, I needed to find ways to recognize teams and people for their hard work and accomplishments. And going one step further, I realized it was important for people to feel comfortable, safe, and enthusiastic about coming to work and being in the office every day.

Since the company was growing, finding and hiring people who *wanted* to be on the team was essential. My hiring practices then were instinctive. It was no secret that IT was male dominated because many of us experienced the imbalance in computer science or engineering programs. But my mother was a programmer and would come home telling me and my brother stories of the challenges she faced at work. She is an immigrant and became a U.S. citizen, and even though she went through English schooling, she isn't conversant as a native speaker. I believe my instinct to hire more women came from my mom, and I always had higher female-to-male ratios on my IT teams throughout my career.

We also had to compete for talent. Back then, we weren't competing with other startups or behemoth tech companies offering outlandish salaries and benefits. In New York City, we were up against Wall Street companies that outbid us and also provided long-term career paths. Our saving grace included more work–life flexibility and the potential to make fortunes. Our startup didn't have grandiose aspirations to change the world, and most of us were just happy not to be working at a big bank or any other large corporation with thousands of people churning out code and surviving the office politics. We sold potential recruits on interesting tech challenges and the opportunity to be a part of a new adventure working for an internet startup.

But we still had to be creative, and I remember getting questioned by human resources (HR) back then when I wanted to offer a quality assurance testing job to an English major who didn't have a computer science degree. My instinct was that we needed someone in the group with strong writing and communication skills, and here she was, an English major with no technical background but an eagerness to learn. HR told me hiring her was a risk, but I thought it was a no-brainer. I was right.

Having a recruiting and hiring strategy is only the beginning of building an effective culture. Building happy, collaborative teams that are open to diverse points of view starts with making the right hiring decisions and continues with nurturing your existing talent.

I was fortunate to address a meaningful challenge in the very early days of agile with several developers on my team, including Bart, Daniel, Alexandra, and Karina. At the time, Bart is still working toward his bachelor's in computer science, but Daniel is mentoring him on server-side software development. Alexandra is a seasoned programmer with a methodical problem-solving approach, while Karina is very new to the group and software development.

They work as two groups of two developers for a while, but as the application gets more complex, they have more interdependencies. Their work is a top priority, so when Alexandra and Karina express their difficulties working with Bart and Daniel, I'm eager to hear what could be slowing them down.

Daniel introduced pair programming several weeks earlier and paired with Bart on some challenging algorithm upgrades. The code was new to Bart, and the two worked well together. I knew algorithm development was a new challenge to Bart, so while I didn't know the ins and outs of pair programming—which entails two developers working together at the same workstation—I gave Daniel the nod to give it a shot.

And it worked. Soon, Bart was ready to go off on his own, and Daniel was eager to take pair programming another step forward. He planned to pair with Alexandra and ask Bart to pair with Karina. Daniel had the best of intentions, hoping to take a practice that worked once and apply it a second time while also addressing some of the coding bottlenecks that were slowing us down.

And that's the issue Alexandra and Karina escalate because they are not interested in working with Daniel or Bart in pairs. They don't like the idea of sitting shoulder to shoulder with them, and they are concerned about whether *their* contributions will be recognized if they pair with another more senior developer.

I listen but don't have an answer. Until then, I cared more about getting the work done, the level of innovation, the code quality, the system's performance, and whether the business was seeing an impact from our efforts.

I had the instinctive reaction that something was wrong, and it wasn't anyone's fault. Daniel had all the right intentions, and Bart was trying to take what he learned and put it into practice. But I sensed something that day. An attempt to get one way of doing things that worked for Bart and Daniel needed more thinking before extending to others in the group. Alexandra and Karina were never part of the discussion, and we were a small enough group back then where they certainly could have been invited to share their thoughts or concerns. Unfortunately, Daniel thrust pair programming on them, and while it was solving the technical problems, it wasn't helping our team dynamic. If Alexandra and Karina had an active part in the discussion, perhaps they would have been more open to pair programming or could have shaped it into something that worked better for them.

That's what creating a way of working is all about. It's the discussion that takes one idea, one agile practice, or one DevOps norm and sees how to apply it again in a larger context. You can't go into team building, defining standard practices, or growing adoption with a what-worked-for-us-will-also-work-for-you mindset. Equally, buying and instrumenting highly prescriptive agile frameworks often robs people of the opportunity to learn, understand why, weigh in, and shape the team's collaborative practices. Digital Trailblazers who want collaborative, diverse, high performance, and high teams with high EQ must invite people to the conversation around standard practices. It's one reason you'll hear diversity *and inclusion* together because leaders must start with diverse teams and then create an environment of open discussion and dialog.

For now, I make a tactical decision. We would use pair programming to train new people. We wouldn't use it as a way of working. We found ways of implementing the pairing without people sitting so close together. It was a practical compromise and one aligned with productivity.

It's during my days of working in startups that I develop my muscles and practices to hire great people first and address skill gaps through learning and pairing. I recognize that having diverse teams isn't sufficient, and I need an inclusive approach to develop standard ways of working that—as I said earlier—help people feel comfortable, safe, and enthusiastic about coming to work and being in the office every day.

These approaches will help you create collaborative teams and agreed-upon ways of working, but there's much more to creating a transformative culture. First, as you gain responsibilities, you'll have fewer day-to-day interactions with teams and people. You'll need ways to measure engagement and sense the organization's morale. You'll need to know how to influence groups, teams, and people, consider individual emotions, and factor in complexities you can't control.

I wouldn't fully understand culture building for another decade when I became CIO for teams in multiple global locations.

There are many ways to think about culture. How you encourage innovation, experimentation, learning, and smart risk taking is critical in transforming organizations. Agile teams committing to their sprint's work is a step away from micromanagement and toward building trust. We expect agile teams to provide honest estimates, and we require product managers to host open discussions to share customer needs and opportunities. DevOps teams adopt blameless postmortems to openly discuss issues and problem root causes without fear of retribution. And we ask everyone to bring data to every discussion, openly discuss insights, and facilitate collegial debates on actions.

But two disciplines stand out from my progression from team leader to global CIO. I needed to learn what it means to be an empathetic leader and then understand how to build a winning leadership team.

Fostering Empathy on Agile Teams

How should I think about team happiness?

Why and how is team happiness important? How should I determine whether and to what extent the team is happy? And what if they're not happy? What should I do about it to make them more comfortable? And what if it's just a few members of the team who are unhappy, but the rest are jolly as can be? Is this a significant issue, or is it just human nature that some team members, at any given time, are probably not going to be happy?

And what should I do if someone on the team starts voicing their unhappiness? They're grumbling to their colleagues or gossiping with friends from other departments, or maybe they're going to human resources with their grievances. How do their colleagues or human resources respond to this information? How will they help an unhappy employee? Will they inform me about the issues? Will they provide suggestions on changes, or will they come in with alarms blazing, assuming that one person's grievances imply that the entire department is in disarray?

These thoughts haunt me when I come into the office every day and especially today. The commute makes my mind wander. Normally I spend the 45-minute ride on the commuter rail reading, listening, or sleeping. But today, my mind won't stop racing. Off the rail, and I could subway to the office, but I elect to walk. It's early and the best time to walk in New York City with few people out to dodge around.

My mind continues its rambling as I think about how to improve my department's culture.

It's not just happiness. There's sadness, loneliness, or a withdrawal that someone might be experiencing. Maybe there's trouble at home? How do I sense this so that I can handle difficult situations with this person appropriately?

Then there's anger.

I'm a driver. I ask a lot from the teams that work with me, and I must assess how hard to push. What's realistic for the person, the team, the department? What are the signs that I'm driving too hard, too much, too fast? Does it overwhelm people, or does it anger them? Are they frustrated at having too much work on their plate, or are they irritated that I ask them to work hard? Are they resisting the changes, and that's causing their anger? Do they want to challenge the direction we are heading and are furious because they would do different things in different ways if they were in charge?

These thoughts haunt me because I'm not an expert at human emotions. I'm closer to a novice. Years of engineering school and problem-solving have ingrained my pathways to drive from listening to problem identification, experimentation, and executing solutions. I work with people, teams, and colleagues to get a job done.

Right? Or so I thought. I was dead wrong.

This mindset of working with people from problem through solution only works to a point.

It works when you're in the weeds and working with teammates on a day-to-day basis. You can then sense their emotions of the day. They came into the office angry at their spouse, not mad at the work you're doing with them. They're happy today because they have challenging work. They're sad because they read about the death of a musician who influences them. You get that level of detail when you're working with the team regularly. You adjust your expectations. You help and accept help. You drive hard but are present to hear everyone's honest feedback.

Agile methodologies help with this significantly. Our teams commit as a team, so if they are stressed out for any reason, they'll commit less. They talk about impediments during the standup and help each other through what's blocking them. Maybe today, someone is just distracted, and a teammate can step in to help. They celebrate the small stuff at sprint reviews and learn from each other at retrospectives.

I *know* that agile practices are one ingredient to the team and employee happiness for these reasons. If a team or an employee is unhappy for long periods, I visit the team and see how their agile process functions. Agile becomes my first long-distance lens into understanding empathy. I use the team's performance and metrics to get a window into their world, and that tells me which teams or people may need some attention.

I also measure engagement qualitatively. Who is asking questions or providing feedback? Are people following up and putting their training and learning to practice? Who is getting their work done and going the extra mile to adhere to standards? Who isn't responding to communications in a reasonable time, filling out HR's employee surveys, or following procedures to update the status of stories and tickets?

Again, these are indicators, and I learn to follow them up with conversations with the employee and sometimes with their managers.

But now, I'm leading a department with multiple teams in multiple locations. I'll get to see some people at the water cooler daily, and others I might only get to see once a year. And even when I see many of them, it is in town halls and large group meetings. Sure, I'll have their attention because I am the CIO. But it still takes many well-chosen words to raise everyone's listening skills and knowledge absorption rates. For the most part, I'll only have their gazes back to tell me whether they understand, agree, are excited, and are ready to drive.

But I know from experience that whatever feedback I get isn't complete or sufficient. Teammates return to their cubes. Their mind and actions go back to their day jobs. They largely continue doing what they were doing before and how they were doing it.

My message needs echoes. My leaders need to reinforce a steady pulse of required changes and adjustments when teammates can apply them to their work. The values, vision, and priorities need to reach the agile team and their teammates when I'm not there.

Developing a Digital Trailblazing Leadership Team

My anxiety increases as I arrive at the office. Today is a big day for me. It's my fiftieth day at this business, and I am halfway into my 100-day plan, a ceremonious time when C-levels are expected to articulate their plans and roadmaps. The tactical parts of this plan aren't the issue, and I'm confident the technical aspects of the roadmap will get done. Getting a leadership team together and turning around the culture is the challenge.

When you get a leadership role, you'll be asked this wonderful question from your mentors. They'll ask about *your* team. Your direct reports. Your lieutenants. They'll say something like, "Make sure you focus on *your* leadership team and get the *right* people working for you." Or something like that.

And the first time you hear it, you might scratch your head on the meaning of the statement and question. Who are the *right* people? What does it mean to *focus* in this context? Then you'll get to the heart of the matter. How should you go about forming a leadership team?

It's not easy, even for those of us who have done it several times before. Every organization is different. Every situation where you are fifty days into the job is different. It starts with hundreds of questions about who is already on this team and then determining whether and to what extent you can make changes.

I do this on day 50, but also day 150 and again and again. I still look at leading organizations and grooming leaders aligned to an agile cadence, though the sprints are not fixed in duration. As a leader, there are times when I can only listen and can make a few tweaks, while other times, I can grab the bull by its horns and drive significant changes.

Today is one of those days, and today is the start of the next fifty days I use to develop my leadership team. In my first fifty days, one leader elected to leave, and the other one, well, let's just say the person wasn't going to work out. I fought to get one additional open position, so now I'm in a race to find the *right* people.

Back to that question on what is *right*. I'm not just looking for leaders to take on responsibilities. These leaders will be closer to the agile teams. They must echo the company's strategy and my vision and have their own voice with their teams and with me. I seek leaders who are great listeners and are ready to make data-driven decisions. They must be collaborators and handle the pressures of driving change. I want drivers, but not bulldozers, because they must seek feedback and seek contributions from everyone. Of course, they need some of the skills I am seeking, but I must pick which skills are critical and which they can learn during the journey.

I hire Donovan to manage operations and Pranav to lead application and agile software development. They need to be driving 30 degrees left and right of the north, but with enough gray area that overlaps their leadership styles, technology acumen, and understanding of responsibilities. It's the overlap that makes them empathetic, collaborative, and often conflicting.

When an application release is 90 percent complete but showing performance issues, who takes charge and drives the *right* decision? When we have only one open position, will they fight for the role without mercy, or will they listen and acknowledge what is *right* for the department and the business? When a developer breaks from standards to reach an innovative solution, how will they collaborate on the *right* balance of activities to support her?

Donovan and Pranav are drivers, and they push their speedboats at 70 miles per hour. The wake they leave behind, which should be the gray area I seek, is wavy and choppy. They argue more often than collaborate, and too many issues bubble up to me. Their boats are moving so fast that the wind prevents them from listening attentively to their teams. There's conflict because the teammates understand the requirements and the agile process but haven't fully embraced why either of them is pushing for specific standards.

And there is even more conflict with our colleagues working in product management. They see the teams' velocity but don't receive communications about the direction, the estimates, and the forecasts. They don't understand why Pranav prioritizes technical debt over features this sprint or why Donovan has to blackout the release calendar for two weeks to support an infrastructure upgrade.

I hire Gracie to take ownership of the project management office, agile practices, and department finances. More important, I select her to create the required balance between speed, agility, innovation, safety, reliability, compliance, growth, operational excellence, empathy, and tough love when required.

I ask her to be *the* active listener and provide feedback to Donovan, Pranav, and me. I want her to make sure the team understands why agile methodologies, when to use NoSQL and not SQL, why bringing an A-game to the change advisory board (CAB) is important, and why we will use several no- and low-code platforms to drive fast and agile solutions. If the team doesn't understand the business direction, then I want her to bring in the right people to explain it to them. I want her to encourage the teams to ask questions and challenge the status quo.

She should lead inclusive discussions on process transformation and improvements and sell me on them. I need her clarity on when to step in and when to get out of the way. Where does the team need air cover? Whom do I need to help get past the proverbial response, "That's the way we always do things"?

I want her to be a team player with our colleagues but also be tough with them. When they ask for too much or don't have their acts together around the requirements, she must say no to them. They celebrate when the teams hit their goals but throw her under the bus when colleagues don't get everything they want. And I am there to support her and the rest of the team because transformation requires prioritization and compromises.

They were two speedboats running 70 miles per hour and an empathetic leader holding them to a formation. We went on to develop five new products together and reshape the business.

As you'll see, feel, witness, and experience, leading transformation is a fast and bumpy journey. A diverse team is required. Thank you, Gracie, Pranav, and Donovan.

Digital Trailblazer Lessons

Fostering High-Performing Teams

Hiring and nurturing diverse teams, creating an inclusive culture, and driving empathy are ongoing needs and essential to transformations. The mix of backgrounds, skills, drivers, and interests all play into how well teams collaborate and manage conflicts. Even when you have the *right* people, you must constantly adjust to whether they're in the right seats with optimal responsibilities and agreed-upon collaboration principles. Organizations transforming and managing shifting priorities must make reviews of leader and team dynamics an ongoing process.

For this chapter, I selected a diverse group of leaders to contribute to the lessons learned:

1. **Cultivate diverse teams to boost innovation and performance.** It bears repeating that companies with above-average diversity had 19 percent higher revenue from innovation than those with below-average diversity.

   When you're looking to fill a position, take stock of your team's EQ, backgrounds, and experiences. Look beyond filling skill gaps and be creative where you target recruiting efforts. Helen Wetherley Knight, co-founder of TechforSocialGood.ca, offers a recommendation: "Seek to hire new leaders from diverse backgrounds. New graduates can breathe fresh life into an established team of experienced leaders, just as a young startup can benefit from the experience of an older leader from a more traditional industry."

2. **Recruit people from different backgrounds, experiences, and places.** I hired people who majored in linguistics, economics, art, communications, and others without a STEM background. A few came from well-known universities, but most didn't, and some didn't have a degree. Paige Francis is CIO of Alliance Support Company, author of *Demystifying IT: A Pocket Guide for the Non-Technical*, and an experienced CIO in higher education. She explains how important it is to challenge the status quo on hiring practices and says, "Professionally, I hire, promote with #DEI-intention.[3] Higher education and advanced degrees are statistically less accessible to underrepresented groups and a basic requirement for a career in higher education. Archaic and counterproductive, given those careers offer degree pursuit as a benefit. I would also say #DEI is the floor, not the ceiling. There is no limit to the heights we can reach with diverse perspectives."

   Jason James, CIO of Net Health, adds that the pandemic should encourage leaders to diversify from where they hire. "Now that a global pandemic has forced organizations to embrace a remote workforce, there's a greater emphasis on hiring for skills rather than for a specific geography. This creates more opportunities to embrace leaders from different backgrounds. Different time zones not only provide expanded coverage when supporting clients but come with their own diversity in regional cultures. For example, would Midwestern pragmatism balance West Coast ambition in development teams?"

And Helen adds this important, pragmatic advice: "Resumes never tell the whole story; you need to get out and meet people in different environments. Try volunteering as a judge at university events or joining a new networking group. Every person you meet has the potential to increase the collective intelligence of your team."

3. **Encourage everyone to contribute to your organization's way of working.** Leaders, and especially Digital Trailblazers, are under significant pressure to drive the organization faster. Maybe you've rolled out agile methodologies at previous jobs or are an expert at instrumenting DevOps. But to succeed in a new organization, culture, and group of people, you must invite them to the discussion, ask for their input, debate options, and decide what's optimal for your organization and situation. It requires open-mindedness. You must seek opinions from a diverse team—not only will it challenge your thinking and ensure you're being an inclusive leader, but it also has the side effect of helping you identify where you can drive faster and when you need to slow down. Kim Wales, CEO of peer-to-peer lending and equity crowdfunding index firm CrowdBureau Corporation and one of my early mentors, suggests, "Allowing leaders to find the 'I' in the 'we' empowers and nurtures thoughtful leadership that fosters ownership, decision-making, and collaboration that drives success."
4. **Engage your leaders to listen and extend your EQ's range.** In Chapter 1, I challenged you to grow beyond the skills that made you successful as an individual contributor. In this chapter, I suggest that your approaches to team building,

listening, partnering, and rallying need to grow when your role extends from leading a single team to leading multiple teams across virtual or global organizations. Your eyes and ears don't extend far enough to experience the pulse of the organization, let alone to understand what's on people's minds and how they are feeling. You must mentor your leaders on where and how you want them to extend your empathetic reach into the organization, with whom to develop relations, what signals to listen for, and how best to help people or struggling teams.

Hybrid working and managing distributed teams add new dimensions to these challenges. You can't pick up people's feelings as easily on Zoom, and there isn't a watercooler to hang out at to listen and set a vibe.

Martin Davis, CIO and managing partner, DUNELM Associates, offers this suggestion: "Make yourself available to your teams, set aside time to have one-on-one meetings, but also encourage them to interact when they have questions or want advice. Be open and share what is going on (where possible). Knowledge is not power in today's world, and we win as a team."

5. **Assign leadership responsibilities and then foster collegial conflicts.** I explicitly define the responsibilities of my leaders so that they know what's expected of them and want them to drive their agendas slightly above their teams' speed limits, say 70 miles per hour. But I also intentionally create some overlap and gray areas to create tension that brings out debate. I want some conflict on my teams because better, thought-through answers come from the debate and discussion. Competition works with hackathons, experiments, and proofs of concept to test different solutions. But I don't go as

far as creating a competitive atmosphere, which in my opinion is a counterculture that has many stressful and avoidable ramifications.

Having a competitive or stressful environment also reverberates to other teams and people you collaborate with regularly. It can create confusion when your colleagues experience the conflicts and don't know how you've assigned responsibilities. And trust me, the last thing you want is to have a competitive culture to ripple up and across the organization, especially if it's in the C-suite. As we'll see in the next chapter, collaborating with leaders has enough challenges without a competitive atmosphere.

■ ■ ■

If you would like more specifics on these lessons learned and best practices, please visit https://www.starcio.com/digital-trailblazer/chapter-8.

Notes

1. "By The Numbers | National Center For Women & Information Technology," 2021, ncwit.org, https://ncwit.org/resource/bythenumbers/.
2. Stuart R. Levine, "Diversity Confirmed to Boost Innovation and Financial Results," *Forbes,* Jan. 15, 2020, https://www.forbes.com/sites/forbesinsights/2020/01/15/diversity-confirmed-to-boost-innovation-and-financial-results/?sh=2c57952ec4a6.
3. "DEI," Dictionary.com, https://www.dictionary.com/browse/dei.

Chapter 9

Selling Innovation to the C-Suite—and Reducing the Stress

I take lots of walks when I work in New York City. My favorite is walking around the block from our offices on Franklin Street, down to Broadway, south to Leonard Street, west to Church, and then back to Franklin. There's an Italian deli on Franklin just before our office where I can pick up a sandwich on a homemade ciabatta roll.

Occasionally, I walk by a movie filming on location, a group of fashion models walking to their next photo shoot, or a musician playing with a case open for donations. I like the musicians, the trumpet players, guitarists, and the occasional cellist. It's often worth pausing, listening to them play, and losing my tensions in their melodies.

Those were the better walks during my career. The overly crowded walks in midtown on 47th Street between Sixth Avenue and Broadway do little to lift the mind. Tables of sunglasses for sale, rotating food trucks, tourists rushing to get to the TKTS half-price ticket stands, and the smell of overdressed executives are not very inspiring. Things went downhill when I relocated to 2 Penn Plaza right in front of Madison Square Garden. There's nothing pleasant about the walks there unless you escape the thirties and make your way to the north end of Chelsea.

Walks help clear my mind, but I seek a bowl of Japanese noodle soup when things get really bad. I still have a soft spot for nabeyaki udon, which I first tasted after interviewing for my first role out of graduate school on Long Island. A piping hot rich broth, shrimp tempura, fish cakes, veggies, an egg, and udon fills the body and comforts the soul. It's hard to find a Japanese restaurant that properly makes this delicately balanced soup, so I settle for Ramen and regularly visit a local noodle shop during the Businessweek sale from McGraw Hill to Bloomberg. McGraw Hill Construction's divestiture was even tougher, and without a great Japanese restaurant around, I settle for cheap sushi, street tacos, and occasionally a burger at an Irish bar. These do nothing for me except afford me the escape from the pressures inside.

Why all the stress and why the need for escapes? When you're part of the team selling a business, you live in several sometimes paradoxical worlds. You're selling the vision to potential owners, which often requires portraying the company as the pot of gold at the end of a rainbow. At the same time, you must manage day-to-day business issues and keep most of the information on the sale and strategic direction a secret from the staff. Then, in the back of your mind, you're wondering whether the outcome is going to be good for you or if you'll soon be hunting for a new job.

Being part of a team selling a business is difficult, but it's not something you're doing every day or year. On the other hand, once you start directing transformation programs, the stress never escapes you. It's not easy leading transformation when you're driving a team and juggling many unknowns.

And the greatest pressures often happen before and after executive meetings.

There are two mindsets I adopt before walking into meetings with the leadership team. My first is survival. Who's my friend today, who's out to get me, and who's just there for the ride? Even when there's an agenda, it's hard to know where everyone stands and what directions the conversation will go in. If there's a crisis, then I've seen executive teams come together, leave their egos behind, and find new ways to work with each other. Other times, it's a shooting gallery of blame, throwing colleagues under the bus, or deflecting attention to some other rotting corner of the business.

In my role as an information and technology officer, the most difficult situation to navigate is when a leader tosses a hot potato onto the table. An issue falls squarely in the middle of the meeting agenda, and there's no clear line of who should take the lead to address the problem. Unfortunately, usually no one wants to take ownership, and it's not my call to say, "Stop," and have the potato land on the right leader. I just know the problem needs solving, and my team must help with the implementation. I also recognize that the business, and often my team as part of it, is suffering because no one wants to take the reins and drive a vision and priorities.

The other mindset when walking into an executive meeting is being the wolf. No, I'm not out on the attack per se, but I am on the agenda to sell something to the executive team. Sometimes it's an investment, a policy change, or to get everyone's agreement on a direction. For example, can I fill an open position, or does everyone agree we make an offer to the candidate I want to hire? Are we ready to sign a deal with a new partner and pursue a joint venture? And so on.

As leaders, the last thing we want is to do all the prep work to drive a decision, only to see our colleagues kick the can down the road and punt on it. It sucks having to go back to the head of IT Ops and tell them we reviewed their pitch for an upgraded IT services management (ITSM) platform, but the leadership team wants to wait before making any investment decisions. Or that they want to delay security training, hold off on hiring a great architect, or revisit the business case to run a POC on new technology.

Sometimes, I use this to my advantage. I always pitch three or four new investments at budget time, but rarely more. And I always advise leaders to start transformations with only one big bet initiative. What's number three or four on the list? It's the ERP that needs an upgrade, but we're not ready to invest in it. Or it's the DataOps platform that should have been in place years ago, but we need more time to research before selecting a technology. When these get shot down, it's more likely that other more critical and planned investments will get the nod. And, when the team is ready to pitch the ERP or DataOps solutions next year, well, there will be less of a surprise.

Selling Innovation and Product Management Practices to the C-Suite

Today, I'm on the executive agenda to review how I intend to establish product management as a disciplined process and align it with an agile way of working. This is no easy task, and I need the executives to fully understand what I'm about to outline to pursue new growth strategies. If we're really going to develop new products, reengineer operations, and evaluate new partnerships, then this is the meeting where I must secure buy-in. Let me walk you through how it played out and outline some key barriers you're bound to encounter as a Digital Trailblazer when you're presenting transformational product ideas or initiatives to leaders.

About a third of the room has been directly involved in developing the framework. It's been a journey helping leaders in the organization understand a disciplined process of developing products and the role of product management. The deck I'm presenting has been through countless revisions. Two other non-executives, including the head of product management, are in the room to explain the function, sell it, and iron out several decisions the executive group must endorse. In fact, I'm only presenting part of the deck, and everyone has a role in selling this transformation.

I first must explain the role of product management and convey that it's not all about developing products and innovations. Product management is a discipline for evaluating market needs, identifying competitive differentiators, proposing target customer segments, defining the vision, and collaborating on a roadmap. I use the word "product" broadly to include products the company sells to customers and the internal products that drive operations and improve employee experiences—like CRM, ERPs, ITSM platforms, integrations, and analytics. These internal products should have selected employee customers and stakeholders and often have nonfinancial success criteria such as adoption, productivity, and quality.

Now, a third of the people in the room have little interest in this presentation. They care about the outcomes, not how the product development factory works inside. But here's the thing: When companies face market disruption, product development outcomes can make or break the business. Some of these leaders will gain new responsibilities, while others will see investments in areas outside of their interests. Transformation doesn't just impact the people working on the products and innovations. It affects the entire company's operating model.

The other third must participate and directly support the product management framework. I can't bring new products to the market without the CFO, the head of sales, and the marketing leaders on board with the approach. I also need the COO, general managers, and operational managers to consider the process changes to support new product offerings.

> *Support* is an interesting word.
>
> Just getting an executive's support in a conference room only amounts to their decision not to confront you. However, if you want that executive to follow through and to go beyond support and endorse followed by action, well then, that's a whole other mountain you're climbing.

Keep that in mind, but for now, at this meeting, the goal is to gain acceptance of the program and input around key decisions. In transformational change, you must reach first base before thinking about running to second base, let alone crossing homeplate.

To get to first base, we need the executive leadership team to agree on the criteria around a new product idea to get the green light for investment. Every company that wants sustainable innovation processes and must adapt to changing customer needs and market conditions faces this challenge.

If you don't set the bar here, new ideas circulate the halls of conversation without any action because no one knows the product development process and what's required to take opportunities, needs, and ideas to the next level. One hallmark of these companies is that without a clear product development process and decision criteria, the staff often resort to sinking their time into building PowerPoint presentations, hoping that an even better deck will garner the necessary support.

Define the bar too low, and the concern is that the organization chases a flood of proposals, under-resources them, and has no big wins to show for it. Pursuing ideas and letting Darwin's rules sort out the winners might work in large technology companies like Google and Facebook, which have more than their share of talent and a healthy cultural acceptance of failing fast. But most organizations are more conservative and have limited talent, so they must be more strategic with their product development and innovation bets.

The other option is to set a higher bar, but this has different challenges. If the bar is set too high, you may demoralize the staff pursuing the innovation because hitting the target is unachievable or takes too long. If it takes six months to draft a deck proving the business cases just to get a pilot approved, then that's probably too long for this day and age of rapid disruptive change.

We're following a process I wrote about in my previous book, *Driving Digital,* that I now help other companies adopt. The basis of the product management process is an agile, iterative approach to planning products centered on answering a series of questions.

It works like this. We identify the idea's *founders*, a term I borrow from startups to help create a sense of ownership and cultivate a culture of intrapreneurship. An idea goes into planning when its founders describe the opportunity with minimal evidence, identify a list of planning questions, and request a timeline and small budget for any research or proofs of concept. The bar for this first step is intentionally low so that passionate founders can pursue new ideas. The main restriction is that individuals can only lead or be a member of one new idea planning team at a time. This restriction places a practical throttle on how many planning initiatives are active, and the approach allows tracking them by timeline, investment, and participants.

At the meeting, we receive no feedback or objection to this first bar. That's not surprising because it's still an idea and the earliest part of the process. No one is really on the hook to support it. Sure, we'll need an innovation budget to cover investments in this phase, but our ask is small and doesn't prove to be a problem. We also clarify that we'll need involvement from sales reps to make introductions and bring us on selected sales calls. But, again, there's no objection from the sales leaders because it doesn't affect their goals and team incentives.

My approach at StarCIO is to set a low threshold for selling new ideas. If someone is passionate about solving a problem or addressing an opportunity, the organization should empower them to invest time to pursue it. We recommend that founders define a vision statement and a set of questions they will answer in their plan. The limitation is that people rarely have the capacity to pursue multiple planning initiatives, so the one-initiative-per-person rule helps prioritize.

The second bar is challenging because it transitions a product from a planning to a delivery stage, and it requires direct investment to bring a product to market. It means allocating one or more teams to work on the product starting from the experimental phases. The group releases early product versions to a subset of customers for their feedback and to evolve priorities. It requires ongoing market research to establish the customer segments, identify buyer personas, define the business model, and propose pricing.

From there, the marketing team needs to develop materials such as branding, prospect messaging, landing pages, and campaigns to find early adopters. Next, operations must adjust their processes to extend and produce new materials required for the product. Finally, there's likely new technology that needs to be evaluated, procured, and instituted. Then, of course, the legal teams must get involved to review pretty much everything, and then there are security reviews, data privacy considerations, financial modeling, compliance factors, and other considerations depending on the industry. In companies and industries where compliance, safety, security, and scale are major factors, legal, financial, and security teams must have roles early in the process.

> Developing new products, enhancing customer experiences, or transforming operations creates more work for everyone. Imagine that! And when leaders realize this, some curl up into a clamshell, not wanting to respond, while others have no issue creating a commotion. I'll talk more about bringing on transformation supporters and handling detractors in Chapter 10. For now, I want you to recognize that not everyone will be happy or enthusiastic to support new ideas because of the added work, long debates, and hard decisions they require.

Some start bickering about how resource-starved they are and whether the funding approved for product development covers their needs to grow their team. Others want to put boundaries and conditions in place to prevent product development teams from requiring them to fulfill tasks completely outside their team's capabilities. Finally, others want more planning done upfront to better assess, plan, and estimate costs for everything they require.

These concerns and objections are manageable if you do your homework. That means talking to these leaders before the meeting and getting their input on how product development impacts their organization. For example, it's common to hear concerns about how the project will add new responsibilities or require skills and capabilities above and beyond what their teams normally do, that is, their definition of "business as usual" (BAU). In many cases, their objections can be overcome by proactively factoring in the funding to address any gaps or additional responsibilities in the project budget.

This review differentiates transformation management from more classic change management approaches. In transformation management, teams seek to learn the current state of impacted operations upfront during planning phases (i.e., how the leader, teams, and individuals understand their BAU processes). Transformation management also calls for active participation from people in the impacted operations in planning and implementing new technologies, processes, and analytics. This approach helps everyone estimate, plan, implement, and guide the transformations needed to fulfill an initiative's objectives and vision.

The fun of this, of course, is that many departments have ill-defined BAUs. Some leaders translate anything you ask them to do as work outside their BAU, while others overcommit and struggle to meet their objectives. Some departments have longstanding and structured processes, but if undocumented, you may need someone with a six-sigma background to review, capture, and analyze their workflows.

We do these meetings with each leader so that they learn and reflect. Sometimes we meet multiple times, and it becomes a negotiation—we give and take a little. This dialog is needed to get everyone involved and committed to the approach, but some lines need to be drawn. I make sure that the team knows that we can't tell leaders what's fully expected of them upfront. Surely, we'll know some of the requirements, tasks, and deliverables, but not all of them. We are planning products in an agile way and learning as we go. That means the product team understands new requirements during the journey, or big surprises require them to pivot the strategy.

> You must stand firm around an agile approach. The more leaders tax the team to understand everything upfront, the less agile you become. It restricts the team and slows things down in the pursuit of perfecting the knowledge around the unknowns. If you don't fight these command-and-control tendencies early, the team will face scrutiny whenever something new is deemed a surprise to a stakeholder.

At some point in the discussion around new products and transformations, you will need to present success criteria in the form of OKRs (objectives and key results), KPIs (key performance indicators), or other metrics. Every organization is different in what they call them, how they align these indicators to strategy, how many they define, and how they measure them.

Often, the heart of the matter falls on financial projections such as revenue, cost savings, return on investment, and the internal rate of return.

You make assumptions on pricing, number of sales, and sales time frames at any point in a product's development. For internal transformations, you estimate the timing and magnitude of operational impacts, for example, estimating reductions in people and hours because of automation.

For product investments in startups, we use a hockey stick growth curve to sell a new round of investment. The first few months after product launch, sales are linear and slow, but there's a magical inflection point to exponential growth. Sure, the venture capitalists (VCs) are interested in your go-to-market strategy, but they all know you designed your spreadsheet on a limited amount of sales prospecting and price testing. The VCs have plenty of data, so if they believe in the team and the product idea, they'll benchmark your hockey stick against other similar and successful product launches.

Large enterprises can pay big consulting houses for this data and market evaluation. But all that means is that you outsourced the methodology and the data gathering. Perhaps it's more accurate or has more credibility than what your in-house team can do. Getting an outside-in perspective can be useful when the evaluations and financial models are grounded in sufficient data, have well laid out assumptions, and include approaches to further validate conclusions.

> However aggressive, conservative, or realistic, the projection is up for debate. How executives use early-stage, forward-looking financial forecasts on new products in making decisions is a governance function that speaks to the heart of the company's culture around innovation and risk-taking. The material question is whether sales leaders support the market, product, and most importantly, the sales expectations projected in the financial model.

Whatever hockey stick you draw based on the data and whoever's credibility is behind it, the product leadership team is asking the sales team—directly or indirectly—to take responsibility for meeting that target. And of course, sales wants to be well compensated for it. Most importantly, they often request unrealistically high expectations for the product. That product coming out of the factory should bear little resemblance to an MVP Chevy Nova and operate more like an Audi Quattro with all the bells and whistles and, of course, an attractive price point.

Getting sales on board with a new product idea in a conservative company, whether it's an enterprise, medium, or small business, is the chasm product leaders must cross. Most companies don't have infinitely deep pockets to invest in new product ideas, and only a percentage have cultures truly open to experimentation and failing. You can buy technology and talent to get you to the finish line, but ultimately, the executives want to believe they can sell it.

Catherine is presenting this to the executive group. She's reviewed the product development process, and we've tag-teamed on answering questions. We're down to the profit and loss (P&L) financial slide, and in preparing for this presentation we had passionate debates about what details to include and exclude. Our objective is to present the P&L as a model that evolves, but as Catherine walks the leadership through the forecasts and assumptions, I can sense everyone's anxieties.

It's a lot easier to present a product development process when you're investing other people's money. But when it comes out of the executive bonus pools, or if it prevents the leaders from hiring people to make their lives easier, then they're likely to be a lot more conservative with spending money on longer term investments.

The questions start coming in around the P&L.

"Catherine, is this a conservative or aggressive revenue forecast?"

Catherine prepared for this softball and replies, “It’s conservative. We only assume one new sale every six weeks for the first six months, and then it increases to one sale per month for the next twelve.”

“Catherine, how did you arrive at the price point?”

Catherine answers, “That came from benchmarking prices from other similar products and then interviewing prospects to understand their values and needs better. Customers who buy the product are likely to generate five times the revenue in the first year from using it. And that’s conservative. Plus, we didn’t include services that we could potentially sell to help customers achieve the goals. That’s a second revenue stream that might materialize and not included the model. Finally, we modeled a price point that’s 80 percent of the target to account for discounts and other incentives.”

I’m feeling pretty good about this now, and the room goes quiet for a bit until one executive speaks up. He decides to test Henry, one of the sales leaders, on his level of *support* and commitment. He asks, “Henry, are you prepared to sell against this model? We will add these sales figures to your team’s sales goals.” He says this while looking over at our CFO in an attempt to get his acknowledgment.

That was the record scratching moment. And I was pissed.

The executive wants to hit it out of the park and get a sales commitment at the same meeting that we’re trying to institute a new way of working. WTF? He knows this is a conservative group, and it took months to get to this point. He knows there are uncertainties along the way of developing and marketing the product before we even get to selling it.

I’ve been preaching a baseball analogy with this team for months. Get someone on base and then let the next batter score the run. Maybe your runner steals a base, or there’s a wild pitch that allows him to get closer to home. Or perhaps the pitcher walks the next batter, and you have a chance for an even better score. Don’t get thrown out running to third with two outs.

Henry waffles, hems, and haws a bit. He supports the plan but doesn't want to sign up for new targets at this meeting before work even starts. His colleague tries to rescue him with a reasonable request. "Let's let the product development start, and then we can further develop a sales plan."

I think that should end the conversation, but I jump in to try closing the deal and provide Catherine with longer term support. My job includes changing the culture, so I don't just want an agreement and then see everyone return to their day jobs. I want them to feel an experimental innovation process at work and to start developing an agile mindset.

So I add, "That's exactly the right idea. We test our assumptions, learn, and adjust our marketing, pricing, pitch, and priorities as we develop the product. That's the nature of running an agile program. We make quick decisions with the information at hand, then use feedback to course correct along the journey. If we hit a speed bump, then we regroup and assess. But analysis paralysis is the death of innovation and progress."

I've seen this discussion play out in several companies, and it's what happens next that can make or break a successful product launch, a significant business process reengineering, or a business model transformation. Or lead to doom.

Let's explore some real-world scenarios.

Scenario one: A new executive chimes in, "Why don't we sell the product first and look to score a few buyers before we invest. We can then use the income to trigger investment in developing the product."

Is this a positive contribution to the culture change or a setback? This idea isn't that ridiculous, and software companies have been doing this for generations. As buying CIOs, we sometimes call it vaporware. You get sold a bill of goods and then wait months for the capability to materialize if it does at all.

But for the software company, it's very hard to sell and even harder to get the buyer to commit. What can be worse is that it puts early adopters into the driver's seat to set priorities and desired capabilities. That's a significant danger considering your early buyers are rightfully selfish and want the product to work for them. Making the product work equally and easily well for their competitors is not their goal.

So, how should you respond? It depends on your organization's culture and talent.

Suppose your organization is already open to risk-taking and has a history of agile execution. In that case, this can be a positive outcome, especially for organizations that overcommit to too many ideas. Selling drives the priority to invest.

But this can be disastrous for conservative organizations. It's a kick-the-can-down-the-road move, putting sales in front of innovation. It requires developing incentives for the sales team, leveraging customer feedback, and executing disciplined agile programs—all unlikely practices in conservative organizations still learning to drive transformations.

Here's my response to this objection: "Our plan includes building a lightweight pilot, demoing it to prospects, and using it to sell them into an early adopter program. But we will need a green light today to build this pilot, and we'll need participation from sales to demo and sell to potential customers. We'll also need to be picky on what goes into the pilot; it needs to illustrate the core capabilities to get feedback, but it can't be the full product with all the bells and whistles."

Note these four highlights of my response: (1) We planned for this objection, (2) we follow best practices by developing pilots off MVPs, (3) we disclose our expectations on departmental responsibilities, and (4) we bring the conversation back to today's decision on whether or not to invest.

Scenario two: A different executive is concerned there will be insufficient funds to invest in areas tied to his line of business. He chimes in, "Can we review all the investment opportunities before we agree to place our bets on this one?"

Baselining a review of the full investment portfolio and potential opportunities may seem like a reasonable request, and it's likely to get support from other executives in conservative organizations. But there are a few reasons to push back on this next attempt to kick the can down the road.

First, it may not be practical to schedule this review, and even if it is, it will add more noise to the decision process. Either the opportunity the executive team is reviewing passes the bar to move forward, or it doesn't, and that's the decision the executive group must make today. Second, they can revisit this decision when there's material evidence requiring a review.

Here's why—it prepares the executive group to make the best decisions with the available information and prepares everyone to run an agile process. Opportunities can emerge at any time, and the exec team should evaluate them against the investment portfolio's current state. And for that matter, teams working on products may uncover customer feedback or new market conditions and require a strategic pivot. These are all real-time decisions and all common and likely.

So, a green light today may turn to yellow or red tomorrow as new information becomes available. That's the scenario the Digital Trailblazer wants to prepare their organization to manage to, and not one where there's analysis paralysis before making any decisions.

Here's how I might respond: "We can review the portfolio whenever we want, but I suggest we do this at a defined interval, say every three months. We can call for a special review if circumstances require it, but the reviews can be time-consuming. Today, I recommend focusing on the program that we're reviewing since we have a team that's put in the hard work to share their goals with us and is ready to move forward. They know we can pivot out plans at any time and stagnating on this decision sends the wrong message when we're asking everyone to deliver faster results.

Scenario three: Here's a scenario that is common for product and operational reengineering programs. A third executive steps in to ask, "If we invest, can we hold off engaging my team in the process until the product is more baked in and we know what changes are required?"

Product teams and companies that agree to this approach are doomed. It allows the leader to return to their BAU without any responsibility to shape how the team plans and executes the initiative. It robs the team working on the initiative of the information needed on their department's requirements and feedback from incremental progress. Absolving these responsibilities often concludes with failed initiatives when feedback emerges too late to enable course corrections and pivots.

> If you're leading a transformation initiative, you must insist on stakeholder participation from the start and seek feedback during the journey. If you aren't getting the required engagement, seek help from the initiative's sponsors and consider pausing work until they address the gap. It's just that important to have a fully engaged agile team, including business participation and feedback from stakeholders.

My response assumes that we did our homework and identified a member of the executive's team to participate in the program. Then, here's how I can respond: "I understand your concern, but with a transformation of this magnitude, I think you would want someone at the table to help steer the ship. And quite frankly, I think we'll be less successful without her contributions. If we start down the wrong path, we'll catch it earlier in the process, and missing essential recommendations from our subject matter experts may slow us down if we have to rework things later on."

If I feel very strongly about having her on the team, I might add, "And starting this transformation without her involvement is a nonstarter."

A form of this scenario happens to us when Catherine gets one more suggestion.

"Why doesn't Catherine sell the product to a handful of customers before we ask sales to participate?"

It's a terrible idea. Not only are we letting sales off the hook, but we're asking Catherine to perform a function outside of her skills and responsibilities. I expect the leading executives to step in and realize this mistake, but they don't. Despite my objections, that's where the executives net out. And it's at that moment when I recognize the initiative is likely doomed.

Great Leaders Rally Everyone on the Vision and Acknowledge Challenges Ahead

Years earlier, I witnessed how leadership teams come together, collaborate, and align on a mission even when there were significant and sometimes nasty conflicts between members.

Sitting in a town hall one day, I recall watching our CEO explain our mission to employees who had been battered and demoralized for months, if not years. It's hard being a medium-sized business within a very large enterprise operating in a blue-collar industry that's foreign to the executive leadership group. People look at their jobs based on their outputs, in this case: a magazine, a data set, leads for jobs, forecasting studies, analyst reports, company rankings, and awards. A small minority of people are passionate about the work—mainly the editors, writers, and long-timers who know the complex intricacies of how business and operations work in the industry. The sales team drinks large quantities of the Kool-Aid and truly believes we offer important and differentiating products and services.

Unfortunately, the truth is that the brand, value proposition, and product offerings are all dated and developed for an era that was fading fast.

At one point, I correctly label our core business as an industry-specific, B2B job board that is less relevant in today's information-rich era. Compared to just five years ago, our customers today don't need our data, leads, and rankings. What's worse is that startups sell SaaS platforms that provide alternative models, approaches, and experiences that compete with our value proposition. They are cheaper and provide workflow and capabilities beyond our data offering.

How long do we have to transform—one, three, five years, or longer? That is anyone's guess. But the CEO knows I need time to engineer new product offerings. More importantly, he knows he must get everyone in the organization involved in our transformation.

The transformation starts with the product, technology, and analytics teams because we must conceive modernized products, develop them, improve them, and propose a whole new way of selling, marketing, and supporting them. That means the CEO needs many employees to excel in today's business, but as we ready a new digital one, they must perform double duties supporting the old and the new. They also must be active contributors to the new business model since institutional knowledge lies in their industry experiences and expertise.

But our experts must also listen and self-reflect because what got us here today and what customers value may not be relevant to their future needs. Bringing what's important from the past, leaving behind sacred cows, and executing an evolving future vision is the heart of transformation. And it only happens when employees buy into the mission and are willing to take on new roles during the journey.

The CEO knows how hard that is because he's done it before, and several of us are in our second round of transforming businesses with him. He knows that beliefs, incentives, mindsets, and culture all play into whether an employee volunteers their insights, or sits in the back of the room, arms crossed, ready to use their knowledge to sink ideas.

The incentive changes come, but leaders pace them with the transformation. You can't realign ad sales commissions overnight when moving from hundred-thousand-dollar print display ads to single-thousands of dollars in digital ads. But you need the sales team to learn how to sell digital before the business model's engines are revving, which takes gaining alignment on mission and vision.

Our CEO asks everyone in multiple offices across the country to gather in conference rooms for our first town hall as a leadership team. He doesn't want people dialed in at their desks, and he wants everyone to feel the energy as he lays out his vision.

"We build bridges, schools, hospitals, and office buildings. We fix roads, upgrade stadiums, and provide affordable housing. We do this by providing our customers with vital information, insights, and knowledge to excel at their jobs and make better decisions. We must do this with integrity, from how we collect data that feeds our platforms, to our editorial excellence in how our journalists report on the news. And we must do this efficiently because we have new competitors, and raising our prices isn't viable when the industry is struggling. We must learn from our customers what they need and how they want to consume our information, and where they want to take action with the data, insights, and editorial that we offer them. We have to identify new prospects that should be interested in our offerings but may need different ways for us to market, sell, and produce products for them.

"And most important, we need all of you to bring you're A game. We must improve what and how we do things today and reconceive a future way of delivering products and services. We must leave some old habits behind and use technology aggressively to shape our future. This transformation won't just be Isaac working with his team, cranking out software and new ways to present our data. We're going to spend more time improving areas vital to our growth and survival, which means we might not be working in your business area on day one. We need all of your inputs, ideas, and contributions, but we also want you to listen, learn, and accept that many of the ways we used to do things are no longer viable in a digital world. That will scare some of you when you see that what you're doing today may not have a future, or it may be a very different one. But if you continue doing it as needed and step up to contribute and learn about our future, you'll already be a part of it.

"Here's my vision of our future."

The truth is, it was a partial vision. We just joined the company weeks ago, and the industry was foreign to us. The writing on the wall was all there, but someone needed to read it to everyone in an honest, and at times, brutal way. We're done if all we do is improve on what we are doing today. And we are going to fall off disruption's cliff if we spend months or years to reconceive our vision. We'll take a stab at it based on what we know and use evidence to adjust it along the journey.

Our vision has baked-in priorities, and our CEO announces it on day one. In some businesses, innovation is prioritized and running in full force, while in others, we will barely keep the lights on. That will upset some people, and we will have to make exceptions at different times, but we make it clear to everyone.

Transformation doesn't mean trying to fix everything at once. That's a recipe for disaster because organizations don't have the breadth of people, funding, practices, and culture to drive transformative changes to apply universally across all aspects of the business. Transformation requires saying yes, no, maybe, do more, do less, pivot, and stop.

As I write this chapter, I'm traveling between two businesses I'm advising on their transformation programs. One is a tiny company with fewer than thirty people, several million in revenue, five strategic priorities, and dozens of critical initiatives. The other is a growing unicorn with around 1,000 employees, multiple product lines, several growth opportunities, and hundreds of priorities that leadership expects to get done over the year.

Both will have some successes and misses. But I guarantee that both will spend an ungodly amount of time debating priorities. Will they prioritize and communicate their big bets, or will they push an all-you-can-eat buffet to the staff and let them sort out how best to respond?

If the executive team fails to debate and communicate priorities, it leads to a bumbling and stumbling transformation fit with restarts and unnecessary failures. But to align on vision and priorities, especially to say yes, no, maybe, do more, do less, pivot, and stop, well, it takes a leadership team that can discuss, debate, argue, console, and decide.

Decide. Decide. It's worth repeating. Just gathering into conference rooms to talk past each other is a fail. Debate without a decision is a fail. Kicking the can down the road is a fail. Saying yes to every opportunity is a fail. The best decision is always to make a decision. Once you decide, then consider when the team leading the initiative should return, discuss progress, and propose updated plans.

Navigating the murky waters of the C-suite starts with an understanding of what goes on behind closed doors and what to do, what not to do, and what may happen when you're invited to present to the group. It's easier not to make decisions, and it's impossible to capture and present perfect information that can drive consensus. It's convenient to push responsibilities elsewhere and go back to business as usual.

Successful transformation leaders know these tendencies. What distinguishes them is the relationships they develop, their deep knowledge of the business, their collaboration with their teams, their empathy to interact with people as individuals, their propensity to prioritize, their desire to communicate an easy-to-understand vision, and their resolve to stay firm on what decisions are needed and where they need people to accept responsibility.

Like many recipes, it's easy to talk about and hard to perform. And it's often stressful. You better plan on taking some walks.

Digital Trailblazer Lessons

Collaborating with Executives

I confess that this was a difficult chapter to write. There are entire books on executive leadership, transformation, governance, developing relationships, and culture. I selected stories and themes that you're more likely to see from the outside-in as you navigate into a transformation leadership role.

I hope you will take away these lessons learned from this chapter:

1. **Find your stress release valves.** As you move up in responsibilities, you're going to have fewer outlets to vent frustration. You'll still be able to go out with your teams and colleagues

but expect them to be guarded even where you have long-term relationships. Share your feelings and be honest with your team, too, but that's often not sufficient for rebounding from the daily stresses of driving transformation. My stress relief rituals included taking walks and indulging in noodle soups. I have colleagues who run, work out, play music, and meditate. Find yours and stick with it. When transformation becomes especially stressful, it's imperative that you continue to take care of yourself, find *your* ways to release stress, and define rituals to maintain your mental health.

2. **Ask for more than support; seek executive endorsements and commitments.** Remember that getting an executive's support without their skin in the game is of very limited value to transformation leaders. An endorsement implies that they will be vocal with their support, but you want more than just their endorsement; you want their commitment to action. Come to the executive with a firm *ask* of what you need and ensure they accept responsibility. Discuss matters such as whom they can assign an active role to the initiative. How will they help define success criteria and priorities? When can you reach out to them to resolve disputes? That's how you know that they are ready to fully sponsor the initiative.

3. **Define and roleplay scenarios around potential objections when selling innovations.** Sales teams rehearse their pitch and roleplay common scenarios where a buyer or a stakeholder may surface an objection. Please make no mistake about it; when you're a Digital Trailblazer and garnering executive buy-ins, you're selling. When you are asking for an investment, seeking to prioritize an initiative, or trying to drive transformational change, you are selling, and there will be objections. While you can't rehearse for every situation, you

can come prepared and practiced. The best way to do this starts by developing relationships with executives and learning their goals, incentives, and biases. Where is there alignment, and can you anticipate where there may be conflicts? Follow this approach with your lieutenants, who should also have assigned responsibilities to develop relationships. Then, gather your leadership team and roleplay different scenarios.

4. **Simplify and share your vision.** In this chapter, I illustrate what happens when leaders kick the can down the road around decisions. Transformational leaders who hold their visions close to the vest and wait for all the evidence to fall into place are just as detrimental. Be prepared to share your vision early and invite others to contribute. Acknowledge that you are still learning and that you will communicate changes to your strategy and goals frequently. The world moves fast, and the goalposts are always changing, but we must provide teams with a sense of direction.

5. **Ruthlessly prioritize and define success criteria.** Agile backlogs have only one No. 1 priority, and teams review the ranked list of priorities when committing to their sprint's work. Transformation leaders and executives must take the same approach when defining strategies, communicating goals, setting OKRs and KPIs, and articulating visions. Leaders who are vague on priorities or convey too many push these decisions down to their teams, who often respond by spreading efforts across many of the priorities. The impact is lots of work in progress, little for the organization to show for it, and often too much unnecessary stress.

   Once priorities are ranked, then articulate success criteria for the top ones. In agile methods, user stories are often written with pass/fail acceptance criteria to set expectations with the teams and establish a shared understanding of when the story is done. For broad initiatives and strategies with many objectives, setting granular acceptance criteria isn't feasible, but sharing success criteria and a select few OKRs or KPIs enables teams to self-organize on solutions with a clearly defined goalpost.

Now that you have a few stories and best lessons on leading initiatives and partnering with the C-Suite, I'll use the final chapter to share my insights on leading transformation programs.

If you would like more specifics on these lessons learned and best practices, please visit https://www.starcio.com/digital-trailblazer/chapter-9.

Chapter 10

Transforming Beyond Crisis and Becoming a Digital Trailblazer

This should feel like a routine flight, but it isn't. As the plane pulls from the gate, I look out the window and am grateful for the on-time departure. It's cold and raining outside, and my mind is wandering between what I just worked on with a client and what I need to focus on when I arrive home in Westchester County, New York.

We were supposed to decide the agenda and select attendees for a workshop to align the incident management, site reliability engineers, and development teams. The organization has many technology operation incidents, not enough time to perform adequate root cause analysis, and the developers resolve too few problems with code fixes. The leadership team is numb to the frequency of bridge calls, the techno-jargon exchanged during them, and the time required to restore services.

The workshop we're planning begins with reviewing the end-to-end process for managing major incidents. We expect to assign roles and responsibilities, define protocols, and make these calls run more efficiently. More importantly, we want to reconsider the severity levels set to incidents, map out a closed-loop process for root cause analysis, and define with the engineering team how they resolve defects.

But we didn't do any of the prep work for this workshop and had to call an audible. Instead, we updated business continuity plans, developed contingency communications, and finalized an order for new laptops. We discussed how we would operate scrum standups and other agile ceremonies virtually and whether some of the more complex architecture work in planning might need reprioritization. I said goodbye, not knowing if I would make it back down to visit them anytime soon.

I see the air traffic control tower as we make our way to the runway. All of this feels surreal and distant until the phone calls and emails come in, and I review the situation. They are preparing because the governor told them to be ready to shut down. The airport is half empty, and I expect Newark airport, near my home, to look like a ghost town.

But the COVID-19 pandemic became personal for me very quickly. I had a full schedule of workshops, keynotes, and dinners scheduled from April through June 2020, and one by one, organizers reached out to either postpone, cancel, or discuss virtual options. I felt like a tired, overmatched boxer taking a left jab, and before being able to regain my posture, a right hook lands and throws me two steps further backward.

The coronavirus pandemic had pretty much killed my next three months of business.

And while my client's offices were very distant from the pandemic, my home was not. New York Governor Andrew Cuomo ordered a one-mile containment zone in New Rochelle, the epicenter of the breakout just outside New York City. My house and kids' schools are less than a couple of miles outside that radius.

As our plane pushes back from the gate, I'm wondering: What does a containment zone mean? And what is life like back in our neighborhood? I call my wife Michele and ask if she has loaded up on groceries.

"Why?" she asks.

I've already read accounts on social media of stores selling out of necessities, including toilet paper. My plan-ahead instincts kick in. I look at my calendar for Friday, March 13, and it is empty, and I decide I will head out first thing in the morning to stock up on the essentials.

Over the years, I've gotten pretty good at trusting my instincts and managing my reactions. When I start seeing signs that the coronavirus is turning into a global pandemic, I move into crisis-management mode. My mind thinks beyond the immediate needs of my family, the illnesses striking many people, and the difficult work facing essential workers. Instead, I focus on what I can control and my new priorities.

Looking at my calendar, I realize that it's not just Friday that's open; pretty much all of next week is suddenly clear because of canceled events. And the week after, I'm supposed to visit this client again, but who knows if they will cancel. April isn't looking good, either.

My mind races some more, and I start adding up the potential impact of a pandemic—job cancellations, travel advisories, lockdowns, rationing, and who knows what else is in store. My mind is focused on my business because anything personal and impacting my family is just too hard to think about and fathom.

In that moment, I make a stark realization. My business largely relies on being in front of people. The basis of StarCIO's primary income is keynote presentations, hosting dinners, facilitating workshops, conducting digital assessments, and consulting on digital practices—all of which require me and my consultants to board planes and work in-person. When I do work from home, I complete writing assignments, participate in social media, and lead advisory calls—a small percentage of my time and even a smaller part of my income.

For a "Driving Digital" business, my business isn't very digital.

Sure, I help organizations with the many aspects of running a successful digital business. Our center of excellence programs help organizations iteratively improve their product management, agile planning, DevOps, and data-driven practices in three-month release cycles. Before COVID-19, this work was largely done in person. We listen, observe, and ask questions. We lead meetings and are flies on the wall during others. We guide organizations through transformative changes, which until now required being on-site, getting to know everyone, building trust, and challenging the status quo.

In between this work with clients, I speak to digital, data, and IT leaders at conferences, events, and dinners. Some of this is for growing technology companies that want my writing, voice, and influence in positioning their products and services to digital and IT leaders. The most challenging events are hosting dinners. I thank Alan Alda for his book *If I Understood You, Would I Have This Look on My Face?* as a key tool for helping me conquer this format.

But now I have an empty calendar. And as companies across the country are going into business continuity mode, well, I don't think anyone will be able to buy StarCIO's in-person engagement services anytime soon. More events to speak at or dinners to host? Unlikely. Workshops and assessments? Nope. For how long? I don't know.

My business would have to go through a transformation of its own.

Learn Your Decision-Making Style from Personal Transformations

The truth is, I've experienced transformations and pivots throughout my career. To fully understand leading transformation, you must experience it, and one way to do this is to reflect on personal transformations that impacted your life and career. It requires differentiating externally driven transformations from strategic transformations, so let me share some key differences with you.

On the one hand, externally driven transformations feel like being on a rollercoaster where you see the upcoming turns, you anticipate the impacts from climbs and drops, and your body proactively braces to respond to the strong g-forces. In externally driven transformations, you are not the spark forcing the change but need to control how you navigate them.

On the other hand, strategic transformations feel like forks in the road where you must make key decisions about your career, life, goals, or priorities.

These are both personal transformations, where you and the immediate people surrounding you, such as your family or your teams, are impacted and influence the transformation.

Let me share some of my personal strategic transformations.

My leap from being a software developer in a biotechnology company to head of software development at a media SaaS company is an example of a strategic transformation. So was my jump to TripConnect, a ground-floor startup where we created a travel industry social network just as Facebook was launching in college dorm rooms, my pivot to leave the world of startups and join McGraw Hill to be a CIO at Businessweek and drive digital transformation, and my decision to transition from executive roles and start StarCIO.

Your personal strategic transformations include choosing your career path, deciding to change jobs, or electing to learn new skills. Think back to when you made big decisions, and you'll remember that you gathered data, sought advice, and then recognized you had to make the best decision with the available information. Procrastination is the enemy because anxiety impacts your mindset, and you are less productive as you mull over the decision repetitively. And while these transformational moments are personal, they are not necessarily irreversible. You can make these decisions, learn, capture feedback, and pivot again as required. Some doors may close after your first decision, but others will materialize.

It can be difficult to make career decisions and embark on a personal strategic transformation, but it's your choice, and you should take some control in deciding your future. Facing a personal, externally driven transformation can be even more difficult because the crisis or change was forced on you, and you must decide how best to respond to the situation.

I faced a personal, externally driven transformation with Michele starting in late 2010.

Jasper, our youngest son, was almost a year old and missing many of his development milestones. He wasn't sitting. He was lethargic most of the time. Having two older siblings that couldn't sit still for five seconds, I thought Jasper was our first "normal" baby. Michele had the mother's instinct, or justifiable paranoia, in recognizing something was wrong and spent the last couple of months taking Jasper to doctors. I kept my head down and stayed focused on work, as I had recently started my role as CIO at McGraw Hill Construction. We launched our first product in October, and a few months later, I made my yearly trip to India with Eleanor (see Chapter 6). All this while Michele was seeing doctors and starting to panic. The latest doctor, a neurologist, set up an appointment to get Jasper an EKG in early 2011.

That was my trigger point. What was the doctor looking for or concerned over that required sending Jasper to the hospital and getting wires stuck to his head?

I went on a hunt through Google, WebMD, and every website that my searches led me. Nothing came up that made sense, and friends and family kept telling me to stop playing faux doctor. I spent days correlating symptoms with prognosis and not finding a connection that made sense.

But I found an answer on YouTube. A baby with a twitch. A fast nodding of his head, just like Jasper was doing. We couldn't predict when he would do it, but we did capture it on video. The neurologist saw the video, and that's why he was sending Jasper for the EKG. He was worried Jasper had infantile spasms, a form of epilepsy. I read everything I could about this disease. No, it's a symptom, not a disease. It's rare, and the prognosis isn't good.

Several weeks later, we were in the hospital for the test. Our neurologist was there. In some ways, I was lucky because I was prepared for when the doctor confirmed Jasper's condition. I broke down crying anyway. Even though I was somewhat knowledgeable, I wasn't mentally or emotionally ready for this news. I certainly wasn't prepared for how it would transform our lives afterward.

That was ten years ago, and Jasper, in many ways, is very fortunate. There were only two drugs with any success stopping or slowing the seizures. He responded to the second one, and after two weeks in the hospital, we brought Jasper home and learned how to administer the drug to him. We were fortunate to be living in New York, where there is funding and a strong program to help developmentally disabled children. His therapists enabled him to sit, stand, walk, talk, eat, and play. Learning is proving to be a much greater challenge, and today Jasper can do some reading but very little math. But he's the happiest 11-year-old you'll ever meet, especially around the holidays. Jasper wants to decorate, bake, and spend time with family. His story is still unfolding, and he is my Superman.

I'll never forget coming back to the office after Jasper's hospital visit. I had no plan on what to say and what not to say to my colleagues. I couldn't lie to them, but I couldn't fathom telling the story to everyone. I had a persona at work. One colleague used to call me "the Energizer Bunny" after the 1980s commercials of the toy bunny that would never drain its batteries. Before taking the job, another colleague gave me a toy bulldozer, knowing that I'd need some heavy machinery to drive organizational change.

At that moment, I felt nothing like a bunny driving a bulldozer. My introvert defense mechanisms took hold, and I kept most of my feelings and what was going on at home to myself. I just couldn't see opening up to the team and showing them my soft side, and I longed for things to be "normal." But I remember telling the story to three colleagues that I trusted.

One was uplifting as he harbored his own struggles with a child's health issues. He had a strong persona, and you never suspected he was living this private and challenging life at home. One was unnerved by the situation and helped me escape the emotions by clarifying that I should listen, learn, and make decisions. The third person warned me that having a developmentally disabled child was hard on families because of the tough choices we'd have to make, the issues we'd have no control over that required our response, and the void in normalcy it would create in our home and family.

I had to adjust to a new normal, and it dramatically changed my leadership approach.

I always strived to be an empathetic leader, but my drive and energy often dominated my leadership style and persona. I got to know people on my teams, but I didn't invest enough energy to learn how transformation impacted them personally. I focused on the goal, the agile steps to get there, and the feedback to help adjust the course.

I didn't know this at the time, but understanding people's goals, needs, motivations, and circumstances confronting them in their personal lives is critical when leading large-scale transformations. And it's why I talk about the importance of empathetic leadership in Chapter 8.

Reflect on the Externally Driven Transformations That Impact Your Business

When considering leading transformations across the business, we must learn from our personal transformations and apply them to teams, departments, organizations, and industries. Like personal transformations, the ones you lead at your business can also be categorized as externally driven, strategic, or what I'll discuss soon—digital transformations.

Let me share an externally driven transformation impacting a business, my business specifically, and how we pivoted in the wake of COVID-19.

So we're on the runway, ready to takeoff off back to New York. I have no playbook on what to do next. 9/11 repeatedly comes to mind. I fear being locked in the house while the rest of the country moves on with normal life.

Within a few months, we start having a better picture of what the "new normal" will look like, and it doesn't involve travel anytime soon. I had to get back to work and consider how to navigate this externally driven transformation in my business.

I rewrite my business plan, redevelop StarCIO's products, and reengineer how we work with clients. We digitize our workshops and launch on-demand virtual courses and instructor-led certification programs.

We develop virtual assessments that provide a framework for benchmarking an organization's capabilities against current business needs and future goals. We design a rating methodology based on five transformational dimensions: smarter, faster, safer, innovative, and culturally transformative. By July 2020, we start having virtual engagements with new clients.

My work style and priorities change, too. I am no longer on planes almost every week and lead all my virtual keynotes, webinars, and webcasts from a small studio in my house.

I speak to hundreds of CIOs, CTOs, and other digital, data, and technology leaders about their shifts to remote working and the urgency to digitize workflows that require too many person-to-person handoffs. Many prioritize cloud migrations, develop applications on low-code platforms, automate complex business processes, and mature how the organization utilizes collaboration tools. Clients in financial services, insurance, nonprofits, and retail must rapidly reposition their products and services because of pandemic-driven shifts in customer needs and demands.

As difficult and painful externally driven transformations are, they do have one point of simplicity. They are happening to everyone within a sphere of impact.

Some impacts may be geographically bound, like that of Hurricane Sandy in the northeast United States, and others are global like the coronavirus pandemic. These transformations may not impact everyone at the same time or with the same magnitude. They require different thinking and decision-making depending on circumstances. But for the most part, there's a lot less explaining and selling of the needed transformations to leaders and employees who might prefer the status quo.

During COVID-19, the enterprise CEO doesn't have to explain why everyone must work remotely. She just needs to convey empathy to those in more dire circumstances and an operational plan to help others adjust to new realities. Retail executives provide little justification for why they invested in more online shopping capabilities, added delivery services, and established in-store pickup options. Hospitals changed many processes, from the procedures to improve essential worker safety to telehealth capabilities to provide less urgent medical services, all with little explanation needed.

A global urgency creates a crisis, and people respond. Leaders from the top and across the organization must be ready to implement changes during externally driven transformations.

But sometimes, the changes are more subtle and harder to read. The financial crisis of 2008 is a good example. You immediately felt the impact if you were working on Wall Street, but it took more time to reach Main Street. The crisis required most companies to conserve cash, prioritize fewer investments, conduct layoffs, and drive efficiencies. But the smartest organizations also considered highly strategic opportunities from the next generation of disruptive technologies, including mobile, social, cloud, and big data.

Externally driven transformations often start with crisis management functions and lead to more strategic transformations. For organizations to survive, leaders must step up to manage the crisis. During these times, employees are more open to responding to top-down leadership because they recognize the situation at hand. As organizations emerge from the crisis, leaders must pivot to more bottom-up direction and employee engagement models to ensure people remain onboard with executing strategic transformation. Under these circumstances, employees are more likely to participate and less likely to become vocal detractors because they understand that the need to transform was driven by the crisis—not the whims of executives.

So, while externally driven transformations are not easy or simple by any measure, they are in some ways simplified because the crisis brought on the pivot and employees recognize that transformation is required.

Top-Down Business Decisions Spark Strategic Transformations

It's important to understand the differences among these three transformation types: externally driven, strategic, and digital transformations.

Strategic transformations are different from externally driven ones because they are driven by fundamental top-down executive and leadership decisions. They can be spearheaded by mergers and acquisitions, business divestitures, global expansions, reorganizations, outsourcing, and other strategic decisions.

One challenge in strategic transformations is to ensure employees understand why leadership is making the decision. Strategic decisions are often made behind closed doors by the senior leadership team and the board. They are often managed by a project management team versed in the objectives. By the time they are announced to the staff, the engines of transformation are already in progress, and it's very easy to alienate employees who can face a range of emotions: shock, anger, depression, bewilderment, for example. Leaders will need specific people to take active roles and responsibilities on strategic transformations, so it's important to have clear communications that cover why the decisions were made and the new expectations.

One marker of strategic transformations is that they can be managed as programs with a defined endpoint followed by ongoing business and organizational adjustments. For example, a strategic transformation driven by acquisitions may be considered complete when key systems are integrated, employees are transitioned to the parent company's HR model, and primary synergies and opportunities meet defined objectives.

Digital Transformations Are Very Different from Strategic Transformations

Digital transformations are driven by competitive, technological, and disruptive forces. Often, multiple external factors drive digital transformation's importance, such as changing market expectations and the impact of disruptive technologies. A crisis may expose the need and importance of digital transformations, but leaders should separate crisis response, which can spur an externally driven transformation, from the digital transformation, which must target future business needs and opportunities.

Digital transformations can't be managed like strategic transformations with clearly defined, set-in-stone objectives, OKRs, operational KPIs, and endpoints. Digital transformations are strategic in their intent but must evolve based on markets, competitors, and technologies, and thus require pivots, resetting of priorities, and reimagining visions.

All businesses must consider digital transformation to accommodate technology-driven evolutions, improve competitive customer and employee experiences, enable faster decision-making, and develop differentiating digitally enabled products from competitors. When you add up these factors, it means that business models must evolve and that many companies must reinvent their go-to-market strategies for a faster evolving world. Some will also update their mission and values to reflect forward-looking objectives, revitalize how customers view the brand, and market worldly missions to potential and existing employees.

> **Digital Transformation is about looking at the business strategy through the lens of technical capabilities and determining how technology can improve the way companies operate and generate revenue.**

There are seven key principles to recognize about digital transformation that I want to detail for you because the term's meaning has muddied over the years. Digital transformation drives investments, so you might hear a colleague label a program as a digital transformation or a vendor try to sell you a technology to accelerate digital transformation. But if digital transformations are going to improve operations, generate revenue, and realign business strategies to new technology capabilities, then here's what you must consider.

1. **They are not just about operational cost efficiencies.** Competitors who outpace your business with digital services, better customer experiences, and dynamic business models—including subscriptions and asset-light marketplaces—will disrupt stagnant companies solely focused on driving down costs.
2. **Digital transformations are hybrid transformations.** Some factors are externally driven, like when an emerging technology creates market disruptions. Others are strategic, like a decision to shift from selling products to offering a recurring revenue subscription service.
3. **It's a mistake to define a prescriptive plan for implementing digital transformation.** Successful digital transformation initiatives require learning customer needs, capturing feedback, experimenting, improving implementations, and adjusting to market conditions. This is why agile methodologies are essential digital transformation practices.
4. **Focus transformation on future market and customer needs.** Some organizations fall into the trap of defining digital transformations based on stakeholder wish lists or issues raised by top customers. But for digital transformation to drive growth, it requires developing outside-in views of potential technology disruptions and business opportunities with target markets. This is why product management disciplines are essential for digital transformation because organizations must prioritize roadmaps based on changing market and customer needs.

5. **Expand technology and data competencies across the organization.** Many industries are in the middle-adoption phases of their transformations, and there's a battle for the required product, technology, and data talent. To woo talent, large enterprises can outbid, startups can provide special incentives, and top brands can out-market, so most businesses must take alternative approaches to hire and retain talent. A strong alternative is to expand tech capabilities outside of IT and empower more people throughout the organization with self-service technology capabilities. This is why low-code and no-code tools, citizen development, and citizen data science are essential digital transformation practices.
6. **Stagnate too long, and you will be disrupted.** Executives often kick the can down the road when pondering strategic decisions, but this mindset can hurt their businesses when considering digital strategies and transformations. Market and customer needs change rapidly, and technology's disruptive impacts can be significant. Fall too far behind, and you're unlikely to catch up. Organizations that promote learning cultures, experiment with emerging technologies, and promote data-driven practices are more likely to find opportunities that entice leaders to invest and transform.
7. **Digital transformations don't have an easy-to-identify endpoint.** These types of transformations are often ongoing because of the fast pace of technology innovations, the ease of funding startup innovations, and the growing number of countries (e.g., China, Israel, and India[1]) competing with digital capabilities. That's why transformation leaders will often say, "Digital transformation is a journey."

Because digital transformations don't have an easy-to-identify endpoint, they must be led and managed very differently from strategic transformations.

Learning is important because new technologies may threaten legacy business models. Leveraging data and feedback is essential to experiment and improve customer and employee experiences. Communications must be ongoing so that existing employees understand any pivots in strategy and to grow the number of people participating in digital transformation initiatives.

The stories and lessons I share in this book prepare you to have a leadership role in digital transformations. To succeed, you'll need the in-the-weeds problem-solving skills discussed in Chapter 2 to fully understand how things work, prioritize the most strategic opportunities, evaluate solutions, and collaborate on implementations. Transformation requires partnering with different disciplines and crafting multidisciplinary teams, and you can use what you learned in Chapters 2 through 4 to better understand the challenges facing those working in software development, DevOps, and product management. The key building blocks of leading transformation require developing agile ways of working, becoming data-driven, leading with a global mindset, and empathetic leadership, all of which are explored in Chapters 5 through 8. Other stories throughout the book—particularly those in Chapter 9—aim to prepare you for developing relationships and partnering with the executives and the C-suite, which will be key to your success. All the stories I've shared should arm you for the challenges you're bound to face.

You can tell from my stories that transformations aren't usually rosy, fun-filled journeys. You face technical debt boulders, data quality minefields, and lots of work to transform into an agile mindset. Sometimes, you must create a blow-up moment to influence new ways of thinking, as I demonstrated in Chapter 4. Very often, you'll find yourself in situations where you must respond to direction changes, unexpected operational issues, and leaders who throw surprise gotchas at you, as I shared in Chapters 3, 7, and 9.

Four Types of People to Influence on Your Digital Transformation Journey

Leading digital transformations is fundamentally hard and grinding work, especially when there isn't a direct threat of disruption driving them. They require asking employees to do twice the work.

Not only are you asking your colleagues to complete today's jobs to preserve the primary aspects of the existing business model, you're also asking them to go above and beyond their daily work to transform the business with new business models, target markets, customer segments, digital products, digitally enabled business processes, competitive technologies, and data-driven organizational practices.

Employees immediately recognize the organization's ask of them to perform double-duty work, and their response usually falls into one of four camps. Some embrace the drive to transform and seek leadership roles even in areas they may not have experience. A second group will go along for the ride and will only stretch themselves when leadership clarifies what's in it for them. A third group will ride with the program, but they loathe the added pressure to execute and sometimes quietly look for new jobs.

The fourth group is the detractors who prefer the status quo and doubt the new vision. Some detractors will vocalize their challenges and resentments and find creative ways to commandeer meetings to spread competing gospels or seed doubts. Others will speak out quietly, often to people they trust and select their objections where they have the expertise or a staked interest. Some detractors hold high ranks in the organization and can directly influence their direct reports and organizations. Others may be high potentials or strong influencers and disrupt the transformation's goals and message.

You might think detractors are the biggest issue in leading transformation because they can disrupt, derail, and slow down programs. But constructive detractors can actually be good for transformations, particularly when they voice concerns or ask challenging questions at opportune moments. Leaders should address these questions because they can expose institutional and dated practices, challenge the status quo, and help others evaluate "how we do things today" from new vantage points. Asking questions is exactly what successful transformations require to get people to ask why, promote blue-sky thinking, and identify new opportunities.

Getting a detractor to become constructive is time-consuming, but it's part of the Digital Trailblazer's responsibilities. So, at the outset, show patience and empathy with detractors. Demonstrate that you're a good listener and a strong collaborator, especially when a detractor shares a valid concern, objection, or fresh idea.

But if the same people raise the same concerns repetitively and without listening and considering leadership's responses, then their behaviors can be destructive. These situations require one-on-one conversations, and if they persist, their direct managers should be involved. If the detractor is an executive or senior leader in the organization, the CEO should address the behaviors. At some point, destructive detractors who fail to listen and persistently disrupt can be considered performance issues and may require human resources' involvement.

But all four groups pose different challenges.

An aggressive early adopter who pursues the latest and greatest technology solutions may drag teams off the strategic course and customer priorities. You want and need these early adopters and emerging leaders ready to challenge the status quo. A goal for transformation leaders is to find the early adopters, mentor them on collaboration skills, and provide them with the teams, processes, and tools to succeed.

That takes a bit of art and science. Where do you provide these innovation leaders with the leeway, self-organizing practices, decision-making authority, and room to fail so that they own and figure out an optimal success path? How do you manage regulatory restrictions, skill sourcing constraints, budgetary limitations, and security factors so that teams understand and work toward them? And where do you require operational standards, technical best practices, alignment on technology platforms, or rigorous KPIs that constrain some of their authorities?

Building Blocks of Digital Transformations Require One-Page Guidelines

There are no right or wrong answers to these questions, except we can safely say that an optimal operating model lies between the two extremes of chaotic self-organization and command-and-control process management. It's an equation that must factor in the opportunity, risks, talents, competitive factors, sunk investments, and impacts of failure. In fact, the biggest problem is that many organizations and their leaders are vague in defining decision authorities and standards, leaving it to the individual leader to figure out.

Transforming organizations address this by developing lightweight governance models and consumable documentation. For example, I always help my clients develop a one-page vision statement that captures the essence of the customer, value propositions, and business strategy. It helps define the goals, objectives, and target timelines that align teams and enable them to plan and execute their objectives with some guardrails. The key is that it's only one page so that it is consumable and referenceable. This one-page requirement also helps sponsors progress the plan without getting bogged down with complex artifacts that will come later, like profits and losses, architectures, user experiences, and detailed timelines, which all require time to plan. The one-pager serves as a problem statement, and when done right, the organization hands the keys to a Digital Trailblazer to use agile practices to iterate on planning and delivering solutions. If you would like a copy of StarCIO's vision statement template, see https://www.starcio.com/digital-trailblazer/vision-statement.

Vision statements are only one form of guardrail. Transformational leaders must consider where other standards, best practices, and centers of excellence can enable scalable execution and innovation. Here are considerations and questions to guide you along the way.

To be successful, you can't let reporting structures become agile execution barriers. Overcome this by understanding and helping define the responsibilities of the various roles in your extended digital organization. That means aligning the agile organizational responsibilities of your product managers, delivery leads, architects, and program managers and outlining the agile team responsibilities of product owners, technical leads, and scrum masters. When planning and executing initiatives, you'll want to create diverse, multidisciplinary teams that include digital marketers, UX specialists, software developers, data scientists, DevOps engineers, security specialists, and others. Ideally, if you ask three people with one of these roles questions around their responsibilities, you want to get consistent answers. You can help facilitate this by developing a simple way to articulate primary responsibilities to everyone on transformation teams—from new hires to long standing employees.

This doesn't mean creating a folder with all the job ads used for recruiting or HR's job description of a role that's often filled with superfluous language. Instead, outline no more than fifteen bullets on key responsibilities of the product owner in the context of working with customers, stakeholders, and in an agile process. You want to know what decision authorities a technical lead has around technology compared to the architect. If an agile team struggles to complete their sprint commitments, what are the product owners, technical leads, and scrum master's responsibilities to get them back on track?

Create one-pagers for each role. One-pagers to describe reference architectures, data models, customer personas, roadmaps, service level objectives, security fundamentals, user experience standards, and style guides—each with a context, scope, and authorities to evolve them over time. Use simple to understand, Twitter-length language. Add pictures and diagrams where they truly simplify a thousand words.

And don't just document them. Talk about these guidelines repetitively and, at the appropriate times, debate where they need upgrades or exceptions. These will only sink in and be used by leaders when ingrained in their understanding and behaviors.

These one-pagers are key artifacts defining the agile principles and operating model for a digital transformation program. They provide the framework for *why* and *how* the organization wants leaders to drive transformation change while building new capabilities.

Successful Digital Transformations Slowly Bring More People Aboard the Journey

Transformations fail when you only have engagement from the early adopter leaders and when an inordinate amount of time is required to address detractors.

The secret to driving sustainable transformation is winning the hearts, minds, and commitment of the middle two groups I outlined above. You'll recognize those employees as the ones riding things out and hoping the flames of change will snuff out. They're the passive-aggressive individuals who look like they are onboard but stick to their day jobs. They're the ones who will only contribute when ordered, called upon, or when they fear their jobs are at stake.

To win these middle two groups over, you'll need to explain the need for transformation in terms they will each understand with the goal of getting them on board so they can make meaningful contributions to the work at hand. This might mean helping the salesperson who has made quota for the last decade by selling a legacy product understand that markets are disrupting and will soon be replaced with a digitally enabled service. It might mean providing the opportunity to the marketer whose expertise is with print advertising to learn and contribute to digital marketing experiments. You might have to help the technologist whose contributions are becoming the organization's legacy systems understand the benefits of learning new technologies and contributing to high-velocity agile development teams. You may need to convince the financial analyst addicted to spreadsheets that it's worth having the patience to learn how to use a self-service business intelligence tool. And you may need to help a business manager understand that just because her team's job function and processes can be easily automated doesn't mean there aren't opportunities for them to take on more strategic work in the organization.

Every organization has people like these, and while leaders should be looking to bring in new people, skills, and perspectives to drive transformations, most companies can't transform without engaging the people who have been instrumental in running the legacy businesses.

So, what can you do as a Digital Trailblazer to bring this group on the journey? How do you increase their engagement, learn from their expertise, and provide them the opportunity to contribute to an evolving and transforming business?

Solutions start by recognizing the challenge. When I educate leaders that transformation requires a bottom-up culture change, the challenge I'm calling out is the need to get more middle adopters on board and contributing to transformation. When you see statistics that as many as 70 percent of transformations fall short of their objectives,[2] it's rarely because of factors like poor strategy or lack of budget. It's because leaders struggle to get the full engagement of the organization on board and contributing.

So, how do you get most of the organization participating and contributing to the transformation?

By engaging one group, one team, and one person at a time.

It starts by helping people understand and invest in themselves by evangelizing a continuous learning culture. Many aspects of how the world is transforming with technology are so fast that it's hard to keep up, but failing to learn is a surefire way of falling behind very quickly.

Learning really is the tip of the iceberg because transformation requires people to apply their knowledge and try things. The organization requires ongoing and continuous experimentation. Try something with a small group, capture feedback, develop insights, and evaluate the next steps. I'm not a big advocate of the adage *failing fast* and would rather see leaders *experiment frequently* and enable customer-driven feedback loops in driving digital transformation.

And how should people experiment? Well, agile processes are at the heart of experimentation! Agile requires taking the visions, data, and feedback-driven learnings, and then using them to realign priorities. It requires team commitment to complete work and continuously plan future work in sprint cadences so that everyone has a short-term, laser focus on the objectives. Product management and agile practices enable teams to better understand customer needs, strategic value propositions, and competitive threats. Organizations that are serious about transformation are developing agile teams that include product management disciplines, data-driven practices, and DevSecOps principles.

And who are these teams, and what are some characteristics of successful agile teams? Well, they are diverse, multidisciplinary teams that ask questions, challenge the status quo, use active listening skills to capture feedback, and work collaboratively on the objectives. Teams no longer must be colocated together. They can be global and use collaboration technologies to share status, debate approaches, and agree on priorities.

And how are these groups prioritizing? Well, the core to a listening culture is to be data-driven, and smart teams will use self-service technologies to capture data from their experiments.

And what are these experiments? They could include the following:

- Building internal workflow applications, integrations, and databases
- Implementing and integrating CRMs, ERPs, marketing automation systems, and other industry-specific platforms that enable workflows
- Expanding the use of dashboards used for decision-making while reducing manual data processing tools
- Converting manual workflows to knowledge-driven experiences with machine learning capabilities and citizen developed applications and hyperautomations
- Improving customer experiences to encourage loyalty, grow usage, and drive satisfaction
- Experimenting with digital marketing capabilities to learn what types of campaigns are most successful with different customer segments and personas

- Updating sales and marketing tactics based on how customers respond to new digital products
- Developing IoT data streams to connect supply chains, manufacturing, and distribution
- Piloting and evolving competitive digital products and services that will be the company's growth platforms

We're moving fast, applying technologies, creating digital centers of excellence, capturing feedback, and transforming the business model.

And we're not doing this transformation just once. It's an evolving process where we'll add new initiatives, reduce the scope of others, and pivot when required. I remind this to teams that have been sprinting through initiatives for one, two, or more than three years. I hope my stories will anchor your understanding of what you may encounter as a Digital Trailblazer.

You'll probably meet people like Phil—the developer who printed out a ream of ETL code—who know the ins and outs of your legacy systems and whom you must influence to become subject matter experts when modernizing. Hire people better than you, someone like Disney-loving Bill, who taught me important IT operational principles, but be sure to help them adapt to the business's culture and standards. I hope you are fortunate to work with innovators like Matthew and Chris and find ways to define your organization's agile way of working. Please keep a global mindset as you work with employees and partners, and plan to visit your teams regularly once travel is normalized. Go out of your way to find Eleanor, Alice, and Donna, the data-driven marketers who will champion your collaboration and partnership. Hire diverse leaders like Gracie and Catherine, who will challenge your thinking and bring new perspectives to your operations. You're likely to work with executives and maybe present to your board of directors along your journey, so remember to answer questions directly and avoid getting into the weeds with them.

And I hope you will reference my lessons learned and then develop your own playbook because digital transformation isn't a linear program. If you seek an agile culture, you'll need a leadership team to debate, decide, and evolve your organization's ways of working. When pursuing a data-driven organization, remember that proactive data governance must be prioritized in parallel to your citizen data science and AI experiments. Establish product management disciplines that balance investing in new capabilities, improving customer experiences, reducing risks, delivering efficiencies, and experimenting with new innovations. To bring more people on your journey, create centers of excellence to guide people on best practices, develop standards to scale technology capabilities, establish self-organizing principles, and promote ongoing experimentation.

Leading digital transformation isn't easy, but it's incredibly rewarding. I hope you are more confident today and ready to be a Digital Trailblazer.

Digital Trailblazer Lessons

Influencing Participants in Digital Transformations

Thank you for reading my stories and learnings in this book. I sincerely hope you have many takeaways and feel better prepared to take on the responsibilities of the Digital Trailblazer.

Here are some of the most important lessons to keep in mind as you blaze your trail:

1. **Evolve your vision statement to align on customer and strategic goals.** Every initiative needs a vision statement so

that teams have a target. Who is the customer, what value are you trying to deliver, who are the threatening competitors, and why does the organization need to invest in the program today, here and now? Remember that teams work hard and focus on solving problems. Without an evolving vision statement, it's easy to get lost on the journey.

It's equally important for you to draft *your* vision statement. Whom will you serve in your quest? What are you trying to accomplish? How is the work you are putting into your career, job, and life important to you? Don't get lost on your personal transformation journey. You can download a copy of StarCIO's vision statement as an example template at https://www.starcio.com/digital-trailblazer/vision-statement.

2. **Find fellow Digital Trailblazers who can lead initiatives.** You are now well on your way to becoming a transformation leader and Digital Trailblazer. But leaders aren't very successful operating on their own. You need peers to collaborate with and learn from, senior people to sponsor your programs, and junior leaders ready to step up and take on new responsibilities. Finding these people and providing them the lessons, tools, and safety to experiment must be a goal of every digital trailblazer. Ships don't steer to port by only the captain turning the wheel.
3. **Accelerate bottom-up transformation and grow middle adoption.** Digital Trailblazers must get more middle adopters to join the journey if they want their organization to succeed in transformation management. You can't easily win people's hearts and minds through town halls, motivational newsletters/emails, or slide decks. Though these are all important, the way to get people to climb aboard starts with empathy and understanding people's goals, incentives, and interests. Bring people onto the ship slowly, then make sure they

comprehend the vision, learn the tools, and are given a role they understand. Market your successes so that more people will want a ticket on the boat, but acknowledge the tough journey ahead because transformation is never easy.

4. **Define your organization's agile principles with easy to consume one-page guidelines.** Transformation requires self-organizing teams; however, keep in mind that giving teams free rein to do what and how they want can lead to failure or unsustainable solutions. The goal should be defining and managing a meaningful selection of standards, but most organizations can't easily define them upfront at the start of their transformations. That's why articulating agile principles is important because they express behaviors rather than hard-to-follow process standards.
5. **Promote learning, experimenting, and outside-in activities to identify pivots.** Once you have a vision, principles, and a team experimenting their way through a transformation, you have another difficult skill to learn—recognizing when to make macro-adjustments, pivot the program, or draft a new version of the vision statement. This requires capturing feedback, observing changing market conditions, and projecting the future implications to your vision. Are the voices of a few customers a trend, a change in customer expectations a new target, a technology disruptive enough to challenge the business model, or a pandemic sufficient to alter the course of businesses? A team needs to review feedback, debate insights, and ratify conclusions. The best transformation teams regularly conduct collegial debates to consider macro and micro conditions and how to pivot their transformation strategies. That's the nature of digital transformation.

■ ■ ■

I wrote this book to help develop more Digital Trailblazers, share my stories, and express the hard-won learnings. I hope more of you are ready to take on the transformation challenges in your organization. Good luck, it isn't easy. And I'm here to help when you have questions.

I am onto the next decade of digital transformation, stories, and learnings. And I hope to see you on the road.

If you would like more specifics on these lessons learned and best practices, visit https://www.starcio.com/digital-trailblazer/chapter-10. You can access the product vision template there and review other templates on agile roles, program management, proactive data governance, citizen development programs, and others.

Notes

1. Theresa Wood, "Global Stars: The Most Innovative Countries, Ranked by Income Group," Visual Capitalist, Jan. 28, 2021, https://www.visualcapitalist.com/national-innovation-the-most-innovative-countries-by-income/.
2. Patrick Forth, Tom Reichert, Romain de Laubier, and Saibal Chakraborty, "Flipping the Odds of Digital Transformation Success," Boston Consulting Group, Oct. 29, 2020, https://www.bcg.com/publications/2020/increasing-odds-of-success-in-digital-transformation.

Epilogue

I'm taking a different type of walk today, a hike actually, on one of the trails winding through Saguaro National Park in Tucson, Arizona. I'm not hiking to relieve stress or manage anxieties. I'm here to enjoy the scenery, breathe the fresh air, and clear my mind after completing Chapter 10 of this book. In a couple of days, I'll be up in Scottsdale finishing my fourth in-person keynote this fall. I'll be talking to IT leaders about how they should prepare for the next wave of digital transformation, or what I refer to in the keynote as digital transformation 2.0.

It hasn't been an easy two years for anyone, and as much as we like to define the "new normal," there are still many unknowns around the long-term transformations in areas like hybrid working, supply chain disruptions, evolving customer needs, growing security risks, and the impact of technologies like artificial intelligence and the Internet of Things that are now more mainstream than emerging tech. These are some of the characteristics of what will drive digital transformation 2.0.

And I see greater evidence of more company leaders recognizing the need to transform, from hospitals with a renewed focus on the patient experience to construction companies seeking to integrate their data and develop predictive analytics.

There is no better time to be a Digital Trailblazer. More leaders recognize the need to transform their business and operating model, and you'll be pushing fewer ropes uphill to get buy-in for investments. Employees have spent nearly two years acclimating to digital workflows, so you're less likely to find detractors holding onto the last decade's legacy practices. While there are myriad technology platforms to choose from, COVID-19 has forced many SaaS and tech providers to improve their ease of use, enable easier integrations, and support citizen development.

But don't get me wrong; while there is no better time for Digital Trailblazers, it's not easy and in some ways, more challenging to drive consensus, plan programs, and lead transformations. You can't easily bring people together in a room to brainstorm innovations and solutions, and the equivalent virtual sessions are less effective. Hybrid working is also driving the "great resignation," which means some of your company's subject matter experts may not be there for you to learn from about today's operating models. And because there's uncertainty around the impacts of inflation, climate change, and the volatile political landscapes, there will be greater debates on which growth markets to target, what emerging technologies to focus on, how to accelerate digital transformations, and what other strategic transformations in the form of mergers and acquisitions and divestitures to consider.

And when you look inside your company and how you will lead digital transformation, Digital Trailblazers will have significant work to align people, processes, and technology. Keep in mind that for the last two years, people and teams have been riding a rollercoaster powered by an externally driven transformation led by the coronavirus pandemic. So Digital Trailblazers must shift people's mindsets from reactive postures to proactive, deliberate, and experimental ones. More specifically, while there is generally a better understanding of core digital practices, including agile, DevOps, product management, and data governance, people's understanding is based on their experiences. The Digital Trailblazers' challenge includes aligning people on terminology, roles, responsibilities, and defining your organization's way of working.

I wrote this book to prepare you for your leadership journey. Every organization will need more people like you to develop digitally enabled products, modernize experiences, democratize data, create tech-driven differentiating capabilities, and drive hyperautomation. They will want empathetic leaders who can inspire diverse, global teams to align on a vision and collaborate on solutions. And your teams will need you to define priorities, provide a safe environment, enable self-organizing practices, and join them in the weeds in your areas of expertise.

Over fifteen years ago, I started my personal journey of sharing what I know and learn through my blog, keynotes, and books. Today, I have published over 800 articles and speak more than fifty times yearly. It wasn't easy for me to prioritize the stories and lessons to include in this book, and I hope the ones I included are memorable and useful. But there are areas I would have liked to cover more: how to balance work between operational needs and innovation, where to shift-left security and testing practices, how to market your transformation successes, and what approaches you can use to select winning digital technologies—to name just a few.

So I hope you will join me in the next decade of digital trailblazing, starting by having the confidence to take leadership roles within your organization. And second, by continuously investing in your learning. I'll keep writing, speaking, and sharing my learnings on my blog, at keynotes, during workshops, in my courses, and with my company's tools. I hope you'll join my community of Digital Trailblazers, and I look forward to hearing about your journeys.

Good luck,

Isaac Sacolick

Find me at https://www.starcio.com/digital-trailblazer/next-steps.

Appendix

Digital Trailblazer Lessons

Chapter 1: Transitioning to a Leadership Mindset

- Reflect on the skills that got you here won't get you there.
- Avoid solving technical problems with proprietary solutions.
- Recognize that communicating with the board and executives is a skill that requires practice.
- Understand the table stakes, then set broader goals.
- Step out of your comfort zone and broaden your perspective by seeking outside-in learning opportunities.

Chapter 2: Navigating Tech Debt's Challenges

- Focus everyone on technical simplicity when developing any kind of new system.
- Let the data be your guide when making decisions, but also trust your instincts.
- Build rapport with your team by acknowledging your own mistakes and failures.
- Lead teams by helping prioritize which questions need solving.
- Demonstrate the business and customer impacts around tech debt and legacy systems.

Chapter 3: Controlling Emotions and Managing Risks

- Be human and empathetic, but control your emotions.
- Develop communication strategies for all severity levels.
- The best technology doesn't ensure high reliability.
- Protect the team and partner with colleagues.
- Take real breaks away from the operations.

Chapter 4: Leading Innovation and Developing Products

- Align on the product vision because roadmaps are rarely straight-line journeys.
- Start with basic agile and scrum fundamentals when establishing new teams or course-correcting struggling ones.
- Begin agile continuous planning immediately after defining the vision and agreeing to pursue a new idea.
- Promote team culture by listening, reserving judgment, asking questions, managing conflict, and just being nice.
- Answer the question before steaming through jargon-filled details, and have some ideas on the next steps.

Chapter 5: Driving Agile Practices, Culture, and Mindset

- Drive transformation by emphasizing the *why* and coach on the *how* and *what*.
- Align with your organization's principles and requirements before changing the culture.
- Develop a shared understanding of product owner, stakeholder, and agile team responsibilities.
- Show me the data before selling me your ideas.
- Reduce technical debt by making it everyone's responsibility.

Chapter 6: Transforming Experiences

- Understand customer experience by reviewing the pain points and desires.
- Partner with marketers on where technology, analytics, and hyperautomation can improve results.
- Promote global team collaboration by helping colleagues learn the culture and foster personal relationships.
- Target supportable platforms because cutting-edge technology may cost you.
- Know the operational issues—and be clear about costs and risks.

Chapter 7: Leading Data-Driven Organizations

- Understand how company culture and norms impact data quality initiatives.
- Focus on meaningful problems because data journeys can be long and complicated.
- Seek easy onramps and avoid selling automation.
- Pick appropriate data technologies aligned to a future way of working.
- Invite experts and colleagues to contribute to your data-driven journey.

Chapter 8: Fostering High-Performing Teams

- Cultivate diverse teams to boost innovation and performance.
- Recruit people from different backgrounds, experiences, and places.
- Encourage everyone to contribute to your organization's way of working.

- Engage your leaders to listen and extend your emotional intelligence range.
- Assign leadership responsibilities and then foster collegial conflicts.

Chapter 9: Collaborating with Executives

- Find your stress release valves.
- Ask for more than support; seek executive endorsements and commitments.
- Define and roleplay scenarios around potential objections when selling innovations.
- Simplify and share your vision.
- Ruthlessly prioritize and define success criteria.

Chapter 10: Influencing Participants in Digital Transformations

- Evolve your vision statement to align on customer and strategic goals.
- Find fellow Digital Trailblazers who can lead initiatives.
- Accelerate bottom-up transformation and grow middle adoption.
- Define your organization's agile principles with easy to consume one-page guidelines.
- Promote learning, experimenting, and outside-in activities to identify pivots.

About the Author

Isaac Sacolick is the president and founder of StarCIO, a technology learning company that guides leaders on digital transformation. A lifelong technologist, Isaac has served in startup CTO and transformational CIO roles. He founded StarCIO with the belief that agile ways of working and data-driven practices can empower diverse teams to drive transformation. Isaac is a writer, keynote speaker, and author of the Amazon bestseller, *Driving Digital: The Leader's Guide to Business Transformation Through Technology*. Recognized as a top digital influencer by HuffPost, Forbes, and IDG, he is a frequent contributor to InfoWorld and CIO.com where he writes about digital transformation, agile management, and other technology and leadership topics. You can find him sharing new insights @NYIke on Twitter, on his blog Social, Agile, and Transformation, or on the 5 Minutes with @NYIke YouTube channel. He lives in Westchester, New York, with his family.

Index

D